TRUSTING THE SIGNS

Finding My Way Along The Camino de Santiago

Elizabeth Hale

deebeebooks.com

ISBN-13: 9781896794198

This book is dedicated to my Aunt Mazie, who role models an authentic life and inspires me to be my best self.

Acknowledgements

I would like to thank my family, friends and work colleagues for supporting me as I prepared to walk the Camino. My endless ramblings and enthusiasm may have been too much at times, but you listened, smiled and encouraged me. Thank you Joanie and Marj, my dearest friends, for taking my hand and leading me on longer than usual walks.

During those 34 days in northern Spain, I met peregrinos from around the world. Whether we spent an hour or a day together, you strengthened my conviction that I was exactly where I was supposed to be. I would like to make a special mention to those who inspired me, made me stronger and with your friendship, helped to carry me along the yellow-arrowed trail. Audile, Andreia, Uno, Antònio, Dave & Cathy, Alfdis & Hermann, Benny, Sampaio, Laurence, Melanie, Julie, Christophe, Ferro, Henrik, Niels & Hannibal, Eleanor, Leen, Jan, Frances & Ann-Marie; you will always have a special place in my heart.

The writing of this book was a journey in itself and I would like to thank the women who took time out of their lives to read my various editions, with a very special thank you to Marj. Not only did she read each chapter of my very first draft, offering suggestions, praise and validation, but she went on to read it through a second time, as I got deeper into the editing process. My deepest appreciation is extended to David Hamilton, of DeeBee Books, who believes we all have a story to share.

My greatest appreciation goes to my sons, Andrew, Tyler and Benjamin, who have been my constant love since the day they each began their own journey. You are my greatest gifts in life and I am so proud to be your Mom.

To everyone who is searching, listening to that little voice and wondering *what else*...I hope my experiences inspire you to take a step.

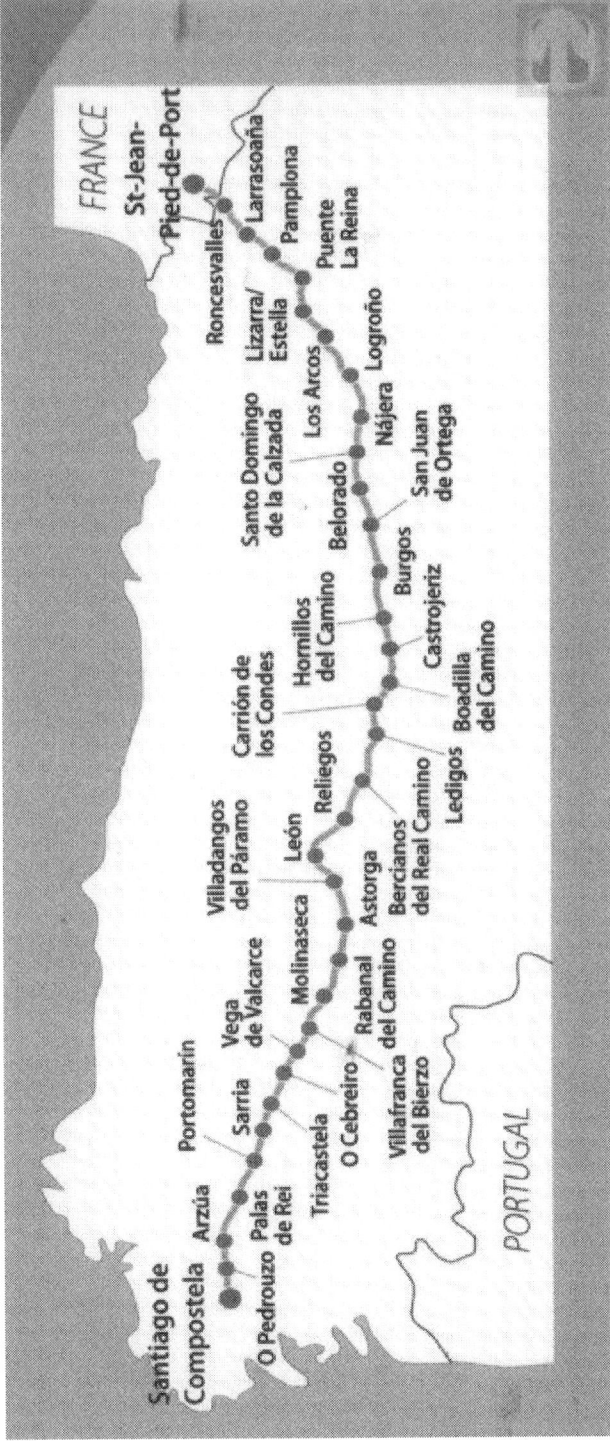

The Camino de Santiago

FRANCE

PORTUGAL

St-Jean-Pied-de-Port
Roncesvalles
Larrasoaña
Pamplona
Puente La Reina
Lizarra/Estella
Los Arcos
Logroño
Nájera
Santo Domingo de la Calzada
San Juan de Ortega
Belorado
Burgos
Castrojeriz
Hornillos del Camino
Boadilla del Camino
Carrión de los Condes
Ledigos
Reliegos
Bercianos del Real Camino
León
Villadangos del Páramo
Astorga
Molinaseca
Rabanal del Camino
Vega de Valcarce
Villafranca del Bierzo
O Cebreiro
Triacastela
Sarria
Portomarín
Palas de Rei
Arzúa
O Pedrouzo
Santiago de Compostela

Prologue: Thumbtack On My Roadmap

Life is a journey of peaks and valleys, straight lines and wrong turns, celebrations and sorrows, and everything in between to ensure we don't get too comfortable. Although taught to embrace the challenges and accept the facts, I was pleading with the universe to let me off this damn rollercoaster before it crashed.

Immersed in a busy, but happy life as a young wife and stay-at-home mom to three sons under the age of five, I didn't catch the signs of my husband's affair until it was too late. He'd made his decision to leave, and I was powerless to change that. My sole mission was to ensure my young sons felt loved, while I attempted to keep my feet planted solidly on the shifting ground. As I volleyed between anger and heartache, I wanted to blame my husband for ruining our family.

But there are two sides to every story, and I knew deep down that I bore some responsibility.

A year later the scars on my heart had started to heal, only to rip open again when my Dad died unexpectedly of a massive heart attack. Those feelings of abandonment and loss returned. The landscape of grief was all too familiar, taking baby steps towards healing.

It took time to adjust to my role as a single mother. Without the confidence to entertain a *Happily Ever After,* I accepted the fact that I was an unlikely *catch* for any eligible bachelor.

Until the day I met Pierre.

While I had been handling the household maintenance with confidence, I knew when I lost heat in my car, that I was in over my head. Entering the lobby of a local automotive service department, I hoped to appear knowledgeable about car maintenance. The last thing I wanted was to be taken advantage of.

The manager attended to my ego with finesse, assuring me that I'd be well looked after. True to his word, I was. As he offered reassurance that the repairs were minor, I couldn't help noticing his natural charm.

Assessing my state of *availability*, he casually inquired, "What does your husband do?"

Matter of factly, I replied. "He lives in Ottawa with his girl-friend!"

Flushed with embarrassment, he apologized. He, too, had recently separated and in his own fragile state, beamed with pride as he showed me a photo of his beautiful two-year-old daughter.

Caught off guard by the storm of electricity our exchange created, my spelling abilities failed when it came time to write the cheque. The left hemisphere of my brain was distracted by the bombardment of endorphins, something I hadn't felt in a long time.

Clearly, the stage had been set.

With a few more visits to the dealership, once sheepishly holding my hubcap in hand, I knew he was as excited to see me, as I him. There was a spark between us, but neither had the courage to take the next step, so the universe offered a little nudge. Months later, while driving home one Sunday afternoon, I recognized Pierre walking along the sidewalk of *my* street. A u-turn had me pulling up beside him. As the saying goes, *the rest is history.*

Within the first year of living together, we experienced two major events that could have easily challenged our new relationship. The boys' dad relocated from our home base of Eastern Ontario to New Brunswick. The thousand kilometre drive made sharing custody on alternating weekends impossible. If that wasn't enough shock for my sons, we sold everything and moved into my childhood home with my mom in Ville Lorraine, a suburb north of Montreal.

Mom's health had diminished after Dad had died, and she needed my support. Having no siblings to rely on, the responsibility to take care of her fell on my shoulders. I hoped the boys would see it as an exciting adventure, but they had to leave their friends and the home they had been growing up in. I was also asking Pierre to move two hours away from his daughter.

While Pierre embraced his role as father figure to my sons, I treasured my time as step-mother. Busy in my daily roles as wife, full-time mom and caregiver to my mother, I still felt something was missing. A search for my own personal interest led me to discover *Mom Writers*, an online community of like-minded women, who supported a shared passion for writing.

Self-indulgent ramblings about the antics of our family life, led to contributions to various online publications. Little did I know that this writing hobby would turn into something far more significant.

Two years after the move, we acknowledged that living in Lorraine was never a viable long-term plan. An open invitation to Mom was extended, and we picked up and moved to a small community just east of Ottawa.

With a taste of online writing and a small income from my contributions, I toyed with the idea of becoming a full-time writer. It was time to finish a neglected undergraduate degree I had started at eighteen. My newfound focus was to major in English.

My professor acknowledged that I had a gift for writing, but pointed out the difficulty in making a living that way, suggesting a teaching career as an alternative. The goal now refocused to include an additional degree, I worked though my undergrad with lightning speed, reading more books in one summer than I had over several years. Life went on hold as I not only ploughed through the reading and assignments, but also prepared for my mom to move in with us.

On the eve of my 40th birthday, I graduated with my Bachelor of Education.

I had found my path.

After my first year of teaching, an opportunity to lead a program for young offenders fell in my lap. Once my hope of *changing the world* wore off, I became frustrated by the restrictions and the deep-rooted attitudes of those youth. The classroom was calling me, an arena where I felt I belonged. However, it seemed that life had something else in store for me.

The longing to keep searching, to go *within* and find my own path was always there. A soft spoken voice kept whispering *what else?*

For the first ten years of our relationship, Pierre and I were a couple in every way except for the walk to the altar. Not averse to marrying again, our delay was *mostly* logistics. In addition to having uprooted our family several times, and being the primary caregiver to my mother, we had also experienced some hiccups in our relationship.

After Mom died, we bought a smaller home and focused on Us, which included an intimate marriage at City Hall. Perhaps we didn't work hard enough, as we continued to struggle with what I felt were serious issues. Deal-breakers breached our foundation and we legally separated a few months after our first wedding anniversary. However, our passion for each other had a mind of its own and we soon found ourselves back together, family unit somewhat restored.

We told ourselves that only soulmates could find their way back to one another, especially after the challenges we had overcome.

Almost two decades into our on-again off-again relationship, Pierre and I were riding the open road of the Trans-Canada Highway, on another of many memorable motorcycle road trips. We were headed towards the northwestern United States, en route to Yellowstone National Park.

There is a sense of freedom when riding a motorcycle and we took advantage of every opportunity to travel, once the kids were old enough to be left at home alone. Riding was a sweet spot in our relationship, and Pierre and I shared the rushes of adrenaline.

Riding, passion and an undeniable synchronicity. *Multiple sweet spots.*

As a couple, we were strong when straddling the iron horse; his left hand squeezing and resting on my calf, leaning back into me with a heartfelt "I love you, baby." A full day of riding would have us arriving exhausted at the nearest cockroach motel. After showering off the road dirt and washing the motorcycle, we would celebrate another successful day on the road with a couple of cold beers.

Our shared enthusiasm for spontaneous adventure kept us strong. There were no troubles in paradise when we rode. But at home, life was not so carefree. With the intense characteristics of a Taurus and Leo partnership, our personal convictions clashed, and opposing views became more than debatable topics. Our values and how we wanted to live our lives, were contradictory enough to cause multiple breakups.

Yet somehow we always found our way back to each other.

Still, that summer road trip of 2014 was the best. We travelled old school, with a large worn road atlas, the route identified in yellow highlighter. Stopping to visit popular tourist venues was not our style; we simply wanted to ride. Every hour or so, we would take a break and use the 10 minutes to fuel up on water and have a well-deserved smoke break.

We loved meeting new people; in that respect, Pierre and I were similar. We were at ease and even drawn to the need to connect with others. Regardless of where we happened to be, you would find us chatting with strangers.

And then, as fate would have it, we met a couple who changed my life.

Not yet out of Ontario, we pulled into a rest stop, backing in beside the only other vehicle. Within minutes we were talking with a couple in their 60s and their younger passenger. Initial conversation covered the *where are you from* and *where are you heading* exchanges.

What started as chit chat quickly turned into listening to their adventures and worldly travels. Happy to have interested ears, they were excited to talk about their upcoming trip to Spain. "We're walking the Camino de Santiago de Compostela."

My attention was caught and I listened intently. I had never heard of the Camino, but made a note of it before we left their company. The first entry in my Blackberry Notes app: *800 km walk, across Spain, Camino de Santiago. Pilgrimage!*

Do you believe in coincidence? That events happen randomly? That we are simply bumping into each other, sometimes connecting with Velcro and other times, just bouncing off without leaving a trace? Do you believe that our paths have been sketched out for us long ago, with the added thrill of free choice to make decisions and learn from them?

Where are *you* on the continuum between chance and destiny?

I *do* believe that events occur in our life to help us find our way, but I've also questioned those challenging and emotional experiences. *Why is this happening?*

Over the years, my belief in the push and pull of life has strengthened. It's been my anchor during storms, offering reassurance when things were painful and difficult, that *this too will pass* and sunnier days are ahead. At times I wondered whether my blind faith was simply a coping mechanism. Was it my way to stay positive when I felt the world start to crumble; an invisible rope I clutched, preventing me from going too far down the dark rabbit hole? *Maybe!* But I've come to appreciate and embrace these connecting-of-dots opportunities as thumbtacks on my personal roadmap.

We said goodbye to the elderly couple in the rest stop, and headed back on the open road, the wind blowing against our weathered, tanned faces. Thoughts of the Camino were tucked away to retrieve at a later date.

We crossed out of Ontario into the States, riding through the Prairies. References suggested the Plains would be boring, but that's the beauty of our unique perspectives. For me, they were as incredible as the Badlands of South Dakota. Views of the patchwork crop fields in shades of auburn, mustard, leaf, and wheat centred me as Pierre fought against the wind to keep the bike upright. As we swayed in rhythm, I was mesmerized by the ebb and flow of wave-like fields.

Each day of that trip offered a new experience: changing terrain, extreme weather, interesting people, and a sense of freedom. But as much as we both thrived on adventure and spontaneity, we were home bodies at heart and rejoiced when we finally pulled into our driveway at the end of this two-week adventure. We were in a good place that summer, and had taken hundreds of photos to allow us to relive the journey.

It is one of my fondest memories of our twenty-year, revolving-door relationship.

A seeker of self-knowledge, I'm always looking for opportunities to learn about myself. Like many others, I've read books on self-improvement while attempting to develop spiritual awareness.

At the end of my 40s, the last of my children had left the nest and I was *still* looking for something, certain there had to be more to my life. Step by baby step, I sought answers, searched for signs and hesitantly asked the universe for direction. Unconsciously, I hung on to the familiar. I felt confident in my knowledge and ability, in being able to anticipate and predict, and I dismissed any signs that might force me out of that comfort zone. A constant tug of war waged between wanting to move forward and trying to find happiness in the present.

The idea of the Camino was safely nestled in a warm spot, waiting patiently for the right time to sprout.

My dear friend, Joanie, ignited the possibility.

Joanie and I had connected through our youngest children when they were in kindergarten. Over the years, our Saturday morning walks became therapeutic. I had allowed her glimpses into my life, sharing only enough that she could support me with a shoulder and an ear. I believe that a large part of what makes our friendship so strong is having some traits at opposite ends of the spectrum. For example, I am impulsive, she is cautious. I can be loud and boisterous, she is reserved and soft spoken. I seek attention, she resists it. We understand and appreciate each other, offering balance and new perspectives.

When Joanie saw that I was focused on something positive, she gave me a video of the *The Way*, with Martin Sheen and Emilio Estevez. *The Way* is an incredibly moving depiction of a motley crew of travellers walking the Camino. Their unique reasons for embarking on the journey create an almost combustible chemistry, but over the hundreds of kilometres and the trials they endure, undeniable friendships develop, bonding them together as they arrive in Santiago.

The movie wasn't an accurate account of the challenges of walking 800 km, but it offered me an opportunity... to test myself, to put my faith in the hands of my Higher Power, and to meet others who also sought answers. Hollywood gave me a peek into something I wanted for myself. Hooked on the idea of walking the Camino, I couldn't put the *why* into words.

Pierre listened kindly whenever I brought it up, but he knew me well enough to assume that this was just another one of my grand plans. You know the kind: big talk, little action. He'd sat on the sidelines of some of my other grand plans: twice attempting to start my own business, a half-hearted attempt at writing, hopping into a teaching career and just as quickly out of it, and now working at a job that no longer challenged me.

I had been walking in circles for years.

Without stating it in so many words, Pierre couldn't understand why I would even toy with the idea of carrying a backpack for 800 km when *we* could ride? He wasn't interested in doing it with me, but also not fond of the idea of my doing it alone. He may have feared I might discover a whole new world that did not include him, but I couldn't get the idea out of my head. Instead, I let it grow on it's own. That was safer.

Although I kept my *Camino Dream* to myself, that didn't stop me from looking for answers. Rather, it awakened me to new possibilities. I needed something, I just didn't know what. Maybe walking the Camino would help solve the mystery of myself.

Ready to Listen
February 2015

Even though I searched for a signal, a direction, *any* confirmation of my own feelings, I didn't trust myself enough to differentiate between what was a *real* sign and when I was over-analyzing. My mind came up with multiple scenarios and reactions to *possible* events I feared and wanted to be ready for. Dismissing what was staring me in the face was not healthy. I fought to hear my inner voice and be true to myself, while ignoring those feelings in the depth of my belly.

Although I preached the benefits of paying attention, I obviously needed to be hit over the head in order to accept what was right in front of me. The indicators had been there for a while, but I wasn't ready to accept them. The screaming sirens and waving red flags contradicted everything I had hoped for and worked towards.

A *Happily Ever After*.

When we disregard our intuition, the universe sends a stronger message. And it's usually something we are not likely to ignore.

In February 2015, our marriage spun out and shot over the cliff, jarring me into numbness. Shocked, I struggled to rationalize or discredit the events, but there was no way to misinterpret *this* sign. The broken pieces were far too many to be glued back together. I didn't even bother.

We had been renting a 3-bedroom townhome that was more than I could manage alone. I needed to focus on finding a new place to live, while dealing with the pain of scraping together the pieces of my life. The two months I spent sorting through, condensing, and packing up my belongings, helped restrain my mind from shooting off in directions I couldn't deal with. All I could muster was a hope that my new surroundings would provide some comfort, while I grieved the loss of my best friend, lover and confidant.

That inner voice reminded me that I was here for a reason.

Alone and on the verge of depression, I kept my misery hidden. Who wants to be pitied or reminded about having to live with the consequences of the choices we've made? Licking my wounds about being so naïve *again*, I fended off concerns from others by pasting on a smile, and showing off my positive attitude. I hoped I was giving the impression that I could handle this challenge and come out ahead. A friend told me years ago to "fake it till you make it," so that's what I was doing.

This was my path and whether I wanted it or not, the universe felt I needed to be here.

Through my darker moments, I wrote in my journal—a red leather portfolio with lined paper I had collected over the years. Every thought I had went down in ink. By letting it all out, I hoped the pressure on my heart and mind would be relieved. Desperate to figure out where we went wrong, the answers I had buried while we were together came out on paper, blurred by my tears.

Everything I couldn't say to Pierre's face and everything I couldn't admit to myself, my fears, frustration and anger, was acknowledged. I relived each reconciliation in my mind, as though past pains would anesthetize my open wounds. We would always start strong with renewed hope, only to fall into old habits even sooner than the time before. We had hurt each other over and over again, the old scars barely healed before we would reconcile.

Even with this insight, I found it hard to let go. How could we have parted ways yet again, when we had survived so much together? *What happened to being soul mates?*

The Camino was calling me, an acknowledgement that I needed to escape, to embrace a new focus, a challenge, a change. I yearned to take steps to find out the meaning and purpose of my life experiences. I would soon be turning 50 and I needed to figure out who I was and what the hell I should be doing. A small tattoo on the inside of my calf is a phoenix rising from the ashes, a constant reminder that this quest was long overdue. Time to sift through the embers and rise up.

Could I get myself ready to walk the Camino this summer?

Reading books and researching online became my mental training until the snow melted. The first book I read was *I'm Off Then - Losing and Finding Myself on the Camino de Santiago*. I could relate to the author, Hape Kerkeling, who felt the need for change and took a leap of faith off his couch and onto the yellow-arrowed route through northern Spain. The discovery of an online forum, with conversational threads ranging from bed bugs to transportation, built my arsenal of knowledge.

Risk-free, I was taking steps forward.

But I found no joy in pounding the hard pavement. A pep-talk was needed to get myself out the front door and taking actual steps. Needless to say, I wasn't exactly dedicated to my physical training. That particular neon flashing sign about my physical fitness, had also been ignored in my heightened enthusiasm for change.

In order to be able to walk an average of 20 km a day, for possibly 40 days, I needed to get into better shape. I had quite the task in front of me, yet had never thought about how challenging the daily routine would be.

When I find myself in a moment of gratitude, I take stock of my blessings, especially friendships. It is fascinating to trace back how fate had our paths cross so we could share each other's lives. In addition to Joanie, I had another friend who supported me unconditionally... and meeting Marj was serendipitous.

Marj and I had connected right away at a networking event and it didn't take us long to develop a kinship. She understands me more than she lets on, her professional insight as a psychologist giving her a deeper understanding of the human condition. She has a way of identifying my fears, helping me find the solutions, and cheering me on to the finish line.

As an avid hiker, she wanted to help me prepare, inviting me to the trails in nearby beautiful Gatineau Park. What started as shorter treks, up and down hills, around and through mud patches, progressed to 20 km hikes with as many pounds on my back.

My excitement grew as I considered losing myself along the Camino.

Register for Spanish lessons. Check.

Request five weeks of summer vacation. Check.

Invest in quality hiking boots and a lightweight backpack. Check.

Research, shopping and occasional hikes was the easy part, but planning made it look like I was moving forward, without making a real commitment.

But who was I kidding? Was I really thinking of travelling to Europe on my own, to hike across Spain with a backpack? I wasn't even comfortable eating in a fast-food restaurant by myself. Was I seeking answers or trying to distract myself? *Probably a bit of both.*

I kept flip-flopping between supercharged *I'm going to do it!* mode and reluctant *Maybe I should wait* moments. The more plans I put into motion, the more I began to doubt myself and rationalize my fears. With more than a few extra pounds on my body, and an overall avoidance of physical activity, I wasn't in the best shape and had only a few months to prepare. Other fears stemmed from contemplating the unknown. To step out of the arena where I knew what to expect, scared the heck out of me. What was I thinking?!

That I needed to escape into the unfamiliar.

The discovery of a Camino planning session with the *Canadian Company of Pilgrims* got my blood pumping. The stones of my path were being laid right before my eyes. Impulsively, I read into events that the universe was speaking directly to me. An email request to be added to the attendance list was quickly returned, with a reply that the session was full. *How could I hit a roadblock so soon?*

As impetuous as I was in the highs, I quickly retreated from a goal at the first sign of trouble. *Maybe the time wasn't right.* My children were also giving me mixed messages.

My oldest son, Andrew, hinted that perhaps I was rushing into too big an endeavour. "Have you thought about training until next summer, giving yourself the advantage of being in the best possible physical shape?" Andrew is a firefighter who trains at the gym every single day, whether he feels like it or not. His physical aptitudes were not inherited from his mother, and he seemed oblivious to the fact that fitness had never been on my list of interests or priorities. I think he was worried I was setting myself up for failure, something he personally avoided.

Tyler didn't have the same reservations. "Sure, Ma, do it if that's what you want." Ty has never been one to dictate to others, and although I'm not sure he understood why I wanted to take this journey, he thought I was capable of making my own decisions.

Ben, my baby, recognized my need for escape and encouraged me wholeheartedly with a "Go for it, Mom!" He is an independent spirit, and I realized we shared a desire for freedom to be ourselves.

Without a doubt, I knew all three would cheer me on, if I actually stepped on the plane.

While still battling self-doubt, I learned that my Spanish course had been cancelled. I admitted defeat... temporarily, reacting to each scenario as it presented itself, instead of sitting back and letting the big picture unfold.

When I submitted a request for five weeks off, I honestly thought it would be declined. I may have been unconsciously hoping it would get refused, giving me a way out. To my shock, the request was granted. Then I found out I could enrol in an alternate beginner language course; I would be learning Spanish after all. If that wasn't enough encouragement, an unexpected email from the *Canadian Company of Pilgrims* had me on the list for a second planning session in late May.

With the plan back on the table and the excitement difficult to control, I still needed someone to tell me I could do this, because obviously my own judgement couldn't be trusted. My friend Jonathan owns a personal training business and I value his opinion. What I wanted was for him to confirm my physical capabilities and emotional strength. To reassure me that this was my time to shine.

"I know I mentioned to you that I'm thinking of walking the Camino. Originally I was going to do it this summer, then I talked myself into waiting, but now I'm giving serious thought to sticking to my original plan. My question is this: do you think I would be able to do it? I was planning to start in Pamplona, omitting the Pyrenees mountains (which is a brutal way to start), leaving me with about 720 km through various terrains. Do you think I'd be setting myself up for failure or do you think it's doable, keeping in mind that I'd be leaving in exactly 6 weeks from tomorrow."

I have a great fondness for Jon, and I knew I could count on him to be honest and to the point.

"I think you should wait a year to do it and train a bit more. My understanding is you walk a half-marathon each day while carrying your backpack. If you think you can do that then you should do it; otherwise I think you should wait."

Jon didn't beat around the bush, but that was one of the things I admired about him. True to my Taurus nature, I was stubborn and headstrong, and I was already planning to take this on, regardless of the push back.

"You didn't tell me what I wanted to hear, but what you did do was challenge me to start walking on a daily basis. I agree that it's like walking a half-marathon each day, but I can walk at my own pace, stop when I want and just 'experience'. As always, I appreciate your honesty, but sometimes we have to do things even when others suggest we wait. It will be out of my comfort zone on so many levels, but I'm being pulled to do it. I keep changing my mind so who knows? After Saturday I'll have a better idea, as I'm going to a day-long information session. It will either deter me or set me full speed ahead."

For once I wanted to listen to and heed that little voice, MY voice. If it was meant to be, the pieces would fall into place.

Any doubts I had walking into the St. Barnabas Church hall quickly evaporated and without hesitation, I registered to become a member of the *Canadian Company of Pilgrims*. With the membership paid, I purchased *my* credential, a pocket-sized Pilgrim Passport bearing my name, that would be stamped at each albergue I stayed at. More symbolic than my hiking boots or backpack, that booklet was just the confirmation I needed.

An older woman sat down right beside me, even though there were numerous empty chairs. She was preparing to walk her *third* Camino, a 1,000 km route, on her own, her husband meeting her at the end in Santiago. She was in her 70s! "You are never alone when you're walking along the Camino."

Over lunch, she explained how she felt drawn to sit beside me, as though we were meant to meet. "I long ago learned to follow those feelings."

Half of the attendees had previously walked one of the routes, and their excitement was evident as they shared plans for their upcoming pilgrimage. I was in the midst of a community that supported camaraderie, love for your fellow man, and a desire for personal growth. Soaking up the positive energy, my body hummed with the electricity. The speakers were veteran *peregrinos,* sharing their knowledge to ensure we would have the best possible experience. From the edge of my chair, I took in every word.

They explained the basics: preparing for the physical demands and how to manage expectations once you're on the road, packing tips to keep the weight down, and recommended equipment. They answered our questions about air and train transportation, the various routes, and the importance of Pilgrim etiquette (removing boots at the door of the albergue, respecting your fellow roommates, and appreciating the volunteers who support the thousands of weary travellers each year). The discussion about the inner journey, how to pay attention and listen to your thoughts, was exactly what I needed to hear.

I floated back to my parked car. There was no doubt in my mind that I would be taking my own pilgrimage this summer.

Not Quite
Complicated Enough

With the decision made, I started looking at flights. My limited experience in overseas travel had me Googling *flights to Spain.* I planned to start in Pamplona, eliminating the challenging trek over the Pyrenees mountain range from Saint-Jean-Pied-de-Port into Spain. The Pyrenees were deemed to be a spectacular climb by all accounts and worth the effort and exertion, but I felt there was great potential for injury early in the trip. Cop out? *Perhaps.*

I had convinced myself that I was being a smart pilgrim, who didn't believe she had to walk the entire 800 km to benefit from the experience.

This adventure would be costly and my bank account was not so flush that I could be frivolous. In my mind, making my own travel arrangements equalled more euros in my pocket, but my inexperience resulted in too many flight searches and an influx of email alerts, heightening my stress level. The time had come to put the details into the hands of professionals.

My original plan was to leave June 27th, returning around August 1st, giving me the month of July to walk (one of the hottest and busiest months along the Camino). As it turned out, an unexpected situation at work delayed my departure by a month, providing extra time to train and mentally prepare. I would have the full month of August, up to and including Labour Day, to find myself.

Norhan at *The Flight Centre* became my new best friend. While I hadn't fully relinquished control, I was using her expertise to make the best decision. She suggested leaving from Montreal, where I could board a direct flight to Madrid and take a RENFE train to Pamplona.

The anticipated total cost including travel, equipment, meals, accommodations and incidentals would be about $5,000. This wouldn't be an all-inclusive week at the beach: I would carry only what I needed, walk until I was tired, make new friends along the way, and hopefully find some personal insights. No one to count on and no one counting on me.

Right around that time, Pierre and I started to rekindle our relationship. We had met a few times—the magnetic pull hard to resist. Although we told ourselves we were just friends, the familiarity, comfort and passion we still felt, were more than we could fight.

In June, Pierre's cousins were tragically killed in a motorcycle accident. He had spent many years of his youth with this couple, and their death was an incredible loss, leaving a void in his heart. That turn of events brought us closer together, and tightened our bond as we tried to make sense of the unacceptable.

The rules of engagement changed and once again, we were a couple. *Sort of.* We agreed to take our time and see where the relationship would go. That was the plan, but neither of us had ever been sensible when it came to reuniting, always picking up where we had left off. I hoped it would be different this time. I said little to the boys, as they had witnessed this picking up the pieces each time Pierre and I had broken up. They couldn't understand why I continued to put myself in that position.

Still, I was ready to take the risk again, holding onto that dream of a *Happily Ever After*. Pierre had given me so much and when times were beautiful, I forgot all that he took away. So yes, I was willing to give it another try, our relationship already set on a new stage. I would be leaving for five weeks. *That would either make us or break us.*

With the final stages of preparation underway, I was pleased with my efforts. Although at times my planning looked quite chaotic to an outsider, I was a great organizer. I shopped for quality items, because this wasn't the time to pinch pennies. If I absolutely needed something along the way, there would be stores in the larger cities, but I wanted to start off well equipped.

The obvious items and must-haves were the hiking boots, backpack and poles. I knew from my hikes with Marj that trekking poles were an absolute necessity. They gave me a solid base to propel up hills and supported my knees on the descents. I'd had knee issues over the last few years, and was just finishing a nine-month rehabilitation strength training program, feeling stronger than I had in a long time.

Due to the anticipated heat, I opted for a liner in place of a sleeping bag. A money belt with an anti-theft lining was a must. The importance of wearing waterproof sandals in the showers was stressed in all my research, with the added benefit of becoming my post-walking footwear. I wasn't thrilled to pay $45 for a pair of Croc sandals, but my feet would be carrying me and I had to protect them. I chose lightweight alternatives whenever possible.

With the option to wash my clothes in a sink and hang them to dry each evening, I only needed two outfits. One to wear during the day, and a second to put on post-shower, which would serve as the clothes for the following day. Both pairs of pants unzipped at the knee, and voilà, I had shorts. One pair was rain and wind resistant to help with any unpredictable weather. One Merino wool t-shirt and another more flattering ultra-light green top. I made the executive decision to bring enough underwear to last several days.

Pierre watched me collect my gear, but I knew he craved a role in my journey (other than being the husband left behind). He had many contacts and proudly told his clients that his wife would be walking the Camino. As fate would have it, a client happened to be a distributor of woolen socks. One day Pierre came home as excited as a little kid, with the most comfortable socks I had ever worn. They were perfect. Not only did they make my hikers feel like slippers, but they also cushioned impact, absorbed sweat and eliminated odour. Once he saw how thrilled I was, he purchased three more pairs.

The temperatures in August could reach the high 30s Celsius, so I had no need for a fleece, but packed one long sleeve shirt, just to be on the safe side. Marj supplied a "little red dress" which she felt was essential for travelling in Spain. This addition to my post-walk wardrobe was most welcome, and I bought myself a complementary ¾ sleeve white shirt, should it get chilly. A black Merino wool tank with my soft, cropped grey bottoms would serve as pyjamas.

Clothing ready. Check.

In preparation for possible inclement weather, I bought a huge blue poncho to cover my backpack and most of my body. I hate wearing hats, but my vanity would be trumped by the preventative measure against sun stroke. This led into the toiletries debate: do I bring enough to last 35 days or do I purchase as needed?

My hair is unruly, and my post menopause curls need conditioner. I solved part of the problem by purchasing a Buff. From all the overnight stays in sleazy motels during our road trips, we had collected a lifetime supply of travel-sized shampoos, body washes, conditioners, lotions and bars of soap. By bringing these along, the weight of my pack would diminish as each bottle went into the trash. Being the smart girl scout, I also bought a bottle of Camp Soap, a liquid detergent that I would wash my clothes with and if needed, use on my body. Add deodorant, a toothbrush and a few mini tubes of toothpaste I'd confiscated from my dentist.

Mairie-Pier, the strength trainer from my rehabilitation program, helped me address my knee issues. She had walked the Camino the previous summer and even knowing my physical limitations, she didn't hesitate to encourage me with an enthusiastic "Go for it." She was emphatic about sharing a few tidbits of information that might be missing from the best guidebook.

"Expect the unexpected. The washrooms *will* run out of toilet paper, so carry a mini roll at all times. With so many travellers the clotheslines could be full, but you can tie dental floss anywhere to hang your clothes. Bring large safety pins so you can hang any still-damp items from your pack while you walk. Your belly will get upset from the lack of sleep and sheer exhaustion, and Mother Nature may call on a long stretch of empty road...bring baby wipes and small doggie poop bags for those emergencies. I'd suggest you pack everything in extra-large Ziploc bags, each with a couple of fabric softener sheets. It makes finding items so much easier, as well as keeping your clothes smelling fresh. Let's face it, hand washing isn't the most effective way to clean your clothes, especially after a day of sweating along the dusty trail."

Each Ziploc bag had a purpose. Bedtime: my liner, pillow case and pyjamas; Clean: the evening clothes and money belt; Laundry: those clothes peeled off before the shower; and Shower: my toiletries. Both the Clean and the Shower bag have a small hole with a shower curtain hook, to keep them out of the stream of possibly cold water.

A comb, sunscreen, tweezers, Band-Aids, antiseptic wipes, mini first aid kit and a full bottle of Aleve were added to my growing collection of necessities. It made sense to carry a light-weight bottle, as I would be passing numerous fountains. A pen was added to the journal Joanie gave me, so I could track my daily adventures. I found a spreadsheet on the Camino forum that contains a town-by-town breakdown of the local lodgings, and downloaded it to my cellphone. Too many books: *Camino de Santiago*, by Sergi Ramis; the John Brierley *Camino Map* pocket book; and a Spanish-English dictionary. A carton of cigarettes would hardly last me the month, but would tide me over until I found a brand that suited my taste.

Smokes. Check.

My prized possession was my FitBit. It would let me know how far I travelled each day and how much time I had left, before needing to get out of bed each morning.

There was still so much to do and the calendar pages were flipping by quickly. My clothes, toiletries and smaller items were laid on the dining room table. Hikers, backpack, duffle bag for transporting my pack and lightweight carry-on pack for the plane, spread over the living room floor like landmines.

I plan to wear my main gear on the plane: my carry-on containing the second outfit, some toiletries, my journal and iPod. If my backpack got lost enroute to Madrid, I would still be able to walk, minus the poles. My kitchen counter was hidden beneath books, Spanish homework, partially crossed-off lists and scraps of paper with important reminders.

Can I bring my supply of Clif Bars into the country?
Sew Canadian badges onto my pack and hikers.
Wrap ribbon around my hiking poles for easy identification.
Purchase euros.
Pack, unpack, remove items, repack.

I would be carrying 24 pounds, excluding the water or any snacks picked up during the day. Rule of thumb is no more than 10% of your weight. I still had too much. The Clif Bars were heavy, as were the multitude of small bottles, but I didn't want to leave anything else behind. On the top of my backpack was a small stuffed bunny, a gift from my co-worker Stephie. She was worried about my going on this adventure alone, and so *Bunny* was to be my protector. Sure.

Had I forgotten anything?

Mid-July I went into panic mode, realizing I hadn't made an accommodations reservation in Pamplona. I needed to ensure my lodgings would be *oh-so-close* to the Camino route that wound through the city. Back into *Google* overdrive, I booked a night stay at the *Hostal Navarra*.

I was ready.

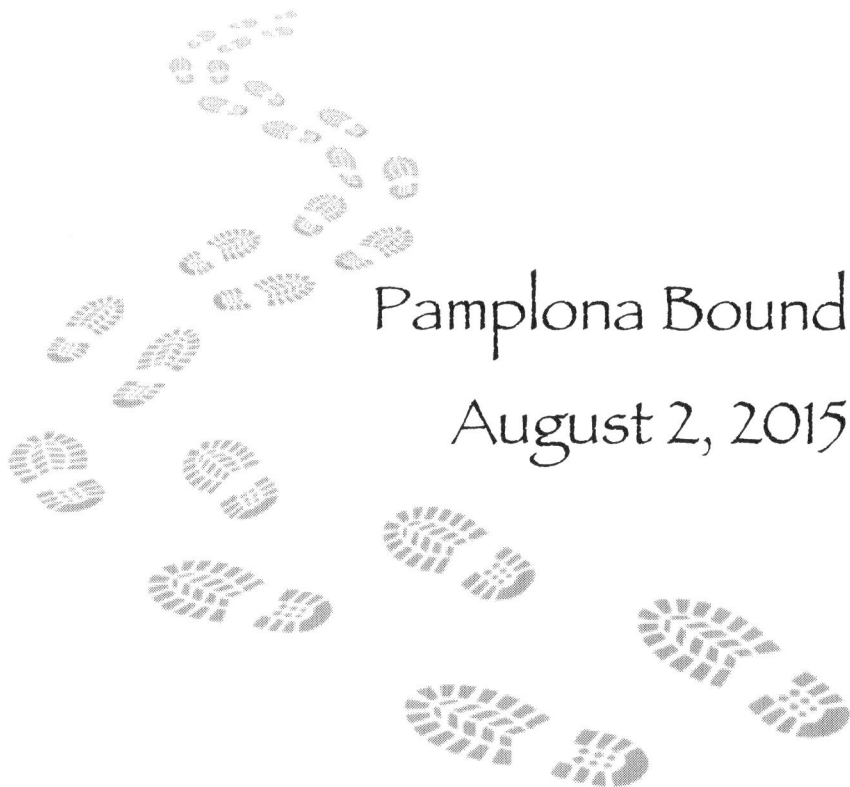

Pamplona Bound
August 2, 2015

It has been an emotional day, every action bringing us one step closer to the two-hour drive to the airport and ultimately the five-week separation. Confident we have plenty of time to get me checked in before we have to say goodbye, my heart sinks at the sight of the line up, snaking its way to the multiple check-in counters.

What am I doing leaving for 5 weeks?

I can still back out if I really want to. *But I don't.* I need this more than I realize. Of course I will miss Pierre terribly, but walking the Camino is part of *my* life's journey, something I want to do just for me. We had the conversation that this isn't about us, but I think he's worried that while I'm finding myself in Spain, I'll come to the realization that I no longer need him in my life.

Two hours pass before I reach the check-in counter. With my passport in hand, I ask, "Do I have enough time to go out for a smoke before I go through security?"

Glancing at the clock behind her, she meets my hopeful gaze. "You have a few minutes."

No pressure.

Pierre has been keeping an eye on my progress, grabbing my hand urgently as I leave the chaos. Picking up our pace, we move towards the automatic doors, hoping to find a quiet spot amidst the taxi traffic and never-ending flow of travellers.

Who am I kidding? I know what this trip could do to our relationship. As we light up our cigarettes, we try to squeeze as much sentiment as we can into five minutes.

"I adore you, Lizzie!"

We lock eyes, and he holds on until I pull away.

As I rush towards the security gate, now blurred with tears, I turn and wave goodbye. *I hope I'm making the right decision.*

An excited energy takes over. I have planned this trip for several months, but my pilgrimage started a year ago on that warm summer morning, when I first heard about the Camino de Santiago.

Security is quick and painless, but when I arrive at the busy boarding gate, I feel alien amidst the buzz of Spanish conversations. Once I am safely settled in my aisle seat, I try to relax. There is no worry about a connecting flight or lost baggage.

My feet in their wool socks and Italian hikers are already starting to fidget, my personal space invaded by the reclined seat in front of me. I don't realize I have dozed off until my head drops forward. Parched, all I can charm from the stewardess is a plastic glass of water, barely enough to quench my thirst. From the air I catch sight of my destination. Anticipation builds as the pilot announces our descent into Madrid.

There's no turning back now.

As I anxiously follow the other passengers across the tarmac, the hot humid Madrid air catches my breath, the outdoor temperature gauge reading 32 degrees. Unable to communicate in Spanish, I smile when anyone looks my way. That's my go-to response when I don't understand: the international smile and nod, laugh when appropriate. Inside the terminal I follow travellers I recognize from the flight. Confident I have found the right carousel, I find the nearest wall and sink to the floor. For a few minutes I take stock of the last year and my arrival in Madrid.

At 50 years old, I am travelling on my own, embarking on what is bound to be a game-changer. Five weeks gives me plenty of time to see this country up close and personal. Spain is known for its architecture, wine and peregrinos. I don't know much about the first two, here or at home, but I've certainly done my research on the latter. The rest will come as opportunities present themselves.

For now, I'm taking one step at a time and I need to get my pack off the carousel and get started. It's time to discover who I am and what I'm made of. *Be careful what you wish for, Lizzie.*

Passport in hand for inspection, I am living on the edge with the dozen possibly contraband Clif bars. Nervously waiting at the front of the line, it's my turn to approach the desk. The Spanish Customs agent says nothing, not even an *Hola Peregrina* offered.

There was no need to worry about security dogs sniffing out my stash of emergency snacks, la policía rushing on site to arrest me for illegal substances. He doesn't even glance at my new passport photo, a source of pride and joy. Relieved but somewhat disappointed, it's not the pilgrim welcome I expected.

Now free to wander within the confines of the airport, I head outside to take a much needed fresh air break. Translation: I need a smoke. *Desperately.* It has been way too many hours since that last, fast cigarette outside the Departures Gate of the Montreal airport.

Mentally patting myself on the back for having made it this far, I smile. I followed through, took the leap, made the plans, and arrived in Spain. My sense of achievement is blurred by having left behind the man I love.

This is not a vacation or a trip for two.

Chain smoking a second cigarette in the humidity invites a wicked head rush, the beginnings of a headache climbing the back of my neck. I'm so thirsty, a drink of anything would help me enjoy my smoke, a habit when I feel rattled. It is 11:30 am Madrid time, 5:30 am Lizzie's time and my hunger, thirst, and nervous energy are nagging at me. *Or is it the fact that I am totally out of my element?*

I have only myself to rely on, and I'm not sure I'm all that dependable. I need to get my bearings and find the airport bus for Terminal 4, so I can catch a ride to the RENFE train station. I'll figure out how to catch the commuter train once I get there.

Don't panic. One foot in front of the other.

At Terminal 4, I head outside again. I'm nervous and the act of lighting up helps me ground myself. *You are stalling, Lizzie. Go find your way!*

When I spy a bank of intimidating self-service machines, self-doubt quickly stands up and identifies herself. Norhan, at *The Flight Centre*, explained that there would be no charge to take the commuter train, because she provided me with a RENFE train ticket. The challenge is to figure out how to obtain that free ticket.

Approaching the ATM style machine with apprehension, it doesn't take long to realize there is a language barrier. My printed train ticket (sans English subtitles), has pertinent instructions that could help, unfortunately I can't understand what is written on the ticket or make sense of the maze on the screen. *Why didn't I take Spanish Comprehension?*

While pushing buttons randomly, I discover there are multiple screens of virtual routes, that look like something only an IT expert or serious gamer could manipulate. I am neither. My proficiency in counting to 100 and identifying my colours is useless. No amount of staring or pretending confidence is going to produce a ticket.

Perhaps one of the lessons I am meant to learn is asking for help.

It is time to surrender to the machine, and join the long queue to the Information Centre. Not advancing fast enough and afraid of the ticking clock, I quickly abandon the line up and walk back to the machine, with a renewed determination.

How difficult can it be? I am a smart woman. Given enough hours and without the pressure of having to catch a train, I could possibly figure it out. Whether the look of desperation on my face or the simple fact that "the Camino *does* provide," out of nowhere my *Terminal 4 Angel* appears.

"Do you need any help?" A lovely petite woman with her hair pulled back in a small bun, and speaking perfect English, smiles as she introduces herself as Anita. "Can I look at your ticket?"

Without hesitation, Anita taps the electronic buttons, scrolls through the maze of routes, producing my ticket like a pro. Then she does the same for herself. There is no possible way I could have done this myself. Taking her hand, I tell her as much, and explain why I am in Spain.

Anita is also headed to the station to catch her train home to Barcelona. She offers to accompany me, ensuring I board the right commuter train, exit at the right stop, hand delivering me into the station. We chat along the way, but I ramble nervously. Once she points out my boarding gate, she hugs me tightly, wishes me a "Buen Camino" and disappears into the crowd.

The gate opens at 3:15 pm and in no time I am plopped in my seat. With three hours to sit and watch the country go by, I *finally* relax. There are no decisions to make, no connections to catch; I am Pamplona bound. My weariness takes over until I hear myself snore.

Disoriented and somewhat embarrassed, I try to regain my composure. Although no one knows me, they have probably figured out I'm a Canadian peregrina, the red maple leafs on the toes of my boots. Thankfully, they cannot put a name to the snore.

The Pamplona station reminds me of those I used to pass on the overnight milk run from Toronto to Ottawa—small enough that you could walk around without needing to enter the building. As my train mates flag down the waiting taxis, I retreat to a bench where I can take some time before my next steps. Grey clouds hover overhead, a light drizzle refreshing me.

By the time I finish my cigarette, all the taxis have departed and the station has cleared.

Oh shit, now what?

A few minutes later, a single cab pulls in.

Fortunately the Spanish language is similar to French, allowing me to converse with my driver. Instead of taking me right to the door, he lets me off at what I feel is a busy metropolitan corner, and points in the direction of *Hostal Navarra*. He searches my face for understanding, so I nod and smile, pay the fare and linger at the corner. Fear of the unknown promotes my anxiety.

Get used to it Lizzie, you are going to be spending a month travelling in a foreign land by yourself. The unknown is all you can expect.

With a café right at the corner, I note that I won't have to go far for food tonight or tomorrow morning. Beside my new favourite restaurant is a nondescript door and a simple sign above, identifying my hostel.

Michael, who had been my email contact, is manning the front desk. While I am delighted to make his acquaintance, the feeling doesn't seem mutual. He's ready to end his shift, but still waiting on another guest. His attitude is cool, but I have Canadian charm and plan to melt this Spanish iceberg. We return to the front door where he demonstrates how to work the key system, stressing that he will be leaving soon.

My room has just enough space for a bed, night table, dresser and a bathroom with shower. I am so tired, I could easily lay down, but I need to find my route for tomorrow morning. Not wanting to get locked out of the building, I double check that I have my room key in my money belt. Back downstairs, I hope my host can provide a map and maybe a smile. Michael's mood seems to have lightened in the last few minutes, and he quickly provides me with verbal instructions.

I know from experience, that this is not the best way for me to retain information. I also know that I tend to nod ignorantly, even when I don't understand. "Do you have a map?" Armed with visual directions, I turn right as I leave the hostel.

Mental notes of the landmarks, I pray I can retrace my steps. According to the map, I am looking for a pretty large green space, but have found myself in a public square, surrounded by old buildings and statues. To avoid looking out of place, I start snapping photos. I had better get comfortable asking for help.

An elderly Señora approaches *me*, asking for *my* help.

"Mi Espanol es poco." I've either said it incorrectly or she doesn't care, continuing to ask me questions. Communicating charades-style, I attempt to redirect the conversation, pointing to my map. She sets the record straight. I had been walking in the wrong direction from my first step out of the hostel. I'm not totally surprised, as following directions is not a skill I have mastered. Thankfully the Camino is lined with yellow arrows.

Señora continues the flow of Spanish conversation until I can finally get a word in and politely excuse myself. I don't want to be a rude Canadian, but I need to know where I will be going in the morning. And at some point I need to put some food in my empty belly because my headache is refusing to be ignored.

Retracing my steps, I watch for the landmarks, and breathe a sigh of relief when I pass the *pharmacia* sign and then the door to my hostel. Map tightly in hand, I find the park Michael had directed me towards. *I know where I am and where I am going.* Back to the now familiar corner, hungry and exhausted, I enter the sweet smelling café. It is time to practice the one important Spanish phrase I know.

"Café con leche, por favor." My body needs more than coffee, pointing to an omelette. My first meal, I don't even balk at the fact that there is tuna in my tortilla.

As the adrenaline wears away, I can feel the weariness of the two days of travel. Ready to call it a day, I'm amazed that I am still standing. Without opening the Ziploc bags, I mentally review their content, more than satisfied that I am in good form. I only need my pyjamas tonight as I have the luxury of a real bed, with sheets and comforter.

Alarm is set for 7 am. Check.

Pierre has sent a few emails since we parted. It's a long week-end at home and he'll be thinking of us while listening to music, and enjoying a few beers. Six hours behind me, he is in the midst of a gorgeous August afternoon while I tuck myself into bed.

Day 1
22 km
August 4, 2015

A full body stretch while still under the covers surprises me by how rested I feel. Without missing a beat and eagerly anticipating that first cup of café con leche, I head into the shower. My morning routine is reversed at home; the shower only comes *after* I've lounged with a coffee or two. But I am not at home. I doubt the residents of Pamplona would appreciate me walking out of my hostel in my pyjamas, sleepily entering the neighbouring café, and retreating to the curb side patio with my coffee in hand. With the number of kilometres I'll be walking each day, I need to be disciplined. I might as well start now.

This is really happening, although I'm not exactly sure what *this* is.

As soon as I get some food in my belly, I'll be walking the famous Camino de Santiago. It's intimidating to say the least. The experience is available to anyone who feels the desire to learn a bit more about themselves, but accepting the invitation sets high expectations. I'm excited and nervous, with no idea what to expect, but I *think* I am ready for it.

It is bound to be physically demanding, but I'm more concerned about being on my own. I have always been comfortable with solitude, but I will want *some* companionship travelling this foreign land, if for no other reason than to ensure I'm headed in the right direction.

If I'm honest, I'm hoping to ignite the spark I know is within me. Let go of past behaviours, find direction, learn to trust my instincts, and maybe find answers to questions I have buried. Before leaving home I told myself I would be open to anything the universe offers.

But first I need my caffeine and nicotine fix.

Repeating my order from last night, I decline the tortilla, and opt for the more inviting chocolate croissant beckoning me from the glass covered dessert tray. My carbohydrate loving brain appreciates a soul search that includes chocolate, but after a couple of bites I realize this isn't what my body is craving.

This will be a memorable trip, but not one I plan on sharing with the world. There won't be any Facebook posts, in fact other than my colleagues, family and a few close friends, no one knows where I am. My photo diary and journal notes will keep my story.

This little café in Pamplona is the ideal location to mark the start of Day 1, but my limited expertise in the art of *selfies* leaves me with a photo that lacks the confident vibe I'm hoping for. Truth be told, I look a bit terrified, with a tense, closed mouth smile. It's hard to ignore the fact that I am out of my element.

Time to get this show on the road.

Buff in place, I look like a cool biker chick, until I add the backpack, iPod and stuffed bunny. Now the cool chick is replaced by an overloaded, middle-aged, barely experienced hiker. That's more like it. All I'm missing is my goofy sun hat. By 9:15 am I am starting toward last night's path.

Here we go!

The shortcut through the park connects me to the Camino Frances. By starting in Pamplona, I shaved off about 80 kilometres. More importantly, I avoided crossing the Pyrenees mountains. Pilgrims can start their journey anywhere along the route, making it easier for those who have less time to commit to the experience. Happy with my decision to start here, I just need to continue through the expansive green space, keeping my eyes peeled for the connecting street.

All guidebooks reassure that the locals are happy to help should I lose my way. They are the shepherds herding the peregrino sheep, pointing towards the right direction. Slowing my pace to refer to my online map, I see two elderly gentlemen notice my hesitation and ask, "Camino?"

As I point to the street I suspect is my turnoff, they nod in confirmation.

"Gracias Señors," I reply with a big smile. All I need to do now is follow the signs.

The sidewalks of Pamplona are lined with silver disced scallop shells, the emblem of St. James the Great. As I walk through well-manicured parks towards the outskirts of the city, the discs are replaced with large stencils in blue and yellow. Everything is laid out for me: it's impossible to get lost.

Gently rolling farmland appears in the distance, rising towards the mountains. Alone on the street, I stop and tilt my face towards the sky. "Thank you for this opportunity."

My goal today is Puente la Reina. According to my guidebook it is 20.1 km, taking an estimated 5.5 hours. It's in print so must be accurate. My FitBit is hooked to the waist of my shorts, accessible for monitoring how far I've travelled. According to my calculations I should arrive around 4 pm, allowing for breaks and lunch. *Seems manageable enough to me.*

I brought along an iPod thinking some tunes would provide a taste of home, as well as help me decompress at the end of the day, but the ear buds keep falling out. Frustrated, I let them dangle in front of my ears. The faint background music is motivating, an occasional song's reference to walking, journeys and following your heart.

Thank you. I'm listening.

Through the rural areas I have to rely on the more informal indicators: yellow spray painted arrows on light poles, wooden posts, and large rocks. One arrow missed and I could be walking in the wrong direction.

The mountainous range becomes more visible in the absence of the morning mist, but I am not intimidated. Instead, I admire the view as I enter Cizur Menor. According to my FitBit, I have already walked 5 km.

A nearby *tienda* awakens my hunger, the partial chocolate croissant long gone. Near the cash is a basket of fruit. Perfect! With two nectarines, an apple and orange, I devour the first before even reaching the neighbouring church bench. The relief is immediate as I remove my pack. *Take a seat, Lizzie.*

The second nectarine goes down as quickly, along with a full bottle of water. My remaining fruit rests at the top of my pack for easy access, should I get hungry down the road. The cool water from the fountain refills my supply.

The trail out of Cizur Menor is rough with loose pebbles, winding aimlessly through open fields. With the terrain flat and unchallenging, it is *almost* like being out for a mid-morning stroll. The 24-pound pack on my back is a reminder that I will be walking for more than a day.

With every step, the view shifts, the mountain more defined. There are plenty of stone markers directing me onto a paved road, then back into the fields. August is supposed to be one of the busiest months for walking the Camino, but I am on my own until I arrive in Zariquiegui, only 10 km into a planned 20 km day.

Even though the walk is manageable, it's no longer flat, the path climbing. As the sun rises higher in the sky, my back becomes sweaty beneath my pack. *This isn't going to be as easy as I thought.*

Whenever I find a bench, a rock or anywhere else that accommodates the seated position, I pit stop. There's still quite a way to go until Alto del Perdón, where the large metal sculptures grace the top of the mountain.

Fortunately, I'm starting to see a few more people, catching up with a group of five women from France. The French language distracts me from the ever-increasing incline, as Audile tells me how she and her friends take a week each summer to walk a section of the Camino.

"Europeans tend to break the Camino into more manageable chunks; either a week or two each summer, or half the trip one year and the remainder another." Proximity is beneficial for those who can't take a month off work.

When I stop for a short break, Audile continues on with her friends. This is no longer an easy walk, and my pace has slowed as my heart rate increases, my breath a little harder to catch. My frequent breaks have brought me in pace with Vicky, who lives in Pamplona.

Fluent in English, she pronounces her name *Bicky*, reminding me of the lesson I learned in my Spanish course. With her sun umbrella in one hand and the flowers she has picked in the other, she tells me that she too will spend a week walking 20 km each day.

"My husband drops me off in the morning and then picks me up at my destination in the afternoon." Today we are heading to the same place.

She is relaxed in her manner, without a backpack to carry and only her water bottle on a belt around her waist. It is as though we are travelling different routes. I am hot, tired and finding the hills a real challenge, but her pace is even, with only the shade of her umbrella on her back. Our English conversation helps to bridge the distance from home.

Both Audile and Vicky were happy to meet a Canadian, asking questions about why I chose this journey and if I planned to walk all the way to Santiago. The first is difficult to answer, but the second is a determined, "Oh yes, absolutely."

Intent on keeping myself going, I lower my head in focus, my poles moving in tandem with my tired legs. I am not the only one struggling, sharing glances with a woman carrying her own large pack, a tall wooden walking staff supporting her efforts. Even with her bandaged knee, she continues to move one foot in front of the other. With only a shared "Buen Camino," a nod and smile, we silently acknowledge the challenge. We are simply two women praying we make it to the top.

Bombarded with thoughts of my naïvety, I didn't think it would be this difficult. I had hiked through the woods with a pack on my back, but this climb to Alto del Perdón is brutal. Between the heat, no lunch, and the exertion, I am stopping often.

My FitBit shows *only* 12 km as I crest the peak. *What in the world was I thinking when I thought this was a good idea?* But I can be an all-or-nothing gal. If I am lost, I'm going out to find my-

self and I'm taking the long, gravel road to do it. This isn't armchair introspection.

The sight at the top of Alto del Perdón makes every racing heartbeat worth the effort. Wind blowing through the larger than life metal figures at the edge of the cliff celebrate my arrival. The scripture highlights the celestial route of this journey: *Donde se cruza el camino del viento con el de las estrellas.* Loosely translated: "where the wind crosses the stars."

A large stone monument provides a place to rest and soak up the view. The beautiful Navarra valley is nestled below the majestic line of wind turbines. On my left, beside the descending trail, is a mobile canteen. Impressive business model. Everyone will need a cold beverage after *that* climb and I indulge in my first Coke while chatting with Vicky.

What goes up, must come down. The climb up was a wicked cardio workout so I'm hoping the trip down is easier on my body. A beautiful, tanned woman athlete arrives at the top of the hill, stands in front of the sculptures to have her photo taken, and then *jogs* down the opposite side. *How hard can it be?*

Relishing my achievement in a way that permits me to delay walking, I wish Vicky an "Adiós Amiga." Once I have talked myself into moving again, I start descending the very steep, loosely stoned path. The struggling peregrina I had passed on the way up is right behind me. We are both taking our time, watching our footing, relying on our poles for support. Descending is different, but not any easier. My new Brazilian friend seems to agree, taking each step with caution.

With my minimal Spanish and non-existent Portuguese, and Andreia's limited English, we attempt conversation. She is obviously hurting, so I *try* to offer her some of my lifetime supply of Aleve, but she appears to be well stocked with medications. When she says, "The Camino is speaking to me," I sense we are on a similar journey.

We continue to pass one another, once sharing a brief conversation with a chipper fellow from Barcelona. With only a daypack on his back, he tells us he is having his backpack transferred to his evening destination. No longer able to keep up with the conversation, I bid them both "Buen Camino" and hang back to stop on a bench.

I need a break, some fuel, and a moment to contemplate how I'm doing on my first day.

There are a couple of albergues in Muruzábal and I am drained, but this would be two towns before my planned destination of Puente la Reina. An executive decision is made while stopping for refreshment at a young boy's lemonade stand outside of Obanos. Puente la Reina will have to wait until tomorrow.

I am done for the day.

The heaviness of my pack has been dragging me down these last 5 km. Only slightly disappointed, I accept that plans are only guidelines. I'm not going to beat myself up over shortening my first day: the Camino has done that for me. By the time I stop it is 4 pm. My excitement keeps me motivated, but the reality is that I am in for a bigger challenge than I expected.

Obanos is a small town with only a couple of streets and I stop at the first hostel I see. It is late enough in the afternoon that I expect at least *some* people onsite, but there is no one. A tiny older Señora opens the heavy wooden door of *Casa Rural Mamerto*, inviting me into the dark and eerily quiet stone building.

As she opens the door to my bedroom, she states the price, which I really don't understand until I hand over 27 euros from my money belt. The cost is more than double the expected rate for a bed to sleep in, but I have more than a bed. I have a private bedroom, bathroom and shower. If I've understood correctly, the included dinner is at 5 pm. Thank goodness, because I've expended way more calories than I consumed.

Washed and sporting my little red dress, I wait in the dining area and write in my journal to pass the time, keeping one eye on the wall clock. The minutes are ticking past, the hostel deathly quiet. There are no dinner smells, no sounds of movement, no sign of my Señora to confirm the dinner hour.

At 6:15 pm I admit I have misunderstood, and return to my room for my water, apple and Clif Bar. Back through the darkened halls, I exit the heavy front door. There isn't even anyone outside, but a bench in the empty church yard has my name on it.

In the absence of others, I feel as though I am the first to arrive in an expedition.

Eating *my dinner* under the shade of a tree, I reflect on my day. *You got through Day 1.*

Now is the perfect time to email Pierre. He'll be waiting to hear how I am doing and I have plenty of news to share, along with some incredible photos.

According to my trusted FitBit, I walked 22 km in the scorching heat, carrying more than 24 pounds on my back. With all my necessary pit stops, it took 7 hours. It shouldn't have taken as long as it did, but the terrain was difficult at times and I stopped often. Sometimes I used my exhaustion as an excuse to have a fresh air break. More than once I had to call upon my inner strength to convince myself that I could continue, having more than my usual conversations with myself.

Not yet 8 pm, I pop an Aleve and crawl under the cool sheets. The sun burn and body aches start to disappear as I doze off. The sounds of muffled voices and dishes clanging wake me. A radio plays softly down the hall. *Dinner was included.* I contemplate getting dressed and joining them, but I lack the confidence to venture into the dining room.

A note on the mental checklist: the Spanish dinner hour is much later than what I am used to.

Day 2
22 km
August 5, 2015

Without an alarm set, my body awakens once it is recovered, and yet an attempt at stretching out my core and limbs alerts my brain receptors to the assault I endured yesterday. *How did I expect to feel?* My out-of-shape body is in shock. A groan escapes as I reach for the bottle of Aleve on the night table, smiling to myself.

Day 2.

The quiet road is lit with sunshine when I exit the empty hostel at 7:30 am. Down the street I notice an albergue busy with activity as pilgrims begin their day. With a wave and an enthusiastic "Hola Amigos," I am on my way smiling from ear to ear. *At least I'm ahead of a few people this morning.*

With new found energy, I am planning a 26 km day towards Ayegui, to make up for yesterday's lost ground. Fuelled with resolve and little research about the day's terrain, I don't even question why I think today will be easier, when I barely got through yesterday.

Puente la Reina is only a couple of kilometres away, bringing me through those hills I looked upon yesterday morning, the patterned green and wheat carpet dips and rises on the horizon. As the landscape shifts between open paths through crops, and narrow dirt trails in high fields, my energy increases. With only a few people on the trail, I have Mother Nature's splendors to myself.

Sunlight has yet to filter through to the dark alleyways of the narrow cobblestone streets of Puente la Reina. Flashbulb memories of a 30-year-old visit to Paris' French quarter come to mind, a one-time visit during a whirlwind tour through neighbouring countries in 1986. I carried a backpack then too, but relied on the train and a Eurorail pass for transportation.

The pit in my belly from last night's Camino dinner had gone unnoticed in my excitement for the new day. As I enter a café, the warmth from the ovens and sweet smell of fresh baking awakens my hunger. The conversational buzz of the locals reminds me I am not at home. Quick to learn some key tricks, I order a larger coffee. "Grande por favor."

With a smile, the plump Señora behind the counter replies, "Si, no problemo."

Fantastico! I'll use it to wash down that tasty looking cinnamon roll.

Seated at one of the tall bistro tables outside, I settle myself and enjoy the ambiance as I watch my fellow pilgrims trek by. A young man exits the café with his own breakfast and limps towards me. "May I join you?"

Always eager to make acquaintances, I don't hesitate to reply. "Of course." Conversations often begin with a first name and nationality introduction, followed by "Where did you start?" Fernando, Lorenzo…something *O*, began in Saint-Jean-Pied-de-Port, and crossed the Pyrenees.

"The scenery is truly breathtaking...but challenging. And now I am walking with my injuries."

We trade cigarettes and compare emergency snacks. He generously offers me one of his granola bars for backup. Although not surprised by the camaraderie, I am partial to the easy conversations on the trail. Compared to life at home, these pilgrims are not too busy to say hello or introduce themselves to strangers. Everyone I have seen so far has offered a wave, a smile and "Buen Camino," the pilgrim greeting of "have a great journey."

Only Day 2, and I am already benefiting from the friendships.

Leaving Puente la Reina under the historical stone arch, I make my way onto the bridge, only to stop halfway to absorb the stillness of the water and the treed rolling mountains. The bridge was built in the 11th century to ease the crossing for those en route to Santiago. This trail for salvation started sometime in the 9th century, the routes adapting over the years. It is humbling to follow a path travelled by so many. There is sure to be lingering energy from the 100,000 seekers who walk it each year.

A crystal blue sky hints at the need to apply more sunscreen and my Buff. My skin was a little tender last night, and with a lack of cloud cover today, I'm anticipating another high 30s afternoon scorcher. Knowing how goofy I'll look, I reluctantly retrieve my new sun hat from the exterior pocket of my backpack. Through farm lands and changing terrain, the fruit laden trail widens, the dirt and pebbles rough beneath my feet.

I am meeting some wonderful people so far, although no North Americans, but I wear my flags proudly on my pack and hiking boots. On more than one occasion this morning I heard, "Oh, you're Elizabeth from Canada."

There is no denying the increase in elevation towards Mañeru. The most challenging section is a narrow path nestled between a wall of rock and a treeline. Walkers and cyclists alike pull into the trees to take a much needed rest period. It's not the increase of pilgrims that slows the pace: it's the difficult climb. Short of breath and starting to feel an unwelcome strain on my knees, I am not alone in my struggles, silently sharing the misery with an older Australian man walking with his wife. We have no desire for pleasantries, only a nodding acknowledgement of distress, his red face mirroring mine. As he winces with each step, I silently thank him for making me feel better about my own suffering.

Head lowered towards the rocky trail, I stop every couple of minutes to slow my racing heart. The heat is unbearable and combined with my limited oxygen, I am starting to worry about passing out. Thoughts of heat stroke and cardiac arrest cross my mind, no longer confident I can make it to the top. Yesterday's hike to Alto del Perdón was easy compared to this.

Relief washes over me as I reach the top, stopping yet again, too exhausted to celebrate the small victory. *Can I keep this up?*

There is no one on the street as I approach town, so I follow the arrow and cross the road completely, right onto the highway. Over the tunes playing near my ears, I can faintly hear something, and turn my head over my right shoulder. With their arms waving frantically, the Australian couple are yelling, "You're going the wrong way!"

Seems I misinterpreted the

yellow arrow.

Back on the route, the Australian couple somewhere ahead, I take advantage of the first water fountain and accompanying bench. I need to steady my nerves as I contemplate what has just happened. *What if they hadn't seen me?*

In and out of Mañeru, the paved road is tucked between rock cliffs on my right and crops on my left. Through and out of fields, I need to pay attention to the signs directing me across the farmers' roads, keeping the haystack in sight as a temporary focal point. Cirauqui is up ahead, completing a 450-metre climb.

My food intake since arriving in Spain has been limited and lacking nutritional sustenance. I need to refuel desperately, feeling weak after this morning's workout. I eat my first bocadillo. It is similar to a sub sandwich with cheese, tomatoes and bacon, although I discreetly removed the meat. I also drink my second Coke since yesterday. I have already consumed more soda in two days than in the last twelve months. This is becoming my go-to beverage when I need a sugar boost.

The older Australian couple with bad knees have arrived ahead of me. I join them at their table and thank them for rescuing me from the highway. With my sandwich settling nicely in my belly, I order a second Coke to bring outside.

At the next patio table is a Swedish mother and her daughter. Mom joins me with her own post-meal cigarette. While her daughter goes in to use the washroom, she leans towards me in confidence. "I would have preferred to travel alone as well, but my daughters didn't think it was safe." Her girls were taking turns walking with Mom. There would be a sibling hand-over in a week or so.

Coming along the trail in the opposite direction is a scruffy, blond haired fellow, who stops to join us and have a drink from his bottle. My curiosity is piqued. "Where are you travelling from?" Having already reached Santiago, he is returning to Saint-Jean-Pied-de-Port.

Really?

With a tired smile he admits, "It's a little more difficult to follow the path back, as there are no yellow arrows."

I am shaking my head in disbelief as he leaves us, less than a week away from a round trip, 1600 km Camino. I'm having a hard enough time going one way, I can't imagine the determination it must take to loopback. Sounds crazy to me, but many people thought I was nuts attempting this. They may not have been too far off the mark.

The meal and conversation has boosted my energy level. With an "Adiós" to my new acquaintances, I continue on alone, mentally and physically stronger than when I arrived.

I meet up and happily keep pace with an older man from Galicia, the region I'll pass through before arriving in Santiago. His English is excellent, the company helping to pass the time and kilometres. Our last stop together is in a street level concrete alcove beneath an apartment building. The shelter is outfitted with a couple of vending machines, wobbly plastic patio chairs and two small tables. Most inviting is the shaded coverage from the inferno I've been walking through.

I am exhausted, but he has already walked 35 km, not yet done for the day. I need to up my game, but this is no easy feat. It is more physically draining that I anticipated and I am out of my depth, the day not yet over. Chasing the craved Coke with an icy cold bottle of water, I restock my supply from the vending machine. I cannot afford to run out of water this afternoon.

The hills are more than I can handle, and I stop often and fight with myself to keep going. I had hoped to walk 26 km today, but that isn't going to happen. When I share my concerns with others, they reassure me that my body will get accustomed within a week. *I have my doubts.* My pack is heavy, I'm not eating well, and the temperature is set to Broil. Thoughts of why I am here keep rising to the surface. I keep moving, slowly, but even sporting my sexy hat, Mother Nature is wearing down my resiliency.

Close to Villatuerta, I begin to feel unsteady.

Up ahead the route turns and I slowly make my way to the stone marker. I have to stop. *Now!* In desperation, I pull off my pack and let myself slide to the ground. My energy supply is depleted and no amount of water is helping. I am unable to even consider how I am going to reach an albergue. Laying on the prickly sun-dried grass, I pull my hat over my face to hide my panic. Peregrinos approach to see if I am alright.

"No Problemo," I reply with a shaky thumbs up. "Muy bien, gracias."

Exhausted and fuzzy headed, I know I am in a precarious situation, in no shape to continue walking, but at risk if I stay under the full sun. Unable to think clearly, I keep my eyes closed and send a message simultaneously to Pierre and my Higher Power.

I know you are with me, but I really need your strength to get me through.

After several minutes of hazy contemplation, the sense of panic lessens and although weak, I am able to sit up and have a drink. *You cannot stay here!* Slowly rising to my feet, I gather my pack and poles. Maybe all I needed was a rest, but I think I received an answer to my prayer. I feel a bit stronger physically, but my confidence is dragging. *I can't do this each day.*

I see Villatuerta in the distance. *You're almost there.*

There is only one albergue in town and I need to find my way to *La Casa Magica*. Unsure where I am headed, I stop at a shaded park to ask some other pilgrims for directions. Out of the sun, the relief is immediate, planting myself beside a young couple from France. Seeing my Canadian badges, they smile knowingly.

"You must be Elizabeth from Canada!" I am probably the only Canadian they have met. We compare walking strategies. Mine is to keep going, with multiple breaks, until I can't go any further. So far I've had a game plan in the mornings, but am realizing I need to be flexible.

"We walk about 20 km, then look for a shaded area like this where we can have a siesta. Once we feel rested, we continue perhaps another 10 to 15 kilometres, depending on the distance to the next town."

They are younger, but then I think of my Galician friend in his 60s, walking more than 35 km a day. I couldn't go any faster or further if my life depended on it. Hanging out with my peregrino peeps, the companionship and cool grass is like a much needed hug. I wouldn't mind stopping right here for the night. I'm out of the sun, I have friends and I really don't know if I can keep on walking, even just another few hundred feet to the albergue. But they will be packing up and continuing on and realistically, I can't spend the night in this little park. That would be absurd. My Magical House is only up the road.

You've stayed too long! There's that voice in my head. Reluctantly, I get up off the grass and say goodbye to the French couple. It has been a long day, much of it spent alone, and I am looking forward to spending the evening with others.

The ongoing question resurfaces like a teenage pimple: *Can I do this for the next 32 days?*

The albergue is tucked into the right-hand corner as the route turns left. Climbing the concrete stairs, I part the beaded entrance with my bulk, happy to be out of the sun once again. There is already another fellow at the desk, so I remove my pack and park myself on the wooden bench. The host turns away from his guest apologetically, looking at me.

"Do you have a reservation?"

Of course not.

Out of the corner of my eye I see the Australians, already showered and looking refreshed after their hard day. We share a wave, happy to know someone here. The host leaves the desk to have a quiet conversation with another volunteer. *Something is wrong.*

The pilgrim who waits patiently looks as beaten as I feel. Sweaty and sunburned, he removes his damp white tank top before pulling out his passports. Pre-work before you can flop onto your bed, is to show your national passport and have your credential (pilgrim passport), stamped and dated. My sweaty friend introduces himself as Uno from Denmark.

"I arrived a few minutes before you."

Once Uno is taken care of, he sits on the bench to await further instructions. The host turns to me and without too much regret, tells me my Magical House is fully booked. "I am sorry, but there is no space available."

There isn't even enough room for Uno, but they were able to find him a bed nearby.

If only.

I hadn't taken so many breaks.

Hadn't collapsed at the crossroad.

Hadn't stopped to enjoy the shade and company.

If only I had arrived 15 minutes earlier, the roles would be reversed and Uno would be wondering where he is going to sleep tonight.

Shock sets in. "What about the park? Am I allowed to sleep there?" It is cool, protected from the hot sun, not a far walk, and what other options do I have? I don't have a tent, only a sleeping bag liner, but my brain is fried and I am at a loss.

The host looks at me like I have two heads and hesitates. "I think so. But I can call you a taxi to take you to Estella," with a hint in his voice suggesting that makes more sense.

It's 4:30 pm and I am absolutely finished.

I heard discussions about a festival in Estella, a mini running of the bulls. What guarantee is there that I will find a bed this late in the afternoon? I can't walk anywhere else. I just don't have it in me. There is no longer a game plan and I can't think clearly. All I can grasp is that I don't have a place to stay. A deep rooted panic takes hold, my brain reeling.

I have no one to brainstorm with, no one to offer support, and the host seems to be getting impatient. Maybe it's just my interpretation of his body language, but I feel I am losing ground with his willingness to help me. The poor fellow is just doing his job. He sees thousands of pilgrims and this isn't the first time he's had to say *No Vacancy*. But I don't care about him. I need to clear the cobwebs and find a solution.

Poor Uno is exhausted and although looking remorseful having just stolen the last bed in town, is probably thanking his own Higher Power for getting here before me.

As I transition into survival mode, a crack of light from the depth of my brain sparks and I pull up the spreadsheet on my cellphone, searching for *Estella*. "Would you be willing to call these albergues to see if any have a bed?"

After three unsuccessful attempts, the last albergue on the list has a couple of beds left. Taking my passport, he makes a reservation. "Hale. Canada." When he hangs up, we all let out a sigh of relief and I fight back the tears. There will be no lonely, damp park for me tonight.

Satisfied that I am going to be alright, I thank the host for his help, give a weak smile to Uno and drag my backpack outside, knowing I am not a guest. Unsure of how long the taxi will take, I sit willingly on the bench outside the beaded door, back under the killer sun. The host comes out, encouraging me to wait inside.

There is a Higher Power at work.

My taxi pulls up at 5 pm. The air-conditioned ride is worth the 10 euros, plus tip, plus a kiss on the cheek after the driver carries my pack in for me. I just saved 4 km. Only my second day and I have taken a taxi. The *hospitalarios* know exactly who I am, offering hugs as they greet me. For 10 more euros, I get to share my bedroom with fifty other pilgrims and I couldn't be happier about it.

I have stopped for the day.

I have a bed for the night.

I have survived a second day on the Camino.

First order of business once I've claimed my lower bunk, is to wash off the day's sweat and dust. The communal showers are a change from last night's private bathroom. Refreshed and somewhat energized, I hand wash my clothes in the large sink. Uncertain how to access the outside clothesline, I reach through a tight window opening near the stove and hang them on the line. It's tricky, but my clothes are drying in the sun, a hint of someone's delicious dinner blowing through.

Embraced by the safety of the others, I could easily go to bed and sleep through until morning, but my weakness pushes me to find something to eat. The volunteers point me towards the main street, where I will have the most luck finding a restaurant open at this time, too early for the traditional Spanish dinner hour.

I don't have far to go, and although a surprise to the owner, he is more than happy to heat up a prepared pasta plate from his refrigerated display case. From my vantage point under the canopied patio, I watch the parade of locals dressed in their bright white shirts, black pants and vibrant scarlet red scarves.

When I return to my albergue, I sit on the park bench across from the front door. Legs crossed, I notice the toes of my left foot peeking through the top of my Crocs. This is the first time I have paid deliberate attention to my feet. The skin around the nail has reddened, but the nail itself has whitened, with a small pocket of pus beneath the cuticle.

Like a loose tooth, I give it a little wiggle. When it wiggles back my tummy pitches. I'm no doctor, but I am going to lose that toenail. Of the many aches and pains over the last two days, the toe reminds me of the uncomfortable sensation when descending the hills. My boots aren't tight enough, my feet sliding forward. It's a sensory overload, not having the stomach to deal with it right now.

Back inside and ready to call it a day, I let the volunteers know I was successful in finding a restaurant. They call over Hermann, a German peregrino, who was also inquiring about a place where he and his wife Alfdis, could have dinner.

Good deed done. Check.

Changed into my pyjamas, my liner and pillowcase unpacked, I lay down. My strength, courage and endurance is being tested, and I still have more than thirty days until I arrive in Santiago. I have come face to face with my ignorance. I wanted a challenging experience, but I am going to have to work for it.

The first one in bed, I expected the sheer exhaustion to pull me away quickly, but my legs are aching, my feet throbbing. I manoeuvre myself in my sleeping bag liner, but it's hard to find a comfortable position. Unable to turn off the mental replay of the day, I am still awake after many of the others come to bed.

God give me the strength to continue.

Day 3
22 km
August 6, 2015

The early morning sounds of my Estella roommates stir me to consciousness. As I take in the scene from the safe cocoon of my sleeping bag liner, I can see others contemplating their day from their own bunks, while more eager pilgrims dress and carry out their packs. Not yet ready to face Day 3, I assess my general well-being. The extreme conditions of the last two days have zapped my strength, leaving me feeling shaky and weak this morning. The sound of my belly growling reminds me that I don't have anything for breakfast, other than a Clif Bar. It's unrealistic to start each day on water alone.

Worming my way out of my liner, my heel catches on the soft stretchy material. There is an aggravated callus on the outside of my right foot, the dead yellow skin looking angry as it masks a reddish-orange bruise. Poking it confirms there's no discomfort. *It can wait.*

A more pressing issue is the state of my toenail that looks ready to separate from the nail bed. With an arsenal of coping behaviours at my disposal, the *Ostrich Stance* is often deployed when I feel anxious over something out of my control. With my head buried in the sand, I wrap my toe in a wad from my roll of emergency toilet paper, hoping it will mend before I remove my boots at the end of the day.

As I leave the albergue I catch sight of a fellow from last night's sleepover, and follow him down the road I travelled for dinner. As I cross the main street toward the yellow-arrowed path, I see Audile.

"How are you, Elizabeth?" She must notice something on my face, as she quickly offers her small pastry bag. "Here, have some."

Her empathy catches me off guard, but I tear a piece from the soft bun, thanking her. Under normal conditions, I would politely refuse the generous gesture with "thank you, but I am fine," but this was no time for pride. *I don't feel fine.*

The nearby gas bar is a chance to address my coffee craving. A twinge of homesickness surprises me. How many mornings did Pierre and I stop to fuel up on coffee before a day of riding? Taking my large coffee to the parking lot, I plant myself on the curb and pull out a Clif Bar. *Breakfast on the road.*

I've stopped for a bit too long. My generous friend and her companions are out of sight, but I am grateful to have seen her this morning. Unexpected pilgrim connections happen regularly, especially as I stop so frequently, but I enjoy their company for however long we are together. There's a good chance I won't see that person again, but I trust that if we are meant to reconnect, we will. I am a firm believer that even the people we meet briefly play a role in our life.

The universe must sense the urgency to reestablish my courage, as the morning's walking so far feels less arduous. With mountains still in view, the terrain is friendlier to my aching body. I am already feeling better when I meet Uno, the lucky recipient of the last bed in Villatuerta. We recognize each other right away and in a gentlemanly manner, he apologizes for leaving me stranded.

"Don't apologize. I kept stopping for a break. Yesterday was a difficult day... but it all worked out as it was meant to."

He, too, is travelling solo and neither of us feel the need to go into detail about why we are here. This isn't Camino dating. For Uno and me, it is simply an arena to get to know ourselves and each other, with the sole purpose of sharing the experience.

The many water fountains along the Camino offer a chance to engage with others, refresh myself, and take a few minutes to recharge. Pilgrims who have done their research are eager to reach the winery and *Fuente de Irache*, the famous dual fountain offering water *and* wine. Built into the stone wall of the *Bodegas Irache*, we are invited to quench our thirst. Regardless of the early morning, we are all lining up to fill our bottles.

The walking continues to be favourable and I'm feeling stronger as we pass beside ploughed fields of red earth, through vineyards and bushes, crossing paved roads to head back into the rural lands. The beauty and calm

of the earth and the company I am keeping, motivates me to keep walking. We can see for miles, the landscape wide open, inviting our arrival.

With limited options to escape the scorching sun, Uno and I head for the welcome coverage provided by stacked bales of hay. Time for an impromptu picnic. We combine snacks and enjoy a well earned rest, as we continue to get to know each other.

At ease in the other's company, we don't need to walk side by side. Uno continues at his own pace when I stop to take a photo or an additional break, knowing I will catch up. Without stating it, we are spending the day together.

The heat is relentless as we continue along the trail. There are no trees along the route, and limited amenities, but a large outdoor café beckons us from the dusty path. A refuge from the overhead grill, this mobile canteen offers a dozen canopied patio sets. Parched and needing my newly favorited sugar boost, I head to the canteen counter.

"Elizabeth!"

Turning toward the familiar voice, I see Andreia, seated with some friends. So far from home and I am already developing a small tribe of friends. With a wave and a smile-filled "Hola, Amiga," I return to the table Uno has secured, cold drinks in hand. He has already removed his boots and socks, and I follow his lead, my bare feet perched on an empty chair to inspect my toe. Still covered, it must be fine.

Andreia comes over to let me know that I'm getting burned, offering me her sunscreen. "Gracias, Amiga." I pull out my own supply, with a promise to re-apply the protection immediately. With a thoughtful gesture, she is watching out for my best interest, as any good friend would do.

In conversation with a group of peregrinos, one fellow eyeballs my pack. "It looks heavy!"

With a laugh, I confess. "It is... 24 pounds!"

He nods towards Bunny, still hanging over the shoulder strap. With a smile, he offers a well intended suggestion. "You may want to ship any unnecessary items home." Of course, I have to share the story of how I came to carry this gift and his response to it surprises me. "There are plenty of us to offer protection."

When Uno and I part ways, the timing seems perfect. He has more kilometres to travel and I will be ready to call it a day in the next town.

Just outside of Los Arcos, a trio of pilgrims lay on the grass beneath a large tree. Laughing in each other's company, they invite me to share the small shade they've claimed. Introducing themselves and their own newly formed friendships, they tell me they met on the Camino, but you wouldn't know that until they start talking. We share our experiences so far, and even though Antònio's English is limited, we are able to share the highs and lows we are all struggling through. My new Italian friend pulls out his iPad and starts taking group shots of the four of us, arm-to-arm on the grass.

Isn't it interesting how quickly strangers bond!

Los Arcos is up ahead and if I can find a bed, I'll be ending another eight-hour day on a positive note, satisfied with the 22 km showing on my FitBit. On the village's main street, I stop to sit on a bench and regroup before searching for an albergue. Within a few minutes, Andreia walks towards me, followed by the trio I left under the tree.

We exchange hugs. Our communication skills are primitive, and yet somehow they understand my anxiety over not having a reservation for the night. After yesterday's nightmare, the thought of full albergues worries me, but not enough to prompt me to call and book one. Without missing a beat, Andreia uses her own cellphone to book me a reservation.

We continue to all walk together and I see a sign for an albergue. Excited about the prospect of the five of us staying together, I point it out enthusiastically and Antònio volunteers to see if there is space. When he returns with a smile and a thumbs up, I am flooded with relief. But then, the light bulb slowly comes on... they won't be joining me. I had forgotten that the trio is not done walking for the day and Andreia's reservation doesn't even enter my mind.

The excitement quickly turns to dread, my anxiety rising as I consider entering the albergue on my own. I could keep walking and stick close to Andreia, but in my mind, that decision also leads to the unknown. There is a bed right here, right now. My goodbyes are hesitant as I leave them to enter the *Casa de Austria II – Fuente de Los Arcos*.

Should I have stayed with Andreia?

The albergue is a busy hive of activity, reminding me of Christmas when we would have a house full of relatives. Staking my claim to a lower bunk in a small bedroom, I head off to explore the main level. A few people are gathered around the dining room table playing cards, while others are taking advantage of the indulgent comfort of the sofas and armchairs in the living room. In the corner is a small bookshelf bulging with reading materials. A full wall near the door to the backyard is plastered in postcards from visiting peregrinos.

That's a great sign!

The backyard is sheltered from the sun. Wooden picnic tables, clotheslines and a long trough with running water and benches on either side, fill the space. Peregrinos are seated along the foot bath, the flowing cold water soothing their aching feet. This is definitely the place where I belong tonight, the nervousness I felt when I decided to stop here, slowly disappearing.

With the day's dirt washed away, and clean clothes hanging on the line, I sit in the garden to update my journal. Each entry starts with the date and the Day, the time I left and the time I arrived, as well as the kilometres walked according to my FitBit. Detailing the motions of my day, I write how I felt in the morning, the towns I travelled through, the events that occured and the people I met. As I read my written words, they help me understand the challenges, while giving me strength to anticipate another day.

Still early in the afternoon and with plenty of energy, I head out on my own to tour Los Arcos. The *Plaza de Santa Maria*, with it's 17th century buildings and row of restaurant options, is already bustling with activity, patrons filling most of the patio tables, musicians and dancers adding to the cultural ambiance. It is a hub of energy with no shortage of eateries.

The corner restaurant boasts spaghetti on their outdoor menu and comfort food is what I am looking for. A handsome older man is chatting in Spanish to the bartender, and although he doesn't look local, he is certainly fluent and comfortable with the fellow pouring his beer.

My server offers to bring out my meal. "Awesome, gracias."

The gentleman turns around with a big smile. "I haven't heard the word *Awesome* in a while!" Dave is *not* a regular. He and his wife Cathy are from the United States, walking the Camino with another couple. Inviting me to join them for dinner, I have the pleasure of two tastes from home: a delicious pasta meal and a side order of English conversation.

"We have our backpacks delivered each day, usually to a private albergue, so we can have a good night sleep and bathroom to ourselves."

Based on my limited yet varied experience, my preference is communal living...but there is *no* privacy.

When I finally return to the albergue, my belly is full and my heart lighter after an evening of laughter and conversation. To my surprise, I find Hermann and Alfdis, the couple from last night, enjoying a glass of wine in the backyard. As they share their bottle with me, we start getting to know each other. Once we cover the usual introductory topics, the conversation flows naturally and in no time it feels like we are old friends who have met up unexpectedly.

Alfdis suggests we soak our feet in the foot bath. While discussing our Camino struggles, I show off my toenail, the callous a new concern. The reddish bruise beneath the dead skin is home to a rather large blister. I don't think it requires draining, hoping the hardened outer layer will protect the tender bubble.

Feet soothed, Alfdis returns to their room to gather first aid supplies. She returns with blister pads and coloured strips of kinesiology tape, confident I will have enough supplies for the next few days. Her tenderness offers an emotional support I didn't realize I needed.

What an incredible day!

Things are definitely looking up and I don't think anything can stop me now.

Day 4
20 km
August 7, 2015

Tired from a restless night of aching limbs and a subpar mattress, I am not in the best shape this morning and in no rush to start moving.

From the edge of my bunk, I examine my feet. Looks like I now have twin toenail issues. The same toe on the *right* foot has a large white blister forcing the nail from its fleshy bed. The left toenail is just for show, hanging on by the cuticle at the top. There is no need to perform another wiggle test. I can tell the right toenail is not quite ripe and let's face it, I'm not ready to face morning surgery. Unsure of the protocol for nail loss, the toes are wrapped in toilet paper, the injuries out of sight. The callus has whitened, but as long as I don't poke at it, there is no pain.

Under the guise of slow preparation, I am stalling my departure with one last trip to the backyard with my coffee. Alfdis is enjoying her own cigarette before she and Hermann start their day.

"How are your feet this morning, Elizabeth?"

Still wearing my crocs, I raise my heel to show off my tape-covered blistered callus. The look on her face suggests concern. "Be sure to take off your boots and socks whenever you take a break." *Yes, Mom.* I certainly stop often enough, but I tend to keep my boots on...maybe fearing I won't put them back on again.

Pack organized, boots laced a little tighter, I feel awake thanks to the continental breakfast offered for a few extra euros. Happy to be in my own company, the now quiet *Plaza de Santa Maria* provides a peaceful corridor to think.

The solitude is part of what drew me to the Camino: the need to be alone, away from the demands of my day-to-day existence, with no expectations from anyone other than myself. This trip encourages me to disconnect from my commitments, while forcing me to look within. After only three days, I realize the importance of celebrating my achievements and accepting help when I need support. My thoughts are a work-in-progress this morning, scattering to the ground for the wind to fit together when the time is right.

There are pilgrims ahead of me and there will be more behind, but I'm walking at my own pace. Whatever the day brings, whether more isolation or company along the way, I am open to whatever the universe offers. It feels so good to release control and just let it happen.

But after my day of walking with Uno yesterday, I realize that sometimes I find the isolation of the Camino lonely. When the path is enjoyable and I'm not struggling or too deep in my thoughts, I wish I had someone to share it with. *Someone to talk to.*

Uno was just what I needed yesterday.

The overcast sky offers a comfortable temperature for walking. The achiness of my feet is enough discomfort to remind me how hard they are working to carry me along. As I walk through rows upon rows of miniature fruit trees, the soil beneath my feet is so dry it's cracked.

In a blink the landscape changes, taking me through wide open harvested fields of cut gold, the path of the tractor still visible, the neatly stacked bales awaiting collection. Mountain ranges ahead welcome me without threat.

How fortunate am I to be able to leave home and work for five weeks, to walk a foreign country in search of myself.

Morning selfies are full of smiles, turning my back to highlight the land ahead of me. My confidence has returned, but I still worry how I am going to manage walking... every day. This is much harder than I anticipated, but that may be exactly what I need.

There are more hikers on the path, but I don't feel the need to slow or increase my pace. A simple greeting is sufficient; my thoughts keep me company. Out of San Sol, the man-made trail of field stones and mortar provides a more stable footing, but like paved roads, there is less shock absorbency than the earth of the fields.

My knees jar on the descents, sharp skewers digging beneath my kneecaps. The physical strain over the last few days is catching up and going down hill is a painful experience.

As I work my way closer into the lush green mountains, the tips of the wind turbines are hidden in a thick mist.

The rocky path opens wider to make space for a garden of *sorrow stones*. I read about pilgrims bringing stones from home or collecting them along the way, letting them go when it feels right. These mini monuments have blossomed through the contributions of pilgrims, one stone at a time.

I, too, have had my share of losses, so I empathize with the need to release them and the welcomed opportunity to just let go. I picked up my own stone on the first day. I'm not sure why it drew my attention, but it did, and I carry it in the small outside pocket of my backpack where I keep my cigarettes. I never considered the extra weight; I felt it belonged with me.

The Navarra country has been energizing me with her fields of sunflowers and vineyards, but during one particularly steep climb, as my body leans forward into the hill, I feel my callus rip off my heel. My stomach flips upside down. With each step, the thick pad of skin scratches the tender raw flesh. I need to find a place to park myself *right now* and deal with whatever mess lies inside my boot.

Ever so gently I pull off my wool sock, avoiding tearing the skin any more. The blister has popped, draining the cushioning fluid, but the callus is still intact! Breathing a deep sigh of relief, I am able to keep moving forward.

The time passes quickly, and I arrive in Viana shortly before 2 pm. My day is done and yet I still have energy to enjoy my afternoon. The *hospitalarios* of the *Albergue Izar* welcome me with a sense of community and celebration. Many of these albergues are run by volunteers, some having walked the Camino themselves and therefore understand the exhaustion at the end of a day. A friendly smile goes a long way in making us feel at home.

Perhaps one day I'll be part of the welcoming committee.

All washed up, I leave my dorm quietly, respecting my weary roommates during their siesta. Following the laughter and conversation coming from the kitchen table, I introduce myself to an enthusiastic American with curly brown hair and an energy I can't resist. He is as delighted to make my acquaintance, introducing himself as Benny, a 30-year-old from California. We share similar comfort levels, opting for a hug instead of a handshake.

"My son's name is Ben, but I call him Bennykins".

With a beaming smile he surprises me. "You can call me Bennykins too, if you want!"

My new young friend, all love and cheer, is a free soul enjoying the ride of life. "Why don't you join me and my friends for lunch? They have prepared an authentic Spanish meal."

Uncertain how to respond to this unexpected invitation, I politely decline even though I am hungry. "Thanks very much, but I've already eaten. Next time!" Lack of confidence, uncertainty, or not wanting to impose... for some reason I retreated from the opportunity.

An icy cold bottle of water from the vending machine in one hand, and my pen, cellphone and pack of cigarettes balanced on my journal in the other, I step through the large patio door and into the enclosed outdoor seating area. In short order others come outside, including Andreia.

This is a first for us and our excitement is evident as we embrace, knowing we have time to get to know each other. It's hard to put into words the connection I feel towards this Brazilian woman. Maybe it's because I met her on the challenging climb to Alto del Perdón or because we see each other every day. Or maybe there is a simple explanation: *we were meant to cross paths so far from home.*

The language barrier only strengthens our desire to connect. In her broken English she explains her journey so far.

She began at the popular Saint-Jean-Pied-de-Port with her friend and travel companion, Sampaio. While crossing the Pyrenees, she sustained an injury that was serious enough to require a detour to the hospital in Pamplona. *If that had happened to me, I would have been rethinking the Camino.* Released from the hospital with a bandaged knee and a supply of medications, Andreia took a taxi *back* to where she had hurt herself and continued walking from there. Others might have continued walking from Pamplona or even gone home.

How many would have backtracked?

She is moving forward, somewhat slower and in agony much of the time, but always with purpose. Regardless of how she feels, she greets everyone with her contagious smile and positive energy. At such an early stage in my own journey, I'm in awe of her determination, faith and strength of character, honoured by the friendship she has offered me.

I remember her first words to me: "The Camino is speaking to me." Andreia intended to listen, growing as an individual, with no intention of letting the challenges beat her. She is facing her struggles as they appear and from what I can tell, takes these incidents as signs.

Sampaio comes out to join us, fresh from his shower, as does Carmen, an Italian woman now living in Spain. The conversation becomes a head-spinning blend of Portuguese, Spanish, French and when all else fails, English. Andreia is documenting her adventure and having a captive audience, asks each of us to share why we are walking the Camino.

"I'll go first!" The words came out before I realized it. "My name is Elizabeth and I'm from Canada. I'm 50-years-old, eager to see the woman I am and what I am made of. I want to see what the world has to offer and what I can offer in return. I feel blessed to have met such wonderful people, including each of you, and especially Andreia, who has inspired me since Día Uno." Covered in goosebumps, I have finally expressed my intention.

After each of us has taken our turn, I am moved by how inconsequential our native tongues are. As more pilgrims come out onto the patio, we invite them to join us.

Laurence is a well-travelled woman from France, who has walked the Camino before. Fluent in Spanish, she is able to join the conversation when I have to sit back and listen. Delighted to be able to practice my *Français* with her, I smile to myself when she corrects my grammar.

"Would you like to join me on the free walking tour of Viana, Elizabeth? We could go for dinner afterwards?"

The town square is busy with those anticipating the tour. While we wait for the guide to arrive we meet 30-year-old Anne, also from France. We are three solo travellers at different stages and ages of life. Impatient with the delay, Laurence makes us an offer too good to pass up. "I toured Viana on my last Camino. Let me take you to the ruins. You won't be disappointed."

Lost in the Parisian language, I follow Laurence as she walks us through the ruins of *La Iglesia De San Pedro.* A patient teacher, she happily explains in English, when I still don't understand. Beneath the weathered and aged ceiling frescos, I am transported back in time. She brings us to stand in front of the stone pillars and points out the unique mason signatures that have become part of history.

Visiting the ruins up close and personal. Check.

Most of the restaurants along the Camino offer a *Pilgrim's Menu,* a selection of main courses, a dessert, wine or water. Affordable prices allow the more adventurous palette a taste of traditional menu items. Hesitant to venture too far from the foods I know, I am eager to try their renowned sausage. Laurence takes matters into her own hands, once again.

"Our friend has never tried chorizo! Would it be possible for you to give her a little sample to taste?" Our waiter returns with enough that we can all share.

I like her hands-on attitude: *if you want something, ask for it.*

At ease with these lovely ladies and proud of my French conversational skills, I jump off the edge of my food comforts and order paella. Perhaps a bit too salty for my taste, but I am happy I tried two new foods today.

This has been the best day so far. A perfect blend of solitude, new friendships and experiences.

I am in love with the Camino!

Day 5
22 km
August 8, 2015

E ven though it's still dark outside, many of my bunkmates are preparing to start their day. Cellphone lights and the noise of backpack organization slowly wake me. With no concept of the time, I reach beneath my black tank pyjama top, into my bra, to check my FitBit. I started wearing my bra to bed in Estella, feeling insecure without support for my 50-year-old girls.

It's only 5:30 am, but I'm fully awake. With my feet planted on the floor, the body aches remind me of the day's expectations, and I'm relieved to feel slightly less wrecked than the other mornings.

Most of the early risers have already started on their breakfast, eager to get out onto the dark streets with their headlamps lit. I'm not so eager, needing time to mentally prepare, to procrastinate, and determine if there is any other way to have this experience... without walking.

Coffee in hand, I head to the already busy patio, taking ownership of a plastic chair. In the pre-dawn hustle, pilgrims gather their still-damp clothes off the racks. The air is fresh without the warmth of the rising sun, the black sky lit only by the glow of the stars above.

Some stop their packing to recline in chairs, or lean back on their elbows on the stairs, to admire the light show. Even with my neck starting to strain, I can't pull my eyes away. As the sky starts to lighten, we all return focus to the task at hand... mine is to sip my coffee and have a smoke.

My eye catches sight of a beautiful young woman in a pink athletic shirt, her long brown hair pulled back in a ponytail. Strong and quite capable of managing her oversized backpack, her facial strain suggests she is trying to keep it all together.

I recognize the look. *I've been there too.*

"Good morning. Your pack looks quite heavy."

She offers a slight smile, her German accent breaking the spell. "It's 28 pounds."

She manoeuvres it onto her back with ease. I would love to continue the exchange, if for no other reason than to see her smile, but this is not the time.

Ready to *prepare* for my own departure, I double check the Ziploc bag sitting at the top of my pack.

Logroño has a post office not far off the route, so with a ceremonial *Adiós Amigo*, I am going to ship home those items *I think* I can do without. The one long-sleeved shirt for cooler weather is still unworn. The temperatures don't warrant it. I'm not going to use the canvas duffle for the trip home, as I can pay to have my pack shrink-wrapped at the airport in Santiago. I'll keep my map book, but the others can go. I'm hesitant to send Bunny home, but I don't think I need any extra protection.

Today's goal of Navarrete begins with a 9 km walk to Logroño. The grey sky releases a welcome sprinkle of rain and after these few days under the hot sun, I'm thankful for the moisture. When the rain becomes heavier, I stop to cover myself with my poncho, feeling like a contortionist, my arms stretched backwards as I try to pull the length over my pack. *My guidebooks never mentioned training for rain gear application.*

Many of the concrete tunnels are adorned with encouraging graffiti. A large blue scallop shell with *Buen Camino* written at the bottom, fills the height of the wall near the exit.

There are plenty of vineyards, the purplish-blue fruit hang dangerously close to the parched earth, inviting a small sample. *Live in the moment, Lizzie. Savour those grapes that were destined to become Spanish wine.*

The woods are becoming my favourite environment, especially when I'm alone. In Mother Nature's warm embrace, I lose myself in the symmetry of the trees, the quiet path inviting self-reflection.

I am feeling strong and capable as I leave behind the Navarra region, and enter La Rioja, real wine country.

Taking shelter from the black sky, I pit stop at the Tourist Office to escape the confines of my poncho and have a smoke beneath the overhanging roof. My Brazilian friends, Andreia and Sampaio, have stopped for information and I wait for them so we can continue across the bridge together, into Logroño.

The headlights of oncoming cars reflect against the wet roads, a subtle sign that I have left the peacefulness of the trail. Although still not pouring, I am wet outside and sweating beneath my poncho, the extra layer twisting around and getting caught up between my legs.

In front of a church, Andreia suggests we take our first trio selfie. Although we don't understand each other all that well, it doesn't stop our attempts at communication. Affection is our language. *How is it possible to feel so connected to strangers?*

Our arrival into the city square is marked by tables of vendors. Fresh breads and pastries, fruits and produce, artisan crafts and books… it makes me think a bit of the Byward Market in Ottawa. If I wasn't so interested in lightening the weight on my back, I might do some shopping. Instead, I ask for directions to the post office.

With a big smile, I hand over my stuffed Ziploc bag to the clerk. "Please send this home." Paperwork completed, bag weighed and padded envelope labelled, I am 1.2 kilos lighter and it only cost me 23 euros. I thought it would be more than 2.5 pounds, but my pack *does* feel lighter.

Bye-bye Bunny! See you in a month.

The Logroño street markers differ from the silver sidewalk discs in Pamplona. They are an imperfect yellow arrow above a scallop shell, and the design of the shell resembles a cloth sack, knotted to a wooden stick. *The backpack from years gone by.*

The path takes me through a children's playground and a well-manicured green space with a man-made pond. Time to rest on the bench and watch the ducks and swans frolic.

More graffiti… a concrete wall beside the road is decorated with a larger than life yellow arrow mimicking the Logroño sign. Through another tunnel, a hand painted map identifies the towns and cities along the route to Santiago. Someone took the time and put their artistic skills toward celebrating the peregrino journey.

Out of town the trail continues towards the lake, where locals are fishing from the roadside. There are more ducks and swans near the entrance to the woods, this time in their natural habitat at the shallow edge. Quietly, I approach a mother duck and her ducklings as they make their way out the water and along the Camino trail. The swans gracefully dip their long necks down into the water, diving out of sight, returning to break the surface. I am mesmerized and taking photos. A woman beside me asks, "Do you have swans in Canada?" She probably thinks I have never seen one.

"Oh yes we do, but I never expected to see any here!"

While taking an extended break, the young pink-shirted woman from this morning's albergue walks by, recognizing me right away.

"Hello again. My name is Elizabeth."

Joining me on the bench, she gives herself a rest. "It's nice to meet you, Elizabeth. I'm Melanie from Germany. I am sorry, my English is not that good."

"Your English is great actually! I was hoping I would get a chance to meet you again."

After covering the introductory questions, we continue chatting as we walk together, headed towards the same town. She is hesitant to speak in English, but I offer plenty of encouragement *and* practice. Other than counting to five, my German is nonexistent. Over the next 10 km we share our journeys to date.

A 34-year-old primary teacher, Melanie started in Saint-Jean-Pied-de-Port. Our conversation covers a wider range of topics than I have shared with anyone else. When she stops with me during my smoke breaks, I know she is enjoying the company as much as I am.

Melanie began this journey with her best friend. She hadn't planned to walk the Camino alone.

Last night her friend dropped a bombshell, announcing that they would *not* be continuing together. Her *best friend* had met a younger fellow she preferred to spend her time with. As quick as that, Melanie is now walking the Camino on her own. Giving her the space and time to share her story, I offer a suggestion to consider.

"Perhaps you're meant to take this journey alone!"

As we approach Navarrete, an older local gentleman stands in the middle of the dirt road handing out flyers. Accepting the pamphlet, our attention is diverted to his small stand of juice and cookies. We grab a couple of juice boxes and some snacks, giving him a few euros for his generosity. The flyer advertises a private albergue *"like no other."* Looking at each other, we shrug our shoulders and smile. *Why not?*

The owners of the *Albergue El Cantaro* have converted their home into a pilgrim lodging. Fewer people per room, a full private bathroom stocked with shampoo and conditioner—we've won the lottery. There is even a small kitchen for our own use, not that I've bought anything to cook or eat. In the 6.5 hours it took me to walk 22 km, I've only had breakfast and the snacks we bought at the roadside. Lunch seems to be the meal I keep missing and I'm taking advantage of the early hour to search out a place to eat.

With map in hand, I manoeuvre my way through the maze of tall houses and narrow streets. It's like walking inside one of those hand-held Dollar Store games I used to buy for my kids when they were young, hoping to keep them occupied for all of five minutes. Only brave enough to venture as far as needed, I spot a restaurant hidden on a lower street. It's a busy place, and the regulars are sitting at the bar watching a soccer game on the small mounted television. Not yet comfortable enough to mingle with the locals and preferring a quieter space, I retreat to the patio with my bocadillo and cold bottle of Coke.

I'm certainly getting better at eating alone. I'm in no rush to leave, simply enjoying the environment. When I return to the albergue, I take the time to update my journal from the comfort of my lower bunk. *Feels like I'm at camp!*

Melanie wants to take part in a church service whenever possible and I definitely want to experience at least one Pilgrim mass. With enough time for a quick dinner, we enter a small eatery just as they are opening. We're the first and only patrons but the waiter, who speaks no English or German, reassures us that it's not too early to get a meal, even though the chairs are still on top of the tables.

That should have been a sign.

Even though Melanie speaks no Spanish, I am confident I can order for the both of us, trying to explain to our server that she is a vegetarian. Without my Spanish-English dictionary or my cellphone, and no pilgrim menu to choose from, I am resorting to hand gestures to let him know she can eat fish. Suffice to say both meals are very unappetizing; undercooked mystery food leaves us needing additional prayers.

It doesn't take many steps into the old church, before my nose picks up on the mustiness of the air. The locals are dressed in their best, using the time before Mass begins to chat with their neighbours. Melanie and I head into the first empty pew, but I feel like an intruder. This is the first time I've been to a church service in many years.

Although I can't sing along to the hymns, the familiar tunes ease my anxiety. I don't believe I need to be in a church to commune with God, but I offer my gratitude for bringing Melanie and me together.

The Pilgrim mass follows the regular service, the priest inviting all of the peregrinos to stand at the front. After stating our first name and nationality, he prays for us, blessing each of us with a Spanish prayer, his hand resting on our head. The goosebumps rise on my arms.

This feels right.

At the end of the service the priest invites his peregrino congregation into closed chambers, to admire the church's collection of old documents and artifacts. If I had a better understanding of religious history it would be educational, but even with my ignorance I feel privileged to be here.

Back at the albergue, a few of us are gathered around the kitchen table when the doorbell rings. No one makes any motion to get up, so I take it upon myself to answer the door. On the other side is a sweaty Irishman in search of a bed. He hasn't made a reservation for tonight and there was no answer when he tried calling.

"Come on inside." As he stands in the entrance, I can't help but ask. "How far have you walked?"

"I'm an ultimate runner. I travelled 70 km today."

"Seriously?"

Using my own cellphone, I reach the owners and attempt to express the urgent need. I'm not sure they realized I was calling from the other side of the wall, but there isn't any room for negotiation. *The albergue is closed.*

Ours is the last lodging before leaving Navarrete and this Irish athlete looks exhausted. Tempted to sneak him in regardless of the owners refusal, he could sleep on the floor if there wasn't a spare bed. I could even be convinced to share my lower bunk with him. After he showers.

"Thanks for your help! I'll run back through town and see if I can find a bed in any of the other albergues."

Day 6
22 km
August 9, 2015

Something is wrong.

Between going to bed last night and waking up this morning, I've lost my courage.

In order to make it to Santiago in time, I'll need to walk more than 22 km each day. I'm obviously not against using transportation if I feel I need to, but with the wisdom of fifty years, I know I won't kill myself to complete this trip. Realistically, I don't think I can walk any more each day than what I'm already doing, especially with the increasing torture to my knees. The down hill descents are taking a toll on my joints and my spirit. My feet are constantly aching and now my legs throb at rest, as though they are still working to keep me going.

Last night's dinner can't be counted as a meal and I'm starved this morning. *I should have shopped for some breakfast items.* The negative self-talk isn't helping; only confirming how inadequately prepared I am.

Not yet out of bed and I don't want to go; my heart is just not on the Camino this morning. How am I supposed to stay strong and motivated to walk another 20 km? And what about tomorrow? And the day after? I've barely started... can I do this for another 28 days?

What the hell is wrong with me this morning? I had a great day yesterday. The walk was long and my body struggled, but I felt good when I finally stopped. For some reason, I woke this morning beneath a dark cloud of dread.

Melanie is in no rush to start her day; we have reversed our morning practices. Being alone will give me time to sort through my thoughts. *I hope.*

For the first two hours I'm tormented by the physical pain. Every step I take, every knife pierce in my knees as I descend a hill, every rip of the blister on my heel as I climb, screams at me. Not so subtle signs.

I'm an emotional mess, and I struggle to move forward. Literally. My pace is slow and reluctant, my body too heavy to carry. My physical state mirrors the storm I feel brewing inside. I've barely started my day, so I'm not sure where this is coming from, but it's impossible to ignore. The lump in my throat hints at my need to cry, but the tears are blocked.

You don't have to be strong for anyone right now. There's no one around, so just sit down, have a smoke and just let it out. My fears, doubts, anxieties, loneliness, insecurities; everything I've bottled up needs release. I cry, but not enough. There's more to come, I can feel it. The sky echoes my feelings, bright blue spots hidden behind the heavy dark grey clouds.

I need someone to talk to.

Moping through the first 7 km, there are no other pilgrims in sight. By the time I arrive in Ventosa, I'm hoping to fuel my hunger and desperate need for companionship. Alone at an outside table, I see Andreia and Sampaio come up the hill, smiling and waving. Their timing couldn't be better, my hugs tight as I hold on a little longer than usual. When I let go, their eyes linger in understanding. While they are inside ordering, Melanie arrives.

In all my reading and researching, the one sentiment that always surfaced was *the Camino provides*. The timing of these strangers-turned-friends allows a glimpse of light to shine on my heart. As we sit around the small patio table, my cellphone beeps. My youngest son Ben, my baby, my Bennykins, has emailed me.

"Proud of you mom, make that mountain your bitch. This is only the beginning, so keep your chin up. Priority number 1 is enjoying yourself, so make sure to stop and smell the roses every now and again. Remember it's just a big hill and hills aren't scary. Sending all the positive vibes your way. Stay strong."

As I read his unexpected, divinely-timed message, the dam of pent up emotions bursts. With blurred vision I read his email a second time.

What are the chances of his note arriving now?

I believe Ben is an old soul and we share a connection that he may not even realize. One stormy winter night 20 years ago, my Mom called to break the news that she had found Dad on the bedroom floor. Shocked and in disbelief, I had to wait until morning to go *home*. With no hope of drowning my sorrow in sleep, I climbed into bed with Ben, spooning his little body that faced the wall. His arm came over to rest on my hip. It seemed like an automatic response, but it couldn't have been a comfortable position for my 3-year-old son.

Dad was sending me a message: *everything would be alright*.

I need to share Ben's words with my friends, not even caring if they understand. My tears let loose again, while they hold me tight. There's no need for words.

Our sandwiches are eaten in silence, but my head starts to clear and the heaviness in my chest lightens. And then the sun starts to shine through the clouds. It's all too surreal, but I'm living this experience.

A small cargo van pulls up beside the restaurant and Melanie doesn't hesitate to see what pastries she can purchase for a couple of euros. I'm inspired by her ability to just go after whatever she wants and I follow her lead. From the the open doors at the back of the van, the smell of fresh baking is the last nudge my mood needs to recalibrate. With too many choices, I end up buying only one soft, still warm cinnamon bun for an afternoon snack.

With their meals consumed, my friends leave before me. They know when I light another cigarette, I want time alone. Now that I am feeling so much better, I want to try and process what happened this morning. Not just the email from Ben, but the thoughts that consumed me and left me feeling so dark and alone. One thing is certain: my spirit is brighter.

The 10 km to Nájera pass quickly enough as I decipher my thoughts. Before I can even think about stopping for a snack, Melanie steps out of a café doorway and calls to me. She's been waiting an hour for me to arrive.

She doesn't take as many breaks as I do, but when she finds herself a restaurant or bar, she'll ask for the WiFi, and send emails and *WhatsApp* status updates, while enjoying a snack and a cold drink. I don't think she usually spends an hour doing it, but something encouraged her to hang around until I walked into town. So early in our friendship, we already feel the mutual benefit being together offers.

My belly rumbles at the sight of a glass display case of appetizers. I order a couple of chunks of baguette topped with cream cheese, tomato, olive oil and spice. So fresh and tasty... I could eat half a dozen, but at least I have something in my tummy to tide me over until dinner.

Whenever that might be.

"If you are thinking of stopping in Azofra, perhaps we should call and reserve a couple of beds." In addition to the lingering fear of having no place to sleep, I really don't want to be alone tonight. Melanie's on board, but speaks no Spanish, so it's up to me to call the municipal albergue. Scribbling a few sentences of Spanish on a napkin, I hope it translates into, "I'd like to reserve two beds for tonight."

Nervous energy runs through me as I wait for the line to pick up. I'm not sure if my question is grammatically correct, but once I start talking the young woman on the other end offers to ease our communications. "Why don't you speak in English."

With beds for tonight, the pressure is off. "High Five."

Reservations made. Check.

Melanie is quicker on the down hills, almost with a hop to her step, but slower on the climbs, hands on her hips as she fights the pain. I am the opposite, finding power going up, but resisting every descending step. Our paces changing, we catch up to one another when the trail is flat, stopping in the shade to snack on our morning pastries.

The *Albergue Municipal de Peregrinos* in Azofra is huge compared to anything I've seen so far. It looks like a recent build and has a large outdoor courtyard with plenty of patio tables and chairs to accommodate the numerous guests. Mini bedrooms line the second floor and face the full length windows. No bunk beds for us tonight, but the two single beds are close together in the closet-sized room.

As I head for the shower, Alfdis and Hermann walk towards me, their arms open for a hug. What an unexpected surprise to see them here. "Why don't you come and join us in the courtyard after your shower?"

Gathered outside, we take shade under the patio umbrellas when we're not sitting along the ledge of the circular foot bath, soaking our feet. Alfdis and Hermann have been married 42 years and lead an active lifestyle through travelling, hiking and camping. When they talk about their five children, I can feel the warmth of their parental love, having been on the receiving line of their compassion.

While Melanie gets to know her fellow countrymen, we catch up, extending the visit to a shared dinner. In no rush, we meander through the streets of Azofra until we find a restaurant with a patio, so Alfdis and I can enjoy the occasional cigarette with our wine. It's not the best pilgrim meal I've eaten, but an improvement over last night, and we toast to the Camino and the friendships made along the way.

As the waiter clears our plates from the table, we invite a German man and his 30-year-old daughter, Claudia, to join us for after-dinner coffees. My German friends try to keep the conversation in English, but with the excitement of sharing their stories, it slowly reverts to their mother tongue. I nod and laugh when appropriate, until someone realizes I don't have a clue what is being said. Back to English... for a while anyway. I don't care if I can't understand; I'm simply content to be ending the day in the company of such wonderful individuals.

Before leaving, I wrap the remaining wedge of baguette from the bread basket, and sneak it over to Melanie. "Would you put this in your bag for me? I'll have it for breakfast in the morning."

Alfdis and Hermann will be taking a tourist break in Santo Domingo tomorrow. It's unlikely we will see each other again, and my heart feels heavy. We have only just started our friendship and I am not ready to let go of this loving couple who have offered me so much.

But this is the way of the Camino.

I haven't quite figured out what happened this morning, but I'm comparing my rollercoaster of emotions to the changing landscape. Sometimes the path is flat and I can walk along and enjoy the scenery, with little worry or stress. Then come the hills and the challenging descents. Sometimes I don't think I'll make it, let alone arrive at my destination, but I find the strength, defying my own expectations.

The people I meet play a huge role in how I feel and how I overcome these obstacles. There's an energy balance, receiving what I need and hopefully offering support in exchange. A smile and wave, a heartfelt *Buen Camino,* and the bonds of friendship that flourish even in the absence of spoken language.

Day 7
26 km
August 10, 2015

It's a later start to the day, but I am patting myself on the shoulder for being somewhat prepared for breakfast. I do only slightly better at home. More often than not, if I am spending the night on my own, I'm grabbing something quick and easy, usually a prepared meal-to-go. Not the best habit, but I seem to be lacking the passion to cook or even plan a healthy meal for myself. That's one of the things I love about Pierre: he loves to cook, especially for others, guaranteeing a fresh, delicious meal when we're together.

The glow of the sun rises over the tops of the houses as I leave Azofra. I am feeling *alright*, but my knees start hurting with the first few steps. Focused on a positive mindset, I tell myself that my body just needs time to wake up; it seems to have forgotten that we still have another day to go. Another four weeks actually.

One day at a time, Lizzie! Don't overwhelm yourself.

I need to walk off the cobwebs and let my body adjust. The first town is Cirueña, 9 km away. I missed my comforting hot beverage this morning, so I will definitely be ordering a *grande*. Maybe more than one, just like at home.

The cloudless sky hints to another hot day of walking through the fields and mountains, but so far so good, as I kick up dust along the gravely trail. Through the crops, the gorgeous warm hues of harvested wheat fields and rows of grapes, make me smile. I feel most content when I am surrounded by nature and all her earthy colours, the contrast of lush green and palette of browns comforting me.

If only there was some other way to get down those bloody hills. Chairlift, donkey, I don't care, but the impact when my foot hits the ground drives spears right into my knees. The right seems to be suffering more than the left, but both are paying the price this morning. Pilgrims that pass me must notice my resistance, as my body is certainly not going with any flow. The hiking poles help to reduce the impact; I know it would be worse without them, but I find I'm clutching them so tightly, my entire body is stiff.

There is sympathy in the eyes of my fellow peregrinos and some even take the time to show me alternative methods for descending. One fellow suggested I walk with my knees bent, in what feels like a squat position, gently bouncing along. He was trying to get me to loosen up. Then a much older fellow in obvious shape, but also with knees that need replacement, suggested I work across the hill, slaloming my way to the bottom. It's a little more time consuming, and can get in the way of others, but does help.

I also try walking sideways, similar to the dirt slalom but more like a hiking slow dance, working my way to one side of the path, then switching directions and moving to the other. I'm not sure if I'm leading or following, or just falling behind the more adept trekkers, but I am appreciative of the tips provided. There is relief, mostly comic, but I'm not laughing.

There have been a number of hills since I started walking the Camino, but it took only a couple of days before my knees started boycotting. Now, as I stand at the top of the hill looking down, I can feel myself resisting. My body is in full blown protest.

I don't want to go down.

Each time my foot hits the ground I can feel my face wince as I brace myself for impact. Half way through the long, steep descent, I'm on the verge of tears. *What's the problem?* My threshold for pain is high; I was in natural labour for twelve hours, pushing a 10 lb 3 oz baby boy out of my body. I shouldn't be reacting this way, but it's not just the agony; it's the discouragement. I should be stronger, better prepared.

I'm not.

My pace slows to a crawl.

Even when the ground is level I struggle to keep moving, wanting to stop ALL THE TIME. Regularly, I peek at my FitBit, hoping I have travelled enough to stop for a break. With one eye on the gorgeous landscape, the other is scouring for a place to park my ass. It may be counterproductive, but it's my life preserver.

No wonder it takes me forever to walk 5 km.

When I stop, I refuel with more than water. Yes, I enjoy a cigarette, even when my heart is pounding and I'm slightly out of breath, that smoke gives me a chance to ground myself, to prepare for the next steps. I'm walking towards my next break. *Not sure I needed to come to Spain to do this, but here I am.*

Cirueña is a modern town and host to my first golf course sighting. Following a pair of older men in their pastel shirts, golf carts in tow, I turn right into the clubhouse as they continue straight to the greens. Welcome to *Cirueña Alta Rioja Golf Club*, home of my morning's first cup of coffee.

A smile to the fellow seated by the window, the familiar surroundings prompt a "Good Morning" rather than a *Buen Camino*.

When I return from the outside with my now empty cup and plate, I go over to say hello. This Scandinavian surprises me. "I passed you while you were taking a break. You had the nicest smile I had seen all morning." I'm obviously benefitting from my numerous mental health moments.

I have crossed more hills that I wished to recall by the time I arrive in Santo Domingo. I'm not breaking any records with the 4 hours it has taken me to walk 15 km. It doesn't bother me that I am slow, nor do I mind the extra time spent on roadside pit stops, but thoughts of quitting this trek are floating around in my mind. While my body fights to take steps, all I can think about is stopping. Perhaps one day I'll return to Spain and tour the cities I am walking through, but today I don't care about the monumental sites.

The only sight I wish to explore is a couple of bags of ice on my knees.

The busy pedestrian corridor is flanked by a stone wall. Hobbling up the steps into a fancy restaurant, I put my hands on the wooden bar top and order a Coke. I would prefer a can over the petite little collector's bottle he produces, but looking around at the dark wood panelling, the bottles of liquor lining the glass shelves behind my bartender, I can see this place is a too posh for cans.

"Hielo, por favor," as I present two of my doggie bags. I have mastered another important Spanish word, *ice*. The server looks at me with disdain.

I'm not asking for a twist of lemon for my Coke sir, I'm looking for First Aid. Pronto! I can't afford to walk away without it, especially having paid too much for my puny bottle of fizzy liquid sugar, that I will guzzle in two big gulps if I can't control myself.

It is time to stand up for what I want, and I want ice. *Now.*

I'm following the lessons I have learned from Melanie, a strong and confident German woman who requests the WiFi before even placing an order. I ignore his frown, pushing the little bags towards him with determination.

"Hielo, por favor. Gracias." Just give me the damn ice. I'm in no mood to use my Canadian charm. I'm well past that.

Maybe he senses potential water works, because he takes the bags, returning them with a few ice cubes each. "Gracias Señor."

Carefully descending the steps back into the pedestrian corridor, I head to an empty table. Pack on the ground, I sit down, defeated. With a bit of strategic manoeuvring, I manage to position a bag on each knee.

Just about noon and only 15 km into the day, I am ready to stop. Maybe permanently. I haven't given up on completing this journey, but my self-pity tosses the idea around. *This might be all I can manage.*

The hustle and bustle of the people milling about grates on my nerves. I need a quiet space to calm myself, but I won't find it here. Melanie spots me from down the street, heads towards my table and plunks herself in an empty chair. She doesn't need to tell me she is having a rough morning; her face and body say it all.

The injuries she started with have been exacerbated by the excessive walking, and her hips and thighs are bothering her. We are quite a pair, empathetic to the other's suffering, silently thankful we have caught up. She gets her own drink from the same restaurant, and we sit quietly, absorbed in our own personal torment.

The waiter who served me inside crosses the lane with menus. "No, gracias," waving him away. Bugger off Buddy, we're not in the mood!

Appearing through the crowd is Alfdis and Hermann, all washed up and dressed as tourists. Over the next day or two they will visit Santo Domingo, embracing the architecture, churches and of course, the shopping. Their original plan was to walk only part of the Camino this summer. They are going camping once home, more than likely returning to finish the Camino another year.

Hermann brings over two more chairs before excusing himself. The waiter, quick on his feet when he spots potential clients, takes Alfdis' order for two coffees.

She looks at me with her motherly love, while I fight to hold back the tears. "Why don't you stop for the day, Elizabeth? Give your body an opportunity to heal."

I look at Melanie, who I know is not prepared to stop, and back at Alfdis, my eyes wet. "I have to keep going." Damn stubborn Taurus! But I need to be with Melanie.

Hermann's return timing with four *Santo Domingo* pastries is perfect. We toast to our friendship one last time. With the bags of melted ice now settled on the back of my neck, I give my German friends one last hug and kiss.

"Thank you for sharing my journey."

My pack feels heavier as I hoist it on my back. Melanie and I keep moving through the throngs of people, and arrive at the Cathedral. There is an interesting legend associated with Santo Domingo. Apparently a pilgrim couple and their son stopped at an Inn en route to Santiago. When the young boy refused the advances of the innkeeper's daughter, she wanted to punish him. After placing a golden goblet into his bag, she identified him as a thief. The penalty was death by hanging. When his distraught parents heard his voice proclaiming his innocence, they went to the magistrate to beg his mercy, disturbing his dinner. The magistrate dismissed the idea, waving his hand and stating, "The boy is no more alive than the cock and hen on this dinner plate." You guessed it! The birds grew wings and flew about the room.

The *Cathedral of Santo Domingo de la Calzada* has installed a golden pen that houses a live cock and hen, and it's said to be good luck if the cock crows in your presence. Melanie and I were both due for a change of pace, not to mention some good luck, but as with so many of the tourist venues, there's a cost to enter. Already feeling jilted by our day, we decide it's not worth it. We are in no mood to support the Spanish tourist economy.

Relieved to get out of the chaos and away from the buildings and people, we accept that we have another 7 km before arriving in Grañón. Stopping at the fountain at the edge of the city, we refill our bottles and soak our Buffs, to prepare for the walk ahead.

The heat of the sun adds to our exhaustion as we climb a steep hill towards one of the few clusters of trees. Dropping our packs unceremoniously onto the grass, we are overdue for a break. With our boots and socks off, we air out our aching feet beneath the cool shade. I haven't done this often enough, but it's hard to motivate myself to put them back on.

Boots equal walking.

We are both ready to call it a day as we arrive in Grañón. We've walked 22 km, much of it in agony. At a small tienda I get another Coke, and chat with the other pilgrims.

"If you are planning on staying here tonight, you should know that the albergue is full. There is, however, an old monastery with space available. A communal dinner is included and there's singing and plenty of camaraderie... but no beds. You sleep on a mattress."

My Californian buddy, Benny, sees me from across the road and rushes towards us. He hugs me tightly before sharing his struggles over these last few days. It is interesting to see how the Camino challenges each of us.

"I miss my Mom!"

My heart breaks for this 30-year-old boy, and I open my arms towards him. "Give me another hug, Benny." I hold onto him as though he were my own son. A free spirit, he is going through his own emotional battle.

"Are you staying at the monastery?"

I don't think so. "My body is in too much pain to spend the night with only a thin mattress between me and the damp cold floor." As much as my spirit might benefit from such an experience, my body won't appreciate it.

"That's too bad. It would be great if you stayed! If you change your mind, I'm sure I can help find some extra mattresses to stack up for you."

"You are very sweet Benny, thank you."

Energized with one last hug, I join Melanie and keep on walking.

No floors for us tonight. Check.

The remaining 4 km are slow, but we arrive at the *Albergue de Peregrinos* in Redecilla del Camino. For only 5 euros, we have a bed for the night; an extra 2 euros gives us a breakfast. A deal by all standards and perhaps because I am so exhausted after a 9-hour, 26 km day, I hug the owner who is surprised by my additional currency.

When Melanie learns there is a municipal pool, the afternoon plans are decided. My girl came prepared; part of those 28 pounds she carries includes her pink bikini.

I sit at the edge of the pool in my little red dress and dangle my legs in the refreshing water, fantasizing about sipping on an icy Pina Colada. Unfortunately, my fantasy is cut short by the lifeguard announcing that because I am not sporting a bathing suit, I have to retreat to the grass.

Really? I want to tell her about my day, the 26 km I walked to get here, how badly my knees and feet need the healing properties of the chlorinated pool.

Relegated to photographer, I take Melanie's cellphone, snapping photos and videos of her enjoying her aquatic paradise. She is the most contented I have seen all day, alternating between the refreshing water and relaxing on the lounge chair.

I'm not interested in soaking up the sun on the grass or being teased by the pool I am prohibited to access. Exhausted from my day, I leave Melanie and return to the albergue to catch up on my long distance correspondence.

Yesterday, I started emailing friends I knew who were thinking of me. I hadn't been keeping in contact with anyone outside of our small family unit, but after yesterday's emotional meltdown, I knew I needed to hear from the people who care about me. My emails may have sounded desperate, and I was. Friends, family members and work colleagues have emailed me, reminding me that I am not alone.

Amongst the emails was a note from Andrew. He's his Momma's boy and had been in touch a few times already. It isn't difficult to read between his lines. Our roles had reversed.

"Glad to hear you're still surviving! So for your feet... having to walk so far each day is certainly not helping them heal. I'll assume you've been taking Aleve, so maybe it would be a good idea if you bussed a few days ahead and took some time off your feet. A day or two to relax in a hotel might do some good, not to mention you're on vacation after all! Let me know what your plan is. You're a trooper. Keep up the positive attitude and work."

He was sending his Momma lots of love and positive vibes across the miles, and I indulge in a little cry while Melanie is still at the pool. I asked for support and it was received.

By the time Melanie returns, we are both famished.

Once we are seated in the compact dining room of a nearby restaurant, we invite a fellow who is alone, to join us. Eduardo is from Brazil. Neither Melanie or I speak Portuguese, Eduardo and I don't speak German. English would be the language of choice and they practice their skills during dinner.

Tonight's first entrée is a tomato sauce bath, topped with a mound of rice and a fried egg perched on the peak. It looks... different; these aren't food combinations I am used to, but it's actually quite tasty. My second entrée is homemade fries and a flattened, marinated chicken breast. Fries are a regular item on the pilgrim menu, but I opt for an ensalada whenever available. Seems salads are the only vegetables I am eating.

With my belly full and ready for bed, I sit on the edge of my lower bunk and consider the journey so far. I have walked 7 days; one week; one-fifth of the way. I'm not sure how I made it or how I will do another month, but I have impressed myself and am proud to have gotten this far.

Week 1 completed. Check.

After all of the kilometres walked today, I know I need to inspect the feet I've been ignoring. Time to check out the status of the loose toenail. Lifting the end of the nail, it raises easily, the meat beneath a bright pink. Almost off and standing at a 90 degree angle, the nail is clinging to a tiny bit of cuticle.

I can't do it and try to put it back down, but I have pulled it too far. My stomach rolls like the high seas as I tear the nail away.

I'm going to be sick.

Day 8
12 km, Bus 50 km
August 11, 2015

The naked nail, covered with antibacterial cream and a Band-Aid, didn't bother me while I slept. This morning I have reapplied the first aid measures, with an added layer of toilet paper to prevent the vulnerable toe from hitting the top of my boot. The blister on my heel seems less of an issue, the green tape holding for now. I'm glad Alfdis gave me the extra supplies.

"Thank you so much for your support last night, Melanie!" As a member of the *Gross Patrol*, she remained calm while I freaked out. Enthusiastically, I tell her how good I feel this morning. "I slept so well last night!"

Her reply is a simple "Yes." She isn't claiming her own good sleep, but simply that *I* slept. "It sounded like there were ten men in the room." We were only two, Melanie sleeping directly above me, with only a thin mattress for acoustic buffering. Obviously tired and recovering from the surgery, I fear my snoring *may* have been amplified.

This might be the last time she sleeps near me.

Melanie and I leave together and the first 5 km are really great. The minimal amount of paved road redirects us back onto the path and through a patchwork quilt of rich golden hues that climb the rolling hills. The changing shades and patterns highlight where one field ends and another begins. The path ahead is swallowed up into the higher crops, taking us with it.

Past the vineyards, the only green spaces are the circling fields near the peak of the hill. The flat terrain lifts my confidence. *So far, so good.*

We catch up to the German dad and daughter, who shared after dinner coffees with us in Azofra. Melanie gets along quite well with them and of course, she is happy to be able to communicate in her mother tongue. She's been talking in English since we've been together and her confidence is growing. I can hear their conversation drift into German when I am ahead or behind the pack.

I'm so proud of how Melanie has embraced the change of her Camino. When we have faith it makes it easier to accept the events we have little control over.

There have been minimal descents so far, and I'm climbing the hills with renewed determination, my pace strong and purposeful, and I often leave my comrades behind.

Then we come to the great decline and it's game over for this peregrina.

It isn't the paved streets or the rocky paths; it isn't the warming sun or any emotional crisis. It's the hills during the last kilometres into Belorado that torture me. My confidence and strength vanish.

The descent is so steep that the invisible knives jab my knees with each step and the tears start to well. My German friends are all ahead of me, looking back to make sure I am still following. Alone on the hill, I make my way down ever so painfully slow.

We stop at the first restaurant in Belorado, and my knees continue to throb. A check of my FitBit heightens my frustration. I'm certain my power and determination had propelled me farther than 12 km. Half of an expected day; this is going to be brutal.

My bocadillo sits untouched while the now regularly requested bags of ice balance on my knees.

Short-fused, I'm refraining from engaging in conversation. All I can think about is stopping. I don't want to go on, but am afraid to voice these thoughts, so instead I withdraw. I contemplate staying in Belorado for the night, but what would I do here all afternoon? I need to keep moving forward, maybe on a donkey or a moped. Maybe a strong biker will come along on his large cruiser, strap my backpack to his top box and bring me. Anywhere. I don't want to keep walking and I don't want Melanie to leave without me. I'm pretty sure I need her by my side, but my heart isn't in it.

As my friends collect their lunch garbage from the picnic table, I know they are ready to resume walking, but I am hesitant to leave. A young woman seated two picnic tables away, gets up and walks towards us. "Hi. I'm Julie from Denmark." Looking at me, she smiles. "We had passed each other a couple of times over the last few days, but had never shared more than a *Buen Camino*. I saw you limping. I guess you have injuries as well."

I don't recognize Julie, but wish I had more time to get to know her.

She doesn't hesitate to tell us that her knees are killing her. "I noticed a bus schedule in the restaurant, so I'm skipping forward to Burgos. I just can't walk anymore!" She needs a break in the worst way and I can see that finding a solution has energized her. "I'm sorry I can't stay longer to chat, but I need to find the bus stop."

As though catching a Frisbee thrown in my direction, my hand shoots up before I can get the words out of my mouth. "I'm going with you!" I said it! This wasn't planned, and I even shock myself, looking immediately at Melanie. I made this announcement out of nowhere and neither of us has time to process what that means for her.

For us.

She is dealing with the unexpected and I might feel the same way if the roles were reversed. Actually, if Melanie announced that she was going to take a bus, I would have my pack on and poles in hand, before she could change her mind.

But at this moment, I am thinking only of what I need. *Right now.*

Melanie is not going to be taking a bus, taxi or donkey for any of the 800 km. She is walking the entire route, regardless of how she feels. I however, am taking advantage of this fleeting opportunity. I wouldn't have looked for a bus myself, but this invitation has come out of nowhere.

Without giving Melanie a chance to say anything, I try to explain my actions. "I hope you are okay with this, because I can't go on!" She knows I'm in agony and she has her own pain to deal with. Disappointment shows on her face, but this is *my* Camino. Perhaps we are meant to go our own way, find our own path.

We hug goodbye, and I know the impact of my decision has yet to register, but there isn't time to waste. Julie knows the bus schedule, but doesn't know where to catch it. The 50 km I am bussing ahead will make it near impossible for Melanie to catch up to me.

I didn't expect it to end this way or this soon, but this is my sign and I am following it. *All the way to Burgos, saving me two days of walking.*

Funny how quickly I can move, sore legs or not, when I feel like I am hurrying to meet up with a long lost lover. My hero doesn't hesitate to ask for direction, and then clarification, to ensure we don't miss the bus. She is a woman on a mission and I am happy to be her co-pilot, arriving at the stop with time to spare. Soon enough we will hand over 3 euros to the bus driver, sit in air conditioning, and fast forward over 50 km of Spanish road.

I am flooded with relief.

Boarding the bus, I can't get over the number of people already seated: sunburned pilgrims, injured pilgrims, tired and dirty pilgrims. We are a buffet of wounded souls, each having surpassed our limits, and thankful for this mobile relief. Julie and I take the empty bench right behind the American couple, Dave and Cathy, who have their packs taxied each day. They look ragged. Across the aisle are two young women leaning against each other, eyes closed, their legs covered in the same colourful bandage Alfdis gave me. Blue, green and purple strips of tape climb their shins, circle their knees, and continue up their thighs.

I'm not the only one struggling on this walk of self-discovery.

While the bus motors along, Julie tells me about her studies and her struggles to figure out what she wants from life. The fact that she can discuss this so easily with a stranger, tells me she is in tune with her inner self. Soul searching, she is looking for answers, hoping to find direction while walking the Camino on her own.

Before we know it we've pulled into the bus terminal. Without the yellow arrows to direct us, we have no idea where we are going. The streets are jammed with tourists and we need to find an

Information Centre to get a map, otherwise we'll be walking aimlessly all afternoon.

My introduction to the beautiful architecture of Burgos begins with a walk under the castle-style 14th century city gate. Buildings line the streets like fashionable models, the colours and intricate designs holding my attention. Further into the bustling city square, the streets become narrow alleyways of a continual flow of people seeming to know exactly where they are going.

To avoid being pulled with the current, Julie and I stop at a corner, getting out of the way of the masses. With a map in hand, we wonder out loud if the municipal albergue is at the top of the hill in front of us. A female voice comes over our shoulders. "The albergue is just up this street."

Turning around quickly, a younger couple is smiling at us. "It's a bit of a steep climb, but well worth it. You won't be disappointed."

Still stunned, we thank them. "We just arrived by bus, so it's all a bit confusing."

As the couple disappear into the crowd, Julie and I look at each other, sharing a smile. There is a greater force at work here and we just experienced one of those talked about Camino phenomenon: ask your question to the universe and someone will answer it.

Thank God the multi-floored *Albergue Municipal de Burgos* has an elevator. It would be cruel to ask anyone to climb so many flights of stairs after a full day of walking. Or even half a day and a bus ride. Our 7th floor accomodations offer 2 bunk beds per cubicle, multiple modern shower stalls and plenty of bathrooms. It reminds me a bit of a college dorm.

As Julie takes the top bunk above mine, I refrain from sharing my *apparent* snoring. Our bunkmates are the two *colourful* girls from the bus, who seem to have rediscovered their strength. There is a wait for the showers, but I'm in no rush; I walked 12 km and covered 62, thanks to Julie and her bad knees. With only a half a day under my hikers, I have the luxury of a full afternoon to re-charge my batteries.

The cathedral, in all its majesty, encompasses an entire block. The architecture is calming, a clean uncomplicated design with fine details and stone carvings on the outer walls, the pinnacle turrets reaching for the sky. Although centuries old, the stonework is clean, only slightly stained towards the top.

The energy of the city square rejuvenates me, and I'm curious to see what Burgos can offer... perhaps the desire to be a tourist for one afternoon.

Where I am accustomed to seeing pilgrims walking with their packs and poles, now I see locals, tourists, families, beautiful clean people passing by expensive boutiques, hotels, and candy stores. It's stimulating, but doesn't aggravate my senses.

The pain in my knees, the weight of my pack, and the worry about when I will find my next meal, is all forgotten as I wander the streets in my little red dress. You couldn't tell that only a few hours ago we were both complaining about not being able to walk any further.

"Why don't we have an early dinner Elizabeth, something special to celebrate our new friendship."

The square has so many restaurants to choose from, but we duck under the canopied tent in the open court. There will be no pilgrim menu for us tonight. With all afternoon to sit and relax, we enjoy a cold beer, toasting Burgos. Our waiter watches for his cue to bring menus, knowing we are in no rush.

Completely at ease with one another, our conversation quickly delves into more personal life stories. Julie is the only pilgrim with whom I have shared the intimate tales of my relationship struggles. She understands, my experiences striking a cord of familiarity. There is no need to elaborate or feel embarrassed. We are in touch with ourselves, connected to others, and searching for answers we suspect are probably already within, just waiting to be discovered.

After dinner, Julie goes off in search of a massage therapist for tomorrow and I seek out a pharmacy to get some advice for my toes and heel.

The sight of my injuries causes the pharmacist to scrunch up her face, but she doesn't offer me a First Place ribbon. I assume she's seen worse. Loaded with antibacterial cream, plasters and blister pads, she also suggests a spray can of cold topical relief. I still have my hefty supply of Aleve, which I pop twice a day, whether I need it or not.

Proactive. Check.

The leisurely pace and change of mindset is helping me understand why the more experienced travellers take the occasional shorter or additional day, to enjoy their surroundings. I'm taking full advantage this evening, but I didn't come to Spain to sightsee, to admire the architecture or study the history.

This is a one-time, much needed break.

From my bench vantage point, I stare at the rows of colourful buildings that stand proud, like soldiers of the busy square. My time in Burgos has removed me from the pressure cooker I felt trapped within and allows more positive thoughts to roam free. How I would love to share *this* experience with Pierre. We'd walk through these streets hand in hand, enjoy a drink on a patio, and absorb the sights as we people watch. Yes, Pierre would find this most enjoyable.

Only four more weeks and I'll be home.

My thoughts are pulled back to the present when an older, local man sits down on the bench beside me. My alarm bells sound when he points to my wedding ring, inquiring if I am married.

"I am waiting for my husband."

To avoid any further conversation, I keep my head down as though reading something on my cellphone. I can feel his eyes on me, probably looking through my little red dress, my radar on alert. Looking up I spy Andreia with Antònio. Abandoning the bench, I rush over to give them both hugs.

My *husband* is probably wondering why my welcome is a little warmer than usual. Poor Antònio looks beaten up, his lips dry and feet blistered in his sandals. We chat for a bit in our blend of English, Italian, Spanish and Portuguese, not really understanding each other, but when we say goodbye, the man on the bench has left.

I return to our dorm just as Julie is coming in. "Are you up for one last coffee, Elizabeth?"

Sitting on the patio at the café across the street, I thank her for rescuing me. Another Camino Angel has appeared in my life, changing the course of my day and helping me shift perspective.

Day 9
23 km
August 12, 2015

It was easier to rewind and replay yesterday's events with a clearer mind. What had started as a strong morning, quickly reversed when confronted with the down hill trek. Cue Julie and my plans changed abruptly. The day ended on such a positive note and a new friend had touched my heart, and yet as I got ready for bed last night, I felt a lingering guilt at abandoning Melanie on the first ride out of Belorado.

Does she understand why I left?

There is no doubt we were meant to meet and share the path, but I had no idea how many days we would walk together; it wasn't something we discussed. We parted each morning at our own pace, and I didn't worry whether I would see her again, confident I would.

Then Julie appeared with her magic bus.

Remember, you chose to walk this path on your own.

It is understandable that at some point Melanie and I would part ways; I just hadn't expected it to happen so soon. It's out of character for me to deviate from the course of the day, but I listened and followed that voice in my head. My actions had implications for Melanie, but I hadn't thought about that. My own needs took priority and I certainly benefited from the bus ride, the friendship, and my tour through Burgos.

As I settled into bed, I remembered that Melanie and I had exchanged email addresses. *Strange when I think of it.* I needed to tell her how much our friendship means to me.

"Have been thinking of you since I left for Burgos. It broke my heart to leave you, but I knew it was the right thing for me. I want you to know how much I enjoyed sharing part of my Camino with you. So many times you changed my mood and spirit, and helped me get through the day. You are such a sweet young woman and I am so glad we had this opportunity. It's possible we won't see each other again, so I want to wish you a Buen Camino my friend. Everything happens for a reason and the way it is meant to be... never forget that. Keep me posted... my plan is to walk again tomorrow. Hopefully the knees stay strong. Sending you a great big hug."

This morning I feel lighter than ever, filled with a powerful optimism. My legs aren't aching as much and I'm not hesitating to get my boots on while my roommates sleep. Julie is just waking up as I put my pack over my shoulder. Reaching up to her on the top bunk, I give her a kiss. "Stay in touch my friend."

There is no rush this morning, nor is there an avoidance to get started, so I cross the street to the café. The bells of the cathedral ring, and other than the shopkeepers and the few pilgrims I watch passing by, the city is still waking up. The soft blue sky and comfortable temperature reflect my inner calm. I'm not sure how far I'll walk today, but I'll continue until it no longer feels good. I have the luxury of time.

The two young gals who slept across from Julie and me, join me with their own coffees. With no more than introductions in our sleeping quarters, I remind them we also shared the bus. In their late 20s and the best of friends, these young women are from Denmark or Germany.

"You could pass for sisters."

They share a secret smile. "We've been told that before." With perfect English they share their 2-stage Camino. "Last year we walked from Burgos to Santiago. This year we started in Saint-Jean-Pied-de-Port."

Eager to head home, exhausted and beaten from their journey, they are proud to have reached their planned destination, and even happier to be catching the first train this morning. They confirm what I suspected when I saw them passed out on the bus: they are emotionally spent.

We get teary-eyed as we share our highs and lows. Meeting new people, making connections you never thought possible, and dealing with the undertow of emotions that seem to spring out of nowhere, knocking you off your feet… we had each experienced our share.

It still amazes me how easy it is to identify with the challenges and struggles of strangers, creating a bond through understanding and empathy. We each choose to walk the Camino, for reasons we may not even recognize, but that single decision to be here connects us. We are tied together from the moment we meet, sharing and being part of each other's journey. Each smile, each wave and each "Buen Camino" pull us closer together.

Now *I am* stalling... I don't want to say goodbye to these lovely young women. My heart is full of love: for them, for myself, for the relationships I've had the good fortune to make, and for the opportunities that still await.

Standing alongside the cathedral, I send out a prayer of gratitude, hoping to absorb any vibrations the universe wishes to grant me.

There's a twinge of excitement as I make my way on my own, keeping an eye open for backpackers. I didn't walk into Burgos, so my sense of direction is absent without the yellow arrows to follow, but the anxiety I felt the morning I left Estella has disappeared. I had so little experience to draw from then; not only travelling experience, but also the inner strength I have since uncovered. Now I can ask for help and direction if I need it, but I can also follow my instincts. As I discovered yesterday, those might be the best directions to follow.

Out of Burgos, the trail leads me back onto the parched earth of the farmland. Crops of sunflowers fill my visual field, the emblem for my journey. *Hope*. Big flowers, small flowers, some a little haggard, others designed with a smile, they brighten the landscape as they face the sun that follows behind me.

Beside a river, I'm drawn to watch the moss floating freely in the shallower spots and follow the flow of the current with my eyes. *There is energy all around me.*

Today I cross over the invisible border onto the Meseta. The Camino desert: 180 km of flat terrain.

Bring it on!

This stage is defined as the most challenging, psychologically, but I'm more confident in my ability to navigate any emotional storms. Reviewers claim the walk is boring, the same scenery day in and day out. Those who are limited in time often chose to bus through this section, but I have no problem with flat and boring. I have been looking forward to the Meseta since the first ache in my knees. Flat terrain and limited hills, this would be the easiest part for me. At 20 km per day, it could take me 9 days, less if I'm able to walk farther. This period will help my body acclimate to the routine.

Good thing I had my coffee and croissant before I left, as the next sustenance stop takes me 10 km, passing through Villalbilla and into Tardajos, where I stop at a restaurant with an outside covered patio.

With a side order of ice for my knees, I am in business, enjoying a snack and well-deserved rest. Chatting with others taking refuge from the sun, I meet Christophe, a French peregrino who is also travelling solo.

Knowing I still have a couple more cigarettes to enjoy before I am ready to leave, I pass on the offer to join them. While they put their packs on their backs, I look out onto the deserted, dusty street ahead of us, wishing I had some other option than walking. Raising my right arm as though flagging a New York City taxi, I call out. "Donkey!" The others laugh, but part of me wishes I could catch a ride the rest of the way.

So far the walk is manageable and I practice my downhill ski techniques as I work my way across each hill. I'm making a conscious effort to flow, rather than resist.

The view changes dramatically, as though my lens has lost its colour. The sight of the dull brown hills with little vegetation, is stark compared to the golds and greens I had come to admire earlier in the week. Thankfully the scenery changes again as I pass through the small town of Rabé de las Calzados, stopping at the fountain to replenish my bottles and soak my Buff in the cold water.

The *Hornillos Meeting Point* albergue is modern and spacious, with a small reception desk near the front door and a couple of wooden benches to remove and store our boots. The kitchen area looks well stocked for those who want to cook, with several long tables set up cafeteria style. Straight ahead is a single glass door leading to the cedar hedge enclosed backyard, an oasis where I plan to spend my afternoon.

My spacious room is at the end of the hall. The only single bed is already spoken for by the blanket covered bulk of a weary pilgrim I recognize. In the lower bunk beside me is an Italian couple. Nestled between her man's legs, his arms wrap around her, whispering in her ear as his head comes around to kiss her cheek. Caught in a trance, I'm unable to pull my eyes away, my own heart aching to be held in Pierre's arms.

Clean and refreshed, I join the others in the backyard. The washing of clothes is quick, not the deep clean of a machine. Everything will need a good wash when I get home. Hanging them on the long line, I relax in a patio chair, updating my journal before sending any emails home. My belly starts to rumble, reminding me that lunch is long gone.

It is a day of comfort foods. Wiping the bowl of spaghetti clean with thick slices of fresh baguette, I leave nothing behind. I've had three meals today.

When I return to the albergue, I spot Christophe passing through the kitchen to head upstairs, surprised he doesn't recognize me. I would love to sit in the backyard and get to know him further. *Not meant to be I guess.*

There are quite a few pilgrims in the kitchen, busy either cooking, eating or cleaning up. It is well stocked with the essential pots, pans, utensils, oils and spices, and all I have to do is pick up the ingredients and create a meal, but it hasn't happened yet. A group invites me to join them, gesturing to the large bowl on the table. This time my excuse is legitimate, thanking them for their kindness, but sitting to join in the conversation.

I'm ready for bed. Although not exhausted, I'm pleasantly tired from the walk and the sun. Plugging my phone in to charge overnight, I see more emails have come through.

How can I fail when I have so many people cheering me on across the miles?

Day 10
20 km
August 13, 2015

A t 5 am the alarms start sounding, followed by 15-minute in-tervals of ringtones, cellphones and flashlights criss-crossing the room. The noise of backpack reorganization and washroom vis-its let me know it is time to rise and shine. By 6 am I am fully awake, despite the restless night. The continuous throb of my ach-ing legs made it difficult to stay asleep for long.

Unplugging my phone, I check my emails. I can always count on a *Good Morning* message from Pierre and the notes of encour-agement from friends. My coworker Ev has sent me an inspirational quote, something she says she will do regularly, as a way of supporting me.

"A journey of a thousand miles begins with a single step."
Confucius

I have time to slip outside in the cool morning air and have a smoke while breakfast gets set up. It's a terrible habit to smoke first thing in the morning, but knowing that doesn't change my routine. Thank goodness there's the option for coffee and something to eat before I leave, as I am obviously still playing Breakfast Roulette. With my toast and jam, orange juice, coffee and biscuits in my belly, I *think* I am ready to start.

Everything is packed up and brought to the bench near the front door. As I get my boots on, Christophe spots me as he heads for the door, does a double take, obviously surprised to see me. I laugh. "You didn't recognize me last night without my Buff."

Why is there a little flutter in my belly as we wish one another a great day? During our chat at lunch yesterday, I picked up on his stress-free attitude, taking the Camino one day at a time, not overly challenged by the physical demands. He exudes a confidence that lacks cockiness.

Too bad we didn't get a chance to talk last night.

My smile lingers as I set out from Hornillos del Camino and within the first few steps I can tell my body is getting the hang of the routine. The knees ache a bit, but my morning Aleve will kick in soon. There are no issues with my feet and I don't even feel the second toenail I know is doomed for removal.

There is something inviting about being alone on the narrow streets, with no sound other than the clicking of my poles as they slide across the smooth stones. I've gotten in the habit of taking a quick selfie once I get myself out of the albergue; this morning I'm looking a little tired.

Out of town, the loose dirt path winds upwards, cutting through the wheat fields. The overcast sky offers respite from the now accustomed early heat, but even under the shade of the clouds, the crops are a beautiful gold. From a distance, the row of wind turbines seem insignificant, but as I get closer I witness their massive stature.

Another monument of sorrow stones, this one piled high, embracing a cross. I take a minute to pay respect to this collection that so many have contributed to. I have a few stones in the outside pocket of my backpack, removing one and adding it to the pile. "May your heart be lightened with one less burden."

Over the first 10 km I notice I am stopping less often, but for longer periods. My FitBit doesn't determine my breaks this morning. I do. Something has changed. A switch has turned on, or maybe off. My actions over the last two days helped unearth the faith I have in my own abilities. *Is it independence? Trusting that it will work out? Taking care of my needs?* Whatever it is, I should probably bottle it up, just in case I need a confidence elixir down the road.

Antònio catches up to me. I haven't seen him since the evening in Burgos, when I pretended he was my husband. He looks a little fragile this morning, his windbreaker held tight to his slim body, his nose peeling from too much sun. The enthusiasm I have come to expect from him is absent. Hopefully my hug and a few kilometres together can boost his spirits.

As we start the steep descent into Hontanas, he moves ahead of me while I slow my pace right down, to tackle the narrow and uneven loose path. My knees get a jolt. *This is just a little blip in the road. Don't get discouraged.*

At the bottom of the hill is an albergue with a restaurant. I've walked 10 km and I'm feeling good, with the exception of the last few hundred feet. *Maybe I should stop. Not push my luck.*

An American I met last night is seated at a nearby table with his own coffee, chatting away, leaving little room for shared conversation. Although friendly enough, his energy suffocates me in a grey cloud. To resist getting caught up in the conversation, I focus my attention on my ham and cheese croissant. He is staying here for the night. *Now is not the time to stop!*

Passing through town, I meet up with Emilia, a woman I have met a few times. A little older than me, Emilia is originally from Chile, now living in Australia. She's easy to talk with, and I have enjoyed the short exchanges we've had so far.

"Elizabeth, you look like you are feeling so much better."

I do feel great this morning.

As I slow my pace to match hers, we approach a small stone building. As Spanish is Emilia's mother tongue, we stop to say "Buenos Dias" to an older wheelchair-bound woman and her caregiver, seated on a bench. These Señoras are enjoying the fine weather, *peregrino watching*. As we say "Adios" to the ladies, I also bid Emilia a "Buen Camino."

Interesting that I pull away from two people this morning, in an effort to serve my own needs. Seems my experiences along the Camino are giving me permission to break ties when it feels right.

The number of buildings in ruin continues to surprise me. The upper level of one home is missing most of its wall, the layers of construction visible like the rings of a tree. There is history in these abandoned homes, perhaps generations of stories to be told.

As I make my way towards Castrojeriz, I hear the familiar sound of approaching footsteps. Maintaining my pace, I wait to turn my head until the shadow comes in line with my own. I offer an enthusiastic "Hola, Amigo" to everyone who walks beside me. If we don't continue walking together, we simply wish each other a "Buen Camino."

This handsome young pilgrim matches my pace. "We have wished each other *Buen Camino* three times. I think it is time for a formal introduction." With a huge smile on his face, he holds out his hand. "I'm Ferro."

This is Ferro's second Camino. At 28-years-old, this Slovakian is walking with his younger brother, Daniel, who is nowhere in sight. "I wanted him to experience the Camino for himself."

Poor Ferro is struggling with the aftermath of having his blisters *threaded*. The trick is to run a sterilized needle through the blister, trimming the thread on both ends. The fluid drains through the thread, releasing the pressure. I came prepared with the tools should it be necessary, but had yet to see it performed.

The only blisters I've had, knock on wood, are the ones around my two toenails and under my callus. They are insignificant compared to the nastiness I've seen on other feet. I'll cross the threading bridge should it come to that, but for now, my blisters are non-existent.

Ferro has a great sense of humour and is particularly interested in learning more about Canadian women. He makes me laugh with his questions, our time together passing quickly. Neither feels any pressure to meet timelines and we enjoy a couple of breaks along the way. One stop has us sharing a Clif Bar while we rest on top of a hay bale, and another has us relaxing on a grassy incline to have a smoke. Ferro rolls his own cigarettes, so I share one of mine, thinking I may be the closest he ever gets to experiencing a Canadian woman.

Before we realize it, the landmark of the castillo comes into view atop the hill, identifying our approach to Castrojeriz, where I hope to spend the evening. As we walk towards the city limits, I tell Ferro how much I enjoyed spending the afternoon with him. He hugs me tightly.

"I can't tell you how much I appreciate walking with you Elizabeth. I was having a miserable day until I caught up with you. Thank you!"

His mood has lightened considerably as we approach Daniel who is laying on a bench smoking his own cigarette, patiently waiting for big brother to arrive. We exchange another hug knowing we will never see each other again.

When I was preparing for this journey, I learned about messages I may receive and the importance of following my instincts. If I felt drawn to head in a certain direction or compelled to stop, I should pay attention. These messages have already started: dismissing Andreia's reservation, taking the bus to Burgos, and laying the stone this morning.

I believe we are meant to listen to these feelings and I certainly don't do it often enough in my day-to-day affairs at home, but walking out here is a great way to learn how to tune into my inner voice.

And trust it.

With 20 km under my belt and feeling great, I decide to call it a day. The large stone entrance to Castrojeriz is all that remains of the ancient San Anton monastery, once dedicated to helping the sick pilgrims on their way to Santiago. I won't be climbing the hill to get a closer look at the 9th century castillo ruins, but the view of the Meseta from the top must be incredible.

The *Albergue de Peregrinos Castrojeriz* is almost empty when I arrive at 2 pm. The sleeping accommodations are crammed with bunk beds, making it feel a bit claustrophobic. As I make my way to select my lower bunk, I pass an exhausted and injured fellow, fast asleep on his cot. I thought I'd had tough days, but this fellow looks beaten, his uncovered feet damaged and blistered from his efforts.

Although the rooms are tight, the rest of the albergue is warm and inviting. The dining area has a cottage feel with plenty of dark wood, a bar countertop and a huge worn table that has probably seated thousands of hungry pilgrims over the years.

After my shower I go exploring to capture the quaintness of this town. Right around the corner of our building is a stone stair-case that climbs towards a small cottage and a mini outdoor foot pool. There is no one around, so I take the liberty of dangling my legs into the cool water, tilting my face towards the sky. From here I can peek at the neighbours house and the multiple attempts at res-toration.

Feet refreshed, I continue towards the centre of town. Castro-jeriz has complemented the historical with newer construction. A modern walkway leads to a lookout that boasts the beautiful valley. My walk encourages me to do some research of the town history when I get home.

Back at the albergue, the bedroom has become a busy hive of activity, making the quarters even tighter. I meet Henrik from Denmark, who notices my toes wrapped in toilet paper. When I explain the loss of one toenail and the impending doom of the other, he digs into his pack, presenting me with the gift of a rubber tip for the toe with no nail.

"Use this Elizabeth. It will keep your toe protected from injury and infection."

Henrik is a handsome man in his late forties, with clear bright eyes and a long beard. He introduces me to his 14-year-old son, Hannibal, and his father, Niels; three generations travelling together along the Camino. I'm fascinated by these men, young and old, who decided to journey together, each with his own set of challenges and expectations.

A Boy Scout, Hannibal wears his shirt and scarf proudly every day, earning himself a few badges this vacation. I can see him being the first one at school to raise his hand and share *how I spent the summer*. He is quite the charmer and a delight to be around. I hadn't expected to see anyone so young, but he impresses me with his knowledge and enthusiasm for this journey, as well as his comfort around fellow travellers.

Niels has a warm smile and kind eyes. He makes me think of my paternal grandfather, who I met only once thirty years ago. Niels is around the age my father would be, but because my dad died younger, I can't imagine him in his seventies. It doesn't take me long to start calling him *Granddad*, which gets me a little nod and smile. Although his English is not as strong as Henrik's or Hannibal's, he understands more than he speaks.

Adopting this family as my own, they become *my Danish Trio*.

While I am sitting around the old dining room table, in walks Christophe. I had left this morning wishing for the opportunity to spend more time with him and here he is. Our conversations to date have been short, but he intrigues me and I have to admit, I am attracted to him.

It's not just a physical chemistry, but something deeper than that, although I can't put my finger on it. He's not much taller than me, obviously fit but not bulky, with a handsome boy next door look. His gentlemanly manner shines through when he is engaging with others, standing up to shake the hand of anyone he meets. *Is it a French charisma?* He's not flashy, nor does he call attention to himself, but there is something about him that has caught my antenna.

There is no shortage of men on the Camino and I've certainly had the opportunity to spend time with a few of them, but never once did I consider those relationships anything other than pilgrim camaraderie. I am not looking for a romantic relationship... but with Christophe there is a little something I wish to explore, feeling conflicted as I consider what it is that draws me to him.

He doesn't speak any English, so I am working double-time on my French skills. He talks quickly and his vocabulary exceeds my francophone library, but I don't let on when I am lost in translation, following the rules of international language.

The more time we spend together, the more enraptured I become, as I try to put the puzzle pieces together. I gather that he was formerly a parachutist in the military, but I get the sense that was in another life. There is certainly a connection and I am overwhelmed by my desire to learn more about who he is, on the inside.

The albergue owners offer an authentic Spanish dinner for a few extra euros. I'm sharing dinner with Christophe, my Danish Trio and another veteran pilgrim, quite possibly in his eighties, but in damn good shape. He is a little quieter, but engaged in our communal conversation. On a tight schedule, this gentleman isn't walking all the way to Santiago, as he needs to return home to attend to his bees! Through this conversation I learn Christophe is *also* a beekeeper.

After dinner our host leads us on an underground tour of the caves. Following the stone stairway, we find ourselves in a dark, damp chamber. The only lights are those built into the old stone walls. One of the guests attempts to translate the host's Spanish into English.

It seems this cave beneath the albergue, now a wine cellar, was once part of a chain of tunnels used as an escape route from the church to outside the city limits. We are going back in time, walking beneath the original 10th century Roman arches. Invited to crouch into a smaller space, I hang back already feeling the walls closing in on me. A small sample of wine ends our tour.

Back upstairs, the energy of pilgrim chatter fills the dining room.

A band of younger travellers, who look like long lost chums, were actually strangers until they met along the Camino. Their laughter is contagious as they retell shared stories for our benefit. John from Scotland, Jacob and Marco from Italy, Sarah and Annie from England, Don from Holland and another fellow from Ireland, crank the energy. The Irish fellow is excited to share that he will be visiting western Canada in a few weeks, to sing with Don Williams.

Is he walking all the way to Santiago, with an upcoming Alberta engagement? I don't have the heart to tell this sweet fellow, whose accent has me hanging onto his every word, that I am not familiar with Mr. Williams. Why burst his bubble!

I have had the most incredible day.

I wonder what other surprises the Camino has in store for me?

Day 11
20 km
August 14, 2015

Last night was my worst sleep so far and I am exhausted from all the tossing and turning, while I tried to find a comfortable position amidst the noise of squeaky springs and pilgrim snores. Up too early, I have to wait for the coffee to brew, but this gives me time to chat with the others as they prepare for their day.

The younger contingent from the United Kingdom are slightly disheveled and still in a daze from the night before. I am nursing my second coffee before the last of them makes it to the dining room. Noticing his limp, I return to my bunk to collect my can of aerosol pain relief.

"Why don't you spray this on your knees and ankles before you leave?"

"Oh, thanks so much. I'll do that!"

Good deed done. Check.

As early as Day 2, people seemed to know who I was before I had the chance to introduce myself. Audile had been talking about me. I realize that I, too, talk about those I've met, whether it's an interesting story they shared or simply how they made me feel when we were together.

This morning, Henrik asks me if I know "Julie... from Denmark." Henrik and Julie walked together a few days ago; she would have benefited from his brotherly warmth and the time spent with my Danish Trio. It's a small world, especially on the Camino!

Over-tired and with no real appetite, I am out the door by 7:30 am, with a couple of coffees under my belt, but only a bit of breakfast. My body feels heavy, as though I am moving through water. Thankfully, the sky is clear and inviting, the sun shining on the golden crops and the wind turbines wishing me *good morning*. There's an influx of cyclists on the trail, moving swiftly along the winding dirt path.

Where my trail gets lost in the fields, there is another snaking up the large hill ahead of me. *Am I walking there?* Distracted by the vibrant yellow sunflowers that worship the rising sun, I try to ignore the magnitude of the hill I am walking towards. *I should have eaten more for breakfast.*

From a distance, the vertical markings of the hill looked like ski trails, but as I walk along the base I see how years of erosion have carved deep crevices into the earth. That might explain why the mountains have rounded peaks.

Obviously the Meseta is not *all* flat and maybe if I read the guidebook I am carrying, I might not have been in for such a surprise. Taking my time, I tackle the gradual climb, stopping often to look back and photograph the trail I am conquering. I'm hoping the view, and my stamina, will impress my family. Amazed I can still breathe, I credit the singsong that surrounds me. I am either following or passing a clan of young Italians who probably belong to a church group, because gospel seems to be the only genre on their *live* playlist.

They have more enthusiasm than my younger friends from last night. Noticing me singing along as they pass, they encourage me to join in. The singing out loud *does* motivate me, but we have a kilometre to travel together, and I'm finding it hard to stay focused while they celebrate this glorious day, oblivious to the climb.

As I arrive at the top, only moments ahead of them, I let out a loud "Woo Hoo!" which momentarily drowns out the full throttle gospel that seems to have gotten louder. The Italians are... enthusiastic about life.

My Danish Trio has already arrived and we take a group photo as we admire the spectacular view of Mother Nature's creation. At the edge of the bluff, I sit down and celebrate my achievement.

The valley below is lined in fields of different colours and stages of harvest, all pieced together like a well crafted puzzle. Some crops are freshly cut, others have had their earth recently turned, and the greens, golds and browns fit together perfectly, with only a few clusters of trees and scattered farm houses around. More mountains lie across to the right, their wind turbines turning

slowly, as though stretching under the bright morning sun. *I am on top of the world.*

Getting off my perch, I swing my pack on my back as though weightless. A few steps forward, the blue of the sky beckons me, but where is the path? I can't see more than a few metres ahead. A few more steps and I know why.

The descent into the valley is not as kind as the climb up, the very steep trail offending my euphoric state. It doesn't take long before my knees wake up like startled babies. It is a long way down, but as Ben had written, *hills aren't scary.* Tell that to my knees!

You can do it Lizzie, it's just a hill, but my self-talk lacks conviction.

I certainly don't attempt to go straight down. I might not make it to the bottom. Starting with the slalom method, I take my time moving ever so slowly. An older Italian man comes up behind me and in his wisdom, suggests I bend my knees and walk heel-to-toe. I am willing to try anything that will make this easier. Focused on the mechanics, I consciously think about every movement, which slows me to a crawl.

"Try moving a little bit faster."

I look at him as though he's suggested I race him down the hill, and maintain my 90-year-old pace. His method *does* reduce the pain in my knees. He continues down the hill, *his good deed done.*

My Danish Trio has moved ahead; they are nowhere in sight.

My fellow comrades are thoughtful with their suggestions and I appreciate all the tips I get. It takes me a bit of time to get the hang of it; I am a slow learner.

I remember when Pierre tried to teach me how to ride a motorcycle. He bought me an old Honda 250cc and once we got it running, he took me into an empty parking lot one Sunday morning. I'd never driven standard, so the concept of the clutch was foreign. Even with his encouraging "feel the bike, Lizzie," I didn't know what I was meant to feel, bringing me to the verge of tears.

Maybe that's why I am so tormented by these hills: I'm frustrated that I cannot meet the challenge. Out of shape, with no real strength in my bulk, and knees that cannot tolerate the impact, I hate that I can be defeated by a damn hill.

You have to get over the fact that this is difficult.

By the time I stop for lunch, my FitBit reads only 10 km and yet I am pooped. The sun is strong, my pack is heavy and my aching legs are waiting patiently for the unending, boring flat the guidebooks promised. I'm blaming my fatigue on the lack of sleep and the assault on my knees.

My plan *was* to walk another 16 km to Frómista, but I don't have that much to give the day. I'll be satisfied if I can do another ten. There are more than a few hills and I am not impressed.

The path changes from dirt trails to pavement, then back into the fields of sunflowers, as though the day is trying to make amends for upsetting me. I continue to meet the challenges, head on, for what they are. Simple tests of my endurance. I won't be taken down by a hill of dirt. There will be no tears today, but there will be plenty of breaks.

Changing regions once again, I leave behind La Rioja and enter into Palencia, the lusher landscape welcoming me. Crops of corn, hay and sunflowers, provide so much visual delight and snapping photos takes my mind off the kilometres still to travel. There is something about these earthy colours that makes the land come alive.

The last few kilometres into Boadilla del Camino are harder to walk, the larger rocks shifting beneath my boots. Satisfied with my 20 km day, I stop at 2 pm, happy to arrive earlier rather than later. I plan to put my feet up and relax with as many Cokes as necessary. The *Albergue Titas* resembles a ski lodge, with a spacious lobby, small convenience store to the right and dining room on the left.

After I register, the owner brings me upstairs to the bedroom, an airy and uncluttered space with plenty of windows and room between the bunk beds. The opposite of the sardine can I slept in last night. There is a private bathroom and shower for women and one for men. *This feels like home.*

Three beds are already spoken for with the occupants enjoying their afternoon siesta, so I choose the one closest to the door. The majority of pilgrims will probably arrive late afternoon, unless they are following the guidebooks and continuing on to the end of the day's stage, in Frómista.

It is a gorgeous day, but I can only take so much of my own company. I'm bored with the quiet. At least when I'm walking, the time passes. If there was someone to talk with I'd stay outside, but there isn't a soul around. When I return to the bedroom, my room-mates have vanished. *Where'd they go?* I never saw them leave, but I have the room to myself.

Desperate to pass the time, I lay on my bunk, but I don't sleep. I fidget.

By 4 pm I am starving, returning downstairs to ask the woman if I can have an ensalada. Her reaction is enough to tell me it's not dinner time. "Una momento," she leaves me to confer with the owner.

The 5 euros is worth the plate mounded high with vegetables and tuna. It is one of the best salads I have had the pleasure to devour. Not so long ago, I would have panicked at the idea of eating out alone, but I no longer feel out of place.

Just lonely.

Two younger women arrive without their packs, stopping because of the ice cream sign in the window. They have already booked themselves into another albergue, but seeing how new this one is, they contemplate joining me. I want to beg them to collect their belongings and move over, but it isn't my place. They both speak English, the Australian carrying the conversation, as she tells me about the American woman who went missing from Astorga in April.

"The woman was on her own, during a month when there are fewer travellers. Reports said that she had been abducted in the early morning and never seen again. When she hadn't checked in with her family, her brother knew something was wrong, prompting a search and investigation. You need to be careful, Elizabeth!"

More often than not, I am truly walking alone. Not in the early hours before the sun comes up, but alone on the empty road or trail, with no other pilgrims in sight. I'm not sure how I missed this during my regular peeping on the Camino forum, but my Australian friend confirms the pilgrim community was in shock. This isn't something that happens here.

The loneliness returns once the girls leave. No other pilgrims have arrived, so it looks like I will be dining alone... again. I miss the camaraderie and energy of last night.

My emails to Pierre are lengthier than usual; I miss him more when I feel lonely. We have a few exchanges and that helps brighten my mood, but it also confirms how much I need to have people around me. Not all the time, but at least in the evenings.

There has been too much isolation today.

I make my way to the dining room, getting the attention of my albergue host. He brings me the first course of my dinner, which isn't great. I decline the second entrée, saying with a smile that I am full. "Café, por favor."

He looks jilted, making me feel like my request is an inconvenience. Waiting on my coffee, I hear the microwave turning. He has poured me a cup of reheated, stale brew. *The Spanish hospitality is lacking tonight.*

Tired of being on my own, I head up to bed for an early night, well aware that I will benefit from a good sleep. Taking a few minutes, I add my end of day experiences to my journal.

Today marks Day 11. I have completed one third of my journey and have walked an incredible, often challenging, 242 km.

*"I may not be there yet,
but I am closer than yesterday.
One step can make all the difference."*
Unknown

I wish I had someone in the next bunk to share this with. I am proud of my accomplishments and I want to tell the world. Plugging in my phone, I see an email from my friend Sabine. The quote she sent encourages me as I turn off the light and close my eyes.

Day 12
24 km
August 15, 2015

The room is dark as my eyes flutter open. It's very quiet, no sound of snoring or movement. Looking around, I see my roommates have already departed, as though I've been alone the entire night.

A great night sleep has rewarded me with emotional and physical strength. I feel well rested and ready to give the coffee another try. With my tasty, hot beverage in one hand and my smokes in another, I sit on the bench outside my albergue. Eager to start my day, I'm slightly disappointed that it's still too dark to venture far. I didn't bring any headgear and I am not about to start walking without any light.

When I ask for a second cup, my host is accomodating and in good spirits. *I bet he had a good night sleep as well.*

With my backpack over one shoulder, I return to the bench that shelters my boots. A fresh Bandaid over the still nailed toe, I pack my Crocs and pull on my wool socks. There's no hesitation to get my boots on and start walking.

With one last check of my emails, I see Ev's quote has arrived early.

> *"With the new day comes new strength and new thoughts."*
> Eleanor Roosevelt

Ready to say goodbye to Boadilla del Camino, I thank my host. "Buenos Dias. I hope you have a great day, Señor."

Even as the sky lightens, the sun is hidden. I'm not complaining, appreciating the cooler morning. With renewed optimism, I begin today's trek towards Carrión de los Condes, a little farther than my normal 20 km, but according to my map, there shouldn't be any hills today, and I'll be reaching Frómista in 5 km.

Trees line the left side of the path, breaking up my visual field. Despite the lack of rain, the water in the canal is almost to the top. This morning's scenery is uninspiring until I reach a new harvest in the early stages of growth. The quilt-like fields catch my attention, my thoughts returning to the northwest Plains we rode through last summer, albeit at much faster speeds than my 4 km per hour.

There are no pilgrims this morning. Boadilla del Camino isn't a popular starting point, so the bulk of pilgrim traffic is already 5 km ahead of me. After yesterday's isolation, I am craving company and the absence of any tugs at my heart. Entering Frómista, I contemplate stopping at the little café.

"Elizabeth!"

Julie is standing outside the café door waving to me. She has been sitting inside, perched on a stool by the front window, watching. "Henrik told me he met you. I was hoping you might pass by before I leave to catch my train to Sarria."

Julie is leaving in fifteen minutes.

Sarria is the 100 km mark for pilgrims wanting to receive their compostela, an official Latin certificate of completion. The Pilgrim Passport, or credential as it's known, is proof you have met two of the three requirements: you walked *all* of the last 100 km and you collected two stamps per day, one from your albergue and the other from another establishment. The third requirement is that you have been walking for religious or spiritual purposes.

Although Julie has made her decision to fast forward to Sarria, she is conflicted, wanting to share her decision with someone who might understand. She isn't the first pilgrim to deviate from the original plan, but that doesn't make it any easier.

Each person is walking their own way, for their own benefit. Changing plans, skipping sections, or ending early does not equal failure. It is part of the journey, which continues long after we return home, whether we arrive in Santiago or not.

Some individuals feel the need to walk the entire 800 km, without resorting to any other form of transportation. Whether it's a personal challenge or a sense of legitimacy, they will struggle through and endure the challenges.

Others, like myself and Julie, don't feel that is as important as the experiences and growth along the way. I will walk for as long as I can, even surpassing my preconceived limitations, but I didn't come to the Camino to walk. I came to escape, to learn about myself, to trust that inner voice whatever it is saying. The walking serves as a tool; the trials and celebrations of each day are part of the process.

Julie is torn between the guilt of letting herself down, and the feeling in her gut that is directing her to Sarria. Only she knows what she needs right now, but I can relate to the inner conflict. Taking a taxi to Estella or the bus to Burgos was never part of my plan either.

There is no right or wrong way to experience the Camino.

Julie feels this is the best decision for her. Nothing else matters.

We hug goodbye as she rushes off to catch her train, leaving me grateful for this unexpected visit.

The canal has reappeared, a tree-lined path leading me towards the locks, the height of the water no more than a foot beneath the short walkway. A leak spills from the worn corners of the block foundation. From the centre of the walkway, I follow the flow of water with my eyes as it travels the wide, man-made steps guiding the energy back to its natural path.

There's a fair amount of walking along highways, through barren fields and drab little towns, but at least the change breaks up the monotony. The cooler weather and lack of hills allow me a decent pace, but company along the way would be most welcome.

Instead of the hikers I hoped to see, there are cars towing small trailers, turning off into the bush. There is barking in the distance and shots fired. Someone had mentioned today is a Holy Day. August 15th is a national holiday; the *Feast Day of the Assumption of Mary*, a celebration of the day the Virgin Mary entered heaven. A strange day to be hunting, but I know little of Catholic practices, at home or abroad.

By the time I make it to Villarmentero, I have walked about 17 km and am starving for conversation. A large yard with hanging hammocks, tables and chairs, a sprinkler and kids toys spread everywhere, seems the perfect spot to engage with others. Tunes are playing on speakers and the wild fowl are patrolling the busy yard.

Although the chickens seem harmless, the geese are eyeing lunches and snacks on the tables, waiting for an opportunity to crane their necks. They are fearless, pecking on backpacks, challenging pilgrims in a dual for their bocadillos.

Henrik, Hannibal and Niels are already mid-way through their lunch. They, too, are heading towards Carrión de los Condes, intending to spend the night at a monastery. "Why don't you join us, Elizabeth?"

Thank goodness! I'm not sure how well I would manage on my own for another night. After they leave, I hang around a little longer to enjoy the entertainment.

There is definitely a sign needed: *Don't fight the fowl!* I laugh, sitting back in my chair, while three young men try to hold onto their bravado in the face of several honking grey geese. The men give up, retreating from their table, their snacks up for grabs.

As soon as I enter Carrión de los Condes, I am on a mission to find the monastery, walking up and down the street searching for a sign. Unsuccessful, I ask a local man for assistance. In the true sense of hospitality to peregrinos, he walks me through the alleyways and maze of streets, pointing down the road. Not sure if we took a shortcut or whether I'll find my way out, but I know I'm headed in the right direction when I see two pairs of hikers up ahead, arriving at the main entrance together.

The two couples speak Spanish, with no English vocabulary. Peeking through the glass window, there's no sign of life in the large marble foyer, but a nun responds to our doorbell ring. More Spanish conversation, which I don't understand.

Into a fancy dining room turned boardroom, the nun gestures for us to take a seat at the long, polished wooden table. She collects her peregrino registration supplies and places them with purpose on the table. *This is serious business.* Once she is seated in front of the albergue stamp, ledger book and small cash box, we are ready to proceed.

She starts with one of the Spanish pilgrims, asking for their passport and credential. She is speaking quickly and assuming I understand her instructions, but all I can offer in return is a blank look. I turn towards the others for guidance; they nod and smile. *Exactly.* I nod and smile at the Sister, who looks like a no-nonsense kind of woman.

The *Albergue Espiritu Santo* has several sleeping quarters, mine housing single beds. I much prefer that, avoiding upper bunks at all cost. My Danish Trio arrived 30 minutes earlier and I select the bed next to Hannibal.

I have found the last two days very lonely, and I'm desperate for companionship. Not waiting for an invitation, I extend my own. "Would you mind if I joined you for dinner?"

Their smiles warm my heart. "That sounds great, Elizabeth."

Dinner for four. Check.

With my clothes washed, I head out to the clotheslines, scanning the large courtyard, mentally reserving a table and chair for one. There are plenty of spots to sit with my journal and more than enough people to chat with.

Can it get any better?

Christophe comes up the ramp just as I pin my last sock. Our reactions are mirrored; surprised and delighted, we hug like long lost friends.

Here come the butterflies.

I motion towards the courtyard. "I was just going to sit at a table."

"Do you mind if I join you?" *The butterflies take flight.*

My French language skills are decent, but don't compete with a Parisian and I cannot afford to resort to the international language. I want to understand everything he is telling me, asking him to slow down and explain further. Sharing stories and catching up on our Camino happenings, we start learning about one another. The existence of the others in the courtyard is forgotten, their conversations background music.

He says a few words in English. *He'd been keeping a secret.* I encourage him to practice, while I work on my French. He's curious about Canada, so I answer his questions, highlighting the different regions, distinguishing the hospitality of the East Coasters, and sharing some of the challenges between Quebec and the rest of the country.

"I would love to visit and maybe even move there. Are you familiar with the process for immigration?"

Flashes of him visiting me at home, and explaining to Pierre why I invited him, whiz through my head. *I can deal with that if the time comes.*

"I know nothing about Immigration processes, but am happy to help in any way I can." Before I can even check my actions, I am tearing a small strip of paper from the back of my journal and writing my email address. *What are you doing, giving him your email? Do you want him to stay in touch once he returns to France?*

The time passes too quickly and then he extends an invitation. "I am going to visit the Cathedral. Would you like to join me? We can get ourselves an ice cream!"

I feel alive, energized, a tingling current flowing through my body. We keep finding each other, but I don't know what it means and I don't trust myself. It has been such a wonderful experience being with Christophe, as though he has flicked on a switch in my heart.

But I had originally come outside to write in my journal and email Pierre, something I look forward to at the end of each day. Pierre and I have gone through so much together and not once have I had any thoughts of wanting anything other than a happily ever after...with him.

Something in the depth of my subconscious steers me away from accepting Christophe's invitation. "I appreciate the offer, but I think I'll write in my journal and send some emails home." My regret is immediate, but it is too late. He goes off to explore town.

The boys are as hungry as I am, so it's an easy decision to dine early. Through the massive tin doors on the opposite side of the courtyard, we follow the street to the first eatery. Brought to the back of the restaurant, we have the mini dining room all to ourselves. As we consider the options on the pilgrim menu, we challenge our waiter with requests of items not listed.

Our evening is filled with laughter and conversation, like any family around the dinner table.

Back at the monastery, the courtyard is busy, but there is no sight of Christophe. Hannibal joins me, a needed distraction from my wandering thoughts. I can always count on an interesting conversation with this 14-year-old Boy Scout.

John, one of the fellows from the European camp and who translated the cave tour, sits down to join us. He is alone this evening, no longer travelling with the others, but I don't ask why. There is no need. That is the way of the Camino. Just because you are together today, doesn't mean you'll be that way tomorrow.

The tone of our conversation has shifted from two nights ago, when we were a crowd of pilgrims having a good time. This is a more personal, one-on-one conversation. John was a teacher, coming to Madrid a few years ago to instruct English, where he picked up his almost fluent Spanish.

"Can I ask how old you are John?"

He is not as young as I thought, closer to forty. *I didn't see that coming.*

As the sun sets and the courtyard empties, I acknowledge that I have lost my chance to indulge and explore my fantasies about Christophe. As though Hannibal can sense my mood change, he alerts me to my coping behaviour. "Are you having another cigarette, Elizabeth? You just put one out, you know!"

I laugh and thank him for monitoring me, making the conscious decision to refrain from lighting up. I have become quite fond of Hannibal. In many ways he is more mature than his fourteen years.

There was too much isolation today, but I received two unexpected gifts: meeting Julie this morning and having one last opportunity to spend time with Christophe.

Day 13
23.5 km
August 16, 2015

Beds squeaking, people snoring; just the normal sounds when sharing your bedroom with 30 other people. I wake in the pitch black, and the urge to pee forces me to check my FitBit for the time. *It's only midnight.* Moving my feet blindly under the bed, I find my Crocs and work my way, arms outstretched, toward the thin crack of light identifying the washroom. By the time I'm finished, the fluorescent glare of the stall has blinded me. With no beacon above my own bed, I need to make sure I don't crawl in with Hannibal by mistake.

I should have counted my steps.

Sleep is only a restless consciousness, until my roommates start to rise at 6 am.

With no vending machines on site, I stretch the last mouthfuls of warm orange juice with small bites of a Clif Bar that resist being swallowed. The quiet of the courtyard is disturbed by the occasional pilgrim exit through the large tin door. I'm not ready yet and it's going to be a while before I exit that door myself, as I have no desire to start walking.

Or even continue.

The gloomy sky hangs heavy, reflecting the weight on my chest. Back inside, my Danish family is in different stages of readiness. Henrik outlines their plan for the day. "Dad is not up for a full day of walking, so he's going to take a taxi the first 17 km. Hannibal and I will join him in Caldadilla de la Cueza."

Grandad is seated on the edge of his bed, shoulders slumped, head down. *I think I know how you feel, Niels. Maybe I should join you in the taxi.* I don't want to walk, but taking a taxi doesn't feel right. I'm going to have other mornings when I feel like this, but I can't start finding excuses. If I am going to do that, I might as well go home.

Henrik feels the dip in my energy. "Do you want me to make a reservation for you at our albergue? You can take your time and meet us there."

Grateful for his empathy, I take him up on his offer. Knowing there is company waiting for me at the end of the day will keep me moving forward.

"I'll send you a Facebook message with the name of the albergue."

With my orange juice finished and the remains of my half-eaten Clif Bar tucked in the outside pocket of my pack, I attend to my feet. The toe with no nail is fine, thanks to the condom Henrik provided within minutes of meeting me. The other one is just about ready to say *Adiós. I'll deal with it later.*

First step over the threshold and I consider stopping at a café for breakfast, or even just a coffee. Depleted of any motivation, I don't bother, and drag myself through the quiet streets. Out of town, the paths are deserted, the landscape ugly. There is no beauty in these barren fields. *How long has it been since any crops flourished here?*

Today has one of the longest stretches with no access to food or drink. That doesn't help my mood or encourage me to pick up my pace. A darkness contaminates my thoughts, and every step is a chore. *I should have joined Niels in the taxi.*

Tucked off the side of the road and hidden by trees is a small mobile food truck. I have walked about 6 km and this canteen is a welcome sight. Dropping my pack and poles at a picnic table, I approach the vendor with a big smile. "Una café con leche, por favor."

My face drops at the size of the *demitasse*, no bigger than a Dixie Cup. I want to ooze all the Canadian charm I can muster and offer him 5 euros to take his own thermal mug from his truck and fill it with coffee. But I don't. *Of course not.* Instead, I flash a forced, all teeth smile, letting him know that I will need a few of these.

"No problemo" he reassures me, offering to refill at no charge.

I point to the sandwich grill on the stainless steel counter and he offers to make me a grilled ham and cheese. While I savour my homemade breakfast, another pilgrim enters from the road. I offer a smile and space for him to join me at the table, and relish the company!

Daniel is from Italy and also started in Pamplona. "I am only walking as far as León this year." He will continue the Camino another time, but his voice lacks conviction. He isn't motivated this morning and we are ineffective in helping each other's mood.

What I am doing here?

It's not an option to sit here all morning, so I reluctantly gather my equipment and leave Daniel to his own company.

The thoughts between my ears are swirling, threatening a wind storm. I had the idea that escaping home and everyone I love, putting myself in foreign environment and walking every damn day for over 700 km, might bring me a little closer to finding... *what*?

Who I am?

What I should be doing?

The negative thoughts consume me. I spend all day, more often than not on my own; forcing my body to walk 20 km so that I can end up in an unknown lodging; maybe have a meal, probably on my own; drink more water than normal and not even pee during the day; spend a restless night fighting the aches and pains... only to start all over again the next morning. *How is any of this beneficial?*

I have been gone for two weeks, still three to go. *Why am I putting myself through this?* My optimism is blinded by tormenting thoughts, the pull towards the dark hole increasing with each step.

The guidebooks state that today's stage of the Meseta is the most challenging due to the never-changing flat trail through the wide open fields, making one vulnerable under the hot sun with little shade and few rest stops for food or water. The concerns are not physical, as the lands are tediously unchallenging. The risk is the effect it has on one's mental state.

I don't mind the flat, I prefer it. But today's sights are discouraging, with little sign of vegetation or people, the scenery barely changing. Other than the unexpected portable canteen this morning, there is *nothing* for 17 km, not even a water fountain to refill my bottles.

All I have is time to let my thoughts go wild. And they are.

Sunflower fields wave in the distance, and my spirit picks up at the only drop of colour on an otherwise grey canvas. Getting closer, I see they too have their heads down. *How's that for a sign?* My own emblem of hope can't even look at me. I'm taking very few photos... there is nothing here I wish to remember. I have seen maybe a dozen people all day. *Where the hell is everyone?*

Every burdensome step is shifting my thoughts towards home. *I am ready to quit this fantasy of a pilgrimage and put an end to the misery.* Hating the routine, the isolation, the struggles... my thoughts fester as I drag myself across the desert. I have no desire to skip ahead to Sarria and walk from there. The compostela was never important to me and it certainly doesn't mean anything, as I plan the most direct route home.

I just don't want to be here anymore. I am so bloody tired of being alone.

It's hard to find any light when there isn't anyone to say those right words to help me see a little clearer. All I have right now are my own dark thoughts and God knows they aren't helping the situation. My mind is racing. I don't see any way out of this torment other than to call it quits. I am not feeling inspired, spiritually enlightened or otherwise benefiting from this journey. That is my justification for ending this *right now.*

I can talk myself into or out of anything. I'm not even wondering if I have given it enough time.

The lonely trek to Caldadilla de la Cueza has dragged on for 11 km since my grilled cheese, giving me plenty of time to plan my escape out of Spain. Stopping at the first and only store, I head for the outside vending machine, slipping my euros in the coin slot.

On the bench I light up a cigarette and think about possible next steps. *Where can I catch a plane? Can I change my departure date? What will people think if I come home early?* I have a long list of reasons for leaving.

A couple exit the store and recognize me from the road. They passed during one of my longer self-pitying smoke breaks and she can tell from the look on my face that I am not doing well emotionally. Sitting down beside me, she encourages me to talk.

She listens while I blurt out what is going on in my head and weighing on my heart. I let it all out, including all the reasons why I want to go home.

Nodding in empathy, a hand on my shoulder, I know she understands. "Have you thought about taking shorter days or breaks in between days, to rest your body? It may help you clear your thoughts and recharge physically. It is difficult to walk so many kilometres each and every day!"

I had heard similar advice, but I'm not buying what she's selling. I have pretty much decided I want to quit and I can come up with more than enough reasons why I can't finish what I started. *I just want to go home.*

"Would you like some company to the next town? Steven and I are stopping in Ledigos." The next town, the end of the day, and maybe the Camino, is another 6 km walk.

Steven falls behind us, while Eleanor and I talk during those 6 km of paved road. Eleanor and Steven are from Swaziland and have 4 children. She is a teacher and he a principal. Steven walked the Camino a few years ago, and neither seem too stressed by the day.

By the time we arrive at the *Albergue de Peregrinos el Palomar*, I am ready to stay with these two wonderful souls who have carried me. There are few people here, and I ask the owner if she has checked in three pilgrims from Denmark. *They aren't here.*

Showered, clothes washed and hanging on the line, I head into the sun-filled backyard. Sitting around the patio table, feeling the warmth on my face, my mind starts to clear now that I have stopped.

This albergue could be much nicer if the owners took a little time to cut the grass, plant some flowers, and fish the dead bird out of the stagnant pool. It would be so easy to fix this into something quite lovely. *I could run this albergue, welcoming weary pilgrims like myself.*

Eleanor's compassion is exactly what I need after 17 lonely kilometres of walking. Steven takes his chair into the shade, giving his wife the space to finish mending my spirit. She pulls a tube of cream from her little bag. "Steven and I massage each others feet at the end of every day. It helps us relax and feel grounded."

That is a word that resonates with me. I certainly didn't feel grounded today: I let the isolation, loneliness, and homesickness pull me away from my intentions.

Looking me in the eye she asks, "Can I rub your feet?"

Her innate desire to support a fellow human through a challenging time shines through. It seems that on the Camino we are unhindered by the restraints that often hold us back from being our best self. Eleanor is proving that we are all equal, connected on this road we travel together.

It takes a few minutes to relax, but she quietly works her fingers, applying pressure until I let go. By the time she has massaged both feet, the tension has released. With a few tears, I let her know that her appearance pulled me away from a dark abyss.

Eleanor is *another* Camino angel that has shown me I am not alone.

Out of respect, I give this couple time for themselves and walk into the neighbouring bar. Ordering a Coke, I inquire about also getting some food. My Spanish hasn't improved and he gestures towards the patio. His indifference feels like he is shooing me away, but perhaps he means to follow with a menu.

From the number of cigarette butts in the ashtray, I'd say more than enough time has passed. Maybe I hadn't made myself clear, maybe he has forgotten me, or maybe he just doesn't care. Whatever the reason for refusing my appetite, I am not impressed. This is not the energy I need to continue my healing. There must be another place to eat and I'm bloody starved.

As I leave in search of a restaurant, I notice a change in my attitude, no longer possessed by my afternoon thoughts. At the end of the street, on the right hand corner, is a bright establishment beckoning me.

Laughter and conversations fill the lounge, as I follow my server into the elegant dining room. White walls are tastefully decorated, the tables are beautifully set; night and day to the bar beside my albergue. The server pours me a glass of cold water and hands me the Pilgrim Menu.

When she returns, I point to a neighbouring table inquiring what the couple are eating. In less than five minutes, Steven and Laura from England, come over to join me.

Seems I was destined to find my way here, sharing the company of this newly married British couple. Unknowingly, they resume the role Eleanor played. After dinner we move into the garden, finishing our wine and wrapping up our evening with coffees.

Our conversation evolves toward the challenges we have each faced, specifically the events of today and how I had worked myself into a lather, ready to find the next flight home. They too had experienced doubts about wanting to continue, but realize after talking with me, that having a partner to share it with helps immensely.

As we get up to hug goodnight, we all agree that tomorrow will be a much brighter day.

Returning to my albergue, I send an email home, copying everyone. It frightened me how quickly my emotions took over, right from the time I woke up. I felt powerless in reeling myself back to a more positive mindset. Then I met some people who helped clear the chaos in my head. I need to share my day and my thoughts about wanting to come home.

I hadn't noticed Ev's email from earlier, but perhaps I was not meant to see it until now.

"A mind that is stretched by a new experience can never go back to its old dimensions."
Oliver Wendell Holmes, Jr.

I have yet to *Google* "How to Escape the Camino," but the only decision I am committing to is to walk tomorrow. I have not given up on myself, but I am allowing myself the option to stop, should I feel it is the right thing.

For me.

Day 14
17 km
August 17, 2015

*W*hat the hell happened yesterday?

In the sunlight of this new day, I have recovered the woman who can replay events with a clearer mind. Perhaps yesterday's doom and gloom needed to occur, leaving me so lost, alone and ready to throw away this journey, that I accepted the help of strangers. I tend to avoid asking for help, feeling it a sign of my own weakness.

Let me be your rock, but don't worry about me, because It's All Good.

It wasn't *all good* yesterday, finding myself heading into the depths of a very dark place. The only way I knew how to escape it was to quit. It wouldn't be the first time I took that route. *Why do I make it so difficult to live up to my own expectations?*

The email to *everyone* last night was a cry for help, but it also justified an earlier departure from Spain, if it comes to that.

I have an out!

I tried to cover the desperation with a bit of humour, jokingly suggesting they hold off placing bets on when I would return. I knew my family and friends would offer encouragement, but the tidal wave of emails that filled my Inbox was unexpected. *Why are you surprised?* The power of love is the best sign of all.

"No one is going to tell you what to do, you're doing this for your own reasons. You've already done quite the feat! We're all going to support whatever you decide to do!"

"I know that whatever is meant to be, will be. And whatever decision you make will be the right one."

"Whatever you decide will turn out to have been the right thing to do. The adventure will continue, no matter what the outcome is."

"You still sound like a believer in the Camino, and that it does provide. You will get the signs you need, to know what to do. After all, it is all about the signs, Lizzie!"

"You are a winner no matter what you decide. Let your heart, mind and body decide your right path."

"No matter what you decide, you've done it!"

"There are no rules."

"You have succeeded in all of our eyes. Do what you feel is best for you."

"In the end it comes down to what you want, what you need and taking one little step at a time in either direction. Wishing you all the strength for whatever YOU decide."

Between my Camino Angels and my cheerleaders back home, the pressure was relieved, their words reinforcing the most important lesson. *I am on this journey for myself.* What others think, or what I might interpret as their thoughts, is not nearly as important as what I think.

In a generous mood, I give the neighbouring bar another chance. With my café grande and a pastry, I sit on the patio with renewed faith in myself.

Before Eleanor and Steven leave, I thank her for being there for me yesterday. "I want you to know how much your kindness means to me. My day would have ended much differently, had I not met you."

Although I am starting off on my own, I am not alone. I will continue walking... with no expectations, no failures, and no worries.

Today I am walking.

In no time I have caught up to a pair of peregrinos I saw at the bar last night. Dad is walking, but his 15-year-old son is riding an adult tricycle, unable to walk. Although my Spanish isn't strong enough for a conversation, I'm grateful for the few shared minutes, reevaluating yesterday's pity party.

The sun is brilliant in a clear sky of baby blue. There are more fields of sunflowers than my eyes can take in. Their colours so vibrant, they look up towards me with a smile. My pack doesn't feel as heavy, my feet aren't dragging, and I have a pretty good pace.

There is no music to be heard, but I catch myself humming out loud. Inept at recalling song titles and artists names, I cannot be sure if it is an actual song or just the music in my heart, the chorus echoing happiness.

With less than 3 km under my feet, I take my first pit stop in Terradillos de Templarios and sit outside with Alejandro, who is from Italy and José, from Burgos, both walking to Santiago.

Like me, they struggled with yesterday's landscape, solitude and the emotions that came with it. When our break is over, we continue walking together. The wheat fields have returned in all of their golden splendour and a crop of sunflowers, with auburn heads bent towards the ground, reinforce the beauty of all living things.

There are no hills that make me cringe, and my pace is strong as I keep up to the men and their long strides. Seeing more sunflowers than any other day, I know it's a reminder that everything will work out fine.

We stop for lunch in San Nicolás del Real Camino and I am already more confident about the rest of the day. When Alejandro and José get ready to leave, I let them know that I will be staying a little bit longer. I want to spend some time in my own company.

Strange that yesterday I was desperately seeking others to fill a void, and this afternoon I am willing to let them leave without me, but we had spent enough time together to know that I can continue on my own. "Buen Camino, Amigos."

As I approach a long-forgotten building, I see cyclist peregrinos taking photos between two statues facing an invisible gateway. Admiring the worn stonework, I'm curious about the ancient structure that seeks to tell its story. Happy to offer my photographic services, I introduce myself to these Italians who have done their Camino research. "This was once considered the halfway mark of the Camino de Santiago. And that," pointing to the remains of the building, "was a pilgrim hostel."

As I walk into Sahagún, a local man hands me a flyer for the monastery. I take it without too much thought, detouring to the sidewalk for a break. I still have another 5 km before reaching Calzada de Coto.

Oblivious to the woman who was walking behind me, I'm surprised when she joins me on the curb, waving the flyer in hand. "Are you staying at the monastery tonight?" I hadn't planned on stopping in Sahagún, but this Spanish woman has appeared out of nowhere, asking if I want to join her. I am going with the flow and accepting the gifts of the universe.

Why not?

As we enter into the *Sahagún Benedictinas,* I can feel a peacefulness wash over me. Quite different from the monastery of two nights ago, pilgrims have access to wander the building. Floors and furniture glisten from polish, cabinets and walls display objects of worship, the Catholic faith echoed throughout. A book-filled library offers a couple of leather chairs.

Yes, there is a comforting vibe here and I welcome it. Or perhaps it welcomes me.

The 16 euros includes a traditional Spanish dinner and continental breakfast in the morning. We are sharing our two-bunk room with Patrice, a 50-year old French cyclist. In no rush to shower, I give my roommates the time to get washed up, while I explore the premises. There's a certain calm I am drawn into and I couldn't ask for a better place to wrap up the day, after yesterday's emotional cyclone.

With the Coke I bought from the front office, I visit the small enclosed garden, finding a table under the stream of sunlight filtered through the roof. I've come prepared to revisit the last 24 hours, bringing my journal, cellphone, and pack of *Winston's.*

This garden is a small paradise with a stone walkway that detours around the colourful plants and flowers. Face towards the sky, I voice my appreciation. "Thank you for giving me another day. I am happy to still be here."

It is with the darkness of yesterday that I can fully appreciate today's light. I need to document my day and the incredible change in perspective. With my feet relaxing on the nearby chair, my skin warmed by the sunlight, I consider the 360 degree change in my

mental state. It hardly seems possible that yesterday I felt surrounded by darkness and today I am glowing.

*"Focus on the journey, not the desti-
nation. Joy is found not in finishing an
activity but in doing it."*
Greg Anderson

I know the hills will return once I am through the Meseta, but
I'm not worrying. Tomorrow is another day, but right now I am
congratulating myself on the incredible accomplishment. I have
walked two of the five weeks.

As I continue to read the emails received this morning, I discover a missed Facebook message from Henrik. How I would love
to see them again, but I sense our time together has ended. My
Brother knows how much he and his family mean to me.

Day 15
18 km
August 18, 2015

When I ask my roommates if I snored, they simply answer "YES!" I've heard that before and know it translates into *you kept me awake all night!* These *Yes* responses make me uncomfortable, but there isn't much I can do about my snoring, other than hope I have new roommates each evening. *Maybe I should stop asking and just appear shocked when anyone mentions it.*

The church bells ring as I don my surgical cap and gown to remove the second toenail. I feel like a pro, pulling back the nail and gently tearing it away from the cuticle at the top. No stomach rolls, no sweats, just removing *another* toenail. As Ben says, *these make for badass stories.*

There are more people on the trail this morning, and I'm happy to exchange a *Buen Camino* with my fellow travellers. I can tell

I'm feeling better; my breaks are merely for a rest when the opportunity presents itself.

I catch myself in a reverie, when I notice shadows beside my own. Turning around in anticipation of another pilgrim, I smile when I discover my company is actually a reflection from the trees I am walking beside. *You are never alone on the Camino.*

Since passing the 400 km mark there are more boulders spray painted with the kilometre-countdown to Santiago. Every step brings me closer.

The trail has been pleasant this morning, and I reach Bercianos del Real Camino in a great mood. A path decorated with various national flags leads the way towards the *Casa del Peregrino*. The owner smiles as I enter the A-framed café, welcoming me. "Good morning."

Not needing my Spanish language skills, I ask for a coffee, "… the largest cup you have, please and thanks." She understands, pointing to a large mug she fills with a frothy café con leche. Eyeballing the tray of baked goods, she proudly confirms, "Yes, they are homemade." Taking my snack to one of the umbrella covered tables, I watch this husband and wife team in action.

A group of Italian cyclists arrives and he welcomes them in their mother tongue, similar to how his wife wished me a *Good*

Morning, not *Buenos Dias*. When all clients are attended to, she comes to sit with me.

This couple met 6 years ago on the Camino. Now they own and operate this gem of a café, hoping to one day walk the route with their young daughter. As pilgrims themselves, they understand the physical and emotional demands, especially through the Meseta. They are not just business owners, but Ambassadors of the Camino. Her husband speaks six languages and they pay attention to their customers, as she did with me, noticing my Canadian flag badges.

"We want you to feel welcome."

I certainly do!

Our conversation turns to those peregrinos who walk for a week or two at a time. "Every pilgrim is searching, but the time spent is not as important as their openness to the experiences along the way."

My own comfort level with this lovely woman allows me to open up about my dark day on the Meseta.

"That is normal and to be expected. So many pilgrims experience similar emotions." With a warm smile she places her hand on my arm. "There is nothing wrong with wanting to go home. The positive is that you are still here today. Every day is another opportunity to grow and learn."

I could easily hang around all afternoon, but I received what I needed.

Before leaving, I head to the little girls' room, a rare need on any given day, as the water I drink seems to evaporate before it has time to pass through my body. Their washroom has hand soap *and* paper towels. *Such luxury!*

The sky, the land, the air... everything seems fresh and bright. The fields are newly turned, sandbars of rich red earth await the next planting season. Other than my hikes through Gatineau Park, I don't think I've ever really stopped to admire the natural beauty of the land. Deep in the fields, I am witness to the growth, energy and abundance. A single sunflower stands strong, alone in an empty field.

After 7 more kilometres and still early afternoon, I decide to stop in El Burgo Ranero. Two lighter days after my meltdown have benefited my body and mind. I'm not overdoing it, nor am I stressing over fewer kilometres walked. I actually love the Camino today.

Don't jinx yourself.

Following an albergue road sign, I divert a couple of blocks off the trail, seeing Dave walking towards me. "Hey Elizabeth! Are you staying here tonight?"

Confirming my intentions, he lets me know he and his wife are here as well, pointing me towards the main street. It looks like a movie set for an old western film; I'm just waiting to see a tumbleweed roll across the empty street. On the right is a restaurant and hotel; on the left, a single building stands alone.

The sign on the albergue indicates it doesn't open until 1 pm, so I have time for a drink across the street. My backpack reserves my seat at an empty table on the patio, while I enter the bar inquiring about the cost of a room. Since it's more than I'm willing to pay, I'm happy to wait until the albergue opens.

There's a nice vibe outside. Everyone's relaxed and enjoying the afternoon sun with a cold beverage. Dave and Cathy come over to join me, inviting me to lunch with their travelling companions, Frank and Sandy. I get the sense that Dave and his wife are leading a more relaxed lifestyle these days, but their friends are on a tighter schedule. Having walked the Camino before, Frank is leading the group towards Santiago.

All too familiar with the challenges, they are having their bags transferred each morning to their evening destination. Dave recalls our shared bus ride to Burgos and Cathy isn't shy to admit, "even without the additional weight of my backpack, this is not as simple as walking every day."

No it isn't.

Across the street, people are gathering outside the albergue. "I'll be back shortly. I'm just going to get myself a bed and then we can order lunch." I'm excited about the afternoon: a good meal, great company and of course, I love the fact that I can speak in English. My Spanish skills have improved *un poco*, but not enough to carry any kind of conversation.

I am the first pilgrim to register at *El Burgo Ranero*; I've made progress since Day 2 when I arrived too late to even get a bed. There is no cost to stay here, since the albergue operates on *donativos*.

The two volunteers welcome me with open arms, one offering to take my pack then pouring me a glass of icy cold water. The other invites me to sit down in front of the small desk. Such warmth and empathy from total strangers. *This was a great decision!*

Distracted by the attention, I climb the stairs to Bed #1, drop off my pack and poles, and return to the front door, eager to join my American friends. The light bulb comes on right in time, and I drop my 5 euros in the donation box. "Gracias, amigos!"

My normal routine is thrown out the window—shower and laundry can wait—I have places to go and people to see. We share our stories over wine, and talk about who we have met and the challenges we have encountered. The hours pass quickly, but now I'm ready to get settled across the street.

When I'm all cleaned up and in a happy place, I take to my bottom bunk to write in my journal. In the room across the hall is a group of weary travellers, exhausted and giggling out of control. As they near hysterics, the conversation centers around their unique aches and injuries.

Each one identifies their stock of colourful pills they will con- tribute to the communal collection and who might benefit. Giggling, they call out requests. It's hilarious and I am having a hard time holding back my own laughter, as I continue to eavesdrop from my bottom bunk. No longer able to resist making a comment of my own, I call out from across the hall.

"Just make sure no one gives him the pink birth control pill!"

Their silence is broken by a familiar British voice. "Is that you, Elizabeth?"

Banging my head on the frame of the upper bunk, I react. "John? Is that you?"

Crossing the hall, I see Melanie, the friend that I abandoned in Belorado on Day 8, standing in the doorway with a look of disbelief. *Can it be?* We're in shock, our reactions delayed. I cannot believe she has caught up to me. With tears in our eyes, we hug each other tightly. John comes into the hall, welcoming me. "It's actually Robert, not John, but you can call me anything you like!"

Out of habit, I continue to call him John, the others laughing each time I say it. We agree on *John-Robert*, at which he smiles. He is an absolute hoot, his British accent adding to his dramatic flare. When John-Robert tells a story, I can't help but laugh.

"You should be in theatre!" He is!

I am introduced to the rest of the group.

Karen is forty and calls Australia home, even though she has been travelling for 4 years. *I thought that was something only 20-year-olds did.* She's been all over the world, working remotely or picking up odd jobs, to keep her in spending money. She's not married, so has the freedom to move about, but I am in awe, and even a bit envious.

Mark is from Switzerland, and is a quieter fellow with a gentle nature. His feet and ankles are swollen, causing him great pain, but still he smiles, making me want to hug him. I can see his friends are a great source of encouragement.

Leen from Belgium has an authenticity that complements her easygoingness and natural sense of humour. Her eyes tell me she, too, is searching this summer.

Each one is travelling solo, having met along the route at different stages. I find it fascinating how groups of strangers connect seamlessly. One person meets another, like Melanie and I had. You enjoy each other's company, maybe travel together for a couple of days. You meet another person, feel the connection, and they become part of the tribe. Late starts or faster paces see the group change, new friends coming into the circle.

The freedom of travelling on your own allows you to continue with others or to part ways, without the pressure of hurting feelings. It's understood that everyone is following their own path, together for however long it is meant to be.

Melanie and Leen take an excursion to the local tienda, so I tag along. This is the first time I am actually shopping, so I have a few items on my list: blister pads for my callus, toothpaste, juice and Coke, and maybe something for tomorrow's breakfast. Walking through the few aisles, my eyes lock on a blue container of body cream. It's a frivolous purchase, but my skin is so dry that I don't think about the extra weight it will add.

The invitation is extended to share dinner with the crew, and it's a meal the United Nations would be proud of. John-Robert has us in stitches as he recounts some of his adventures, inviting everyone around the table to share and celebrate. We each have our own horror story, and the sharing brings us closer together.

Walking back to the albergue with a full belly, I feel blessed to have had such an incredible day. Not yet ready to enter, I stop at a bench to have a smoke, check my emails, and read the quote Ev has sent.

"Travelling tends to magnify all human emotions."

Peter Hoeg

Someone has pitched a tent close by and several people have gathered around to sing along to a softly-strummed guitar, the community and camaraderie warming the evening. As it starts to get dark, a fellow joins me on the bench. I ask him about the weaved bracelet he wears on his wrist.

"My daughter made it for me. Wearing it keeps her near."

We talk about family and what has brought us here, and I share the struggles I've had. He can relate from his own personal experiences, expressing his hope for this journey along the Camino. "I needed to rediscover what is important to me, and the only way I felt I could do that, was to escape from the busyness of what my life had become. I needed to step into a simpler way of being. To live simply."

He leaves me with the now familiar sentiment: "It's not about whether you walk to the end. It's about the experiences along the way."

More than ready for bed, I walk through the common area, the tables pushed together to accommodate about twenty enthusiastic souls. I offer my services as photographer extraordinaire, gathering multiple cellphones before mounting the bench in front of the window.

"Where I come from, we say *SEX* when we take a picture."

When I have everyone in the frame, giggling and smiling, I start clicking, repeating the process with each cellphone. Entertained, they invite me to join them for dinner, but I politely decline. They are just starting to celebrate.

There are only two more days through the Meseta and then it's back to the hills. I'm not looking forward to that, but will cross those mountains when I get there. I may need to find myself a pilgrim with a donkey.

Day 16
24 km
August 19, 2015

The midnight revellers were loud. Who to blame? The gang hanging around the tent, the group I photographed downstairs, or the locals?

Even after the noise died down, I wondered if my body cream was laced with caffeine, as my eyes popped open each time my bunkmate rolled over his plastic covered mattress, the bulk of his form stretching the thin supports that kept us from sharing my lower bunk.

The sun is rising later and it's still dark as the morning activities begin. Pleased with my breakfast provisions of a carton of orange juice and the unidentified pastry I bought last night, the first bite lets me know I patted myself on the shoulder prematurely. The *bun*, that looked so inviting in the store display, is a tasteless, too crunchy meringue mass. Tossing it in the garbage, I cross the street in my jammies.

There are already a few people sitting inside the bar, but I take my not-quite-large-enough coffee and croissant outside to the cool, still damp patio chair.

I'm not shy to admit that my diet over the last year has been questionable, mostly processed foods and bags of snacks I couldn't resist, but not as rich in white carbohydrates as my Camino diet. The fact that my shorts are starting to loosen confirms I am burning more calories than consuming, but I couldn't sustain this routine for more than my allotted five weeks.

I'm a creature of routine. At home I enjoy a few coffees with Pierre, shower, fix my hair and makeup, get dressed for work, and have one last cigarette before I head off to begin my day.

Here, I have a similar routine.

Coffee, if it's available; several cigarettes to assist with contemplation; scan the premises for any sturdy livestock willing to carry me; dress and organize my backpack; prep my feet; work my way reluctantly to where my boots are parked, hoping they've been stolen; lace up the boots no one wanted; and, sit outside with my pack and poles to contemplate a bit more with another smoke.

Someone suggested this would be a good time to quit smoking. *Hell No!* This is a good time to be a smoker. *Non-smokers just don't get it.*

By the time I have gone through all possible options for stalling, Melanie and her gang are already on the road, but I'm not worried. I haven't reunited with my German Sister, only to lose her after the first night. We have more time to share together, and I suspect Mark will be walking gingerly this morning, the girls slowing their pace to keep him close by. *I'll be able to catch up.*

The deep orange-pinkish hue of the rising sun is spectacular and moments like this remind me how fortunate I am to be here.

The trail *should* be relatively flat again today, just a couple of hills to keep things interesting, but my knees are aching more than usual and my back is sore. As I get closer to León the terrain will change, and that makes me a little anxious, but I'm not focusing on that this morning. Instead, I'm admiring the horizon and the sun-kissed gold of the wheat fields.

Keep walking Lizzie!

Thankfully there is a dirt path that follows alongside the highway, as the asphalt offers little to cushion the impact of my steps. My numerous breaks this morning are opportunities for selfies and I'm all smiles.

After 12 km, I reach Reliegos, the first town of the day. From the road I see Mark, Melanie and Leen seated outside a café. Melanie is on her cellphone, probably updating her *WhatsApp* status; Mark looks distressed, his feet elevated on an empty chair; and Leen seems unaffected by this morning's hike. I can't resist calling out to them. "Hola, Amigos!"

They echo back in unison.

I need to get some ice and food—I'm starving, my croissant long gone and my knees are really bothering me. Surrounded by friends, I am not letting the pain bring me down.

"What's your plan for the rest of the day?" asks Leen.

Translated: *how far am I walking?* Ideally, I'd like to call a cab and drive to Santiago, but that's not an option. "I am hoping for at least 20 km."

Melanie and Leen are planning a good day of walking as well and with my commitment voiced, we will continue together on the remaining 12 km towards Puente Villarente. As for Mark, he has decided to stop after 6 km, in Mansilla de la Mulas.

Those 6 km will torture him, his feet and ankles terribly swollen. Melanie and Leen don't want to say goodbye, but he is determined. There is no room for discussion. He must be feeling pretty desperate to let his friends continue without him.

Before we say Goodbye, I ask Mark to use my cellphone to secure us beds for tonight. Melanie and Leen don't speak a word of Spanish and mine is barely comprehensible, but Mark is fluent.

We gather together to share in Leen's Camino tradition, taking an 11 am group selfie. It is easy to see that my friends are thinking about this time tomorrow, when Mark will be absent. As he falls behind once we start moving, it's obvious he doesn't want company as he struggles with his laboured walking.

Melanie, Leen and I arrive in Mansilla de la Mulas, stopping for a Coke at an outdoor patio. The narrow street is crowded with pilgrims, the air buzzing with the electricity of human interactions. A handsome young man joins us and Melanie introduces me to Patrick.

He started his own journey from his homeland of Germany and has been on the road for the last three months, working his way to Santiago. From there he plans to go on to Finisterre and then catch the Portuguese route, eventually arriving in Morocco!

He is tanned, and his hair appears uncut since he started. He has the beginnings of an untrimmed beard on his face, and looks to be in his early twenties. Retrieving an apple, wedge of cheese and tearing a chunk of baguette from the top of his pack, Patrick uses his pocket knife to prepare his lunch. An impressive and industrious young man, it was his tent pitched beside the albergue last night.

"Can I ask you why you slept in your tent, when our albergue was donativo?"

He could have stayed at no charge if money is an issue, but it isn't.

"I prefer to be on my own. I love being outside...unless the weather is nasty. Then I might stay in a hostel." He is a free spirit and quite self-sufficient, but there's also a peaceful air that surrounds him. He is living life on his terms.

"How old are you, Patrick?"

He smiles as he lets out a little laugh. "Older than I look. I'm almost 40."

His lifestyle is treating him well. I admire his desire to wander, to explore and experience, to live simply. He has no time frame for returning home, just seeing where his travels bring him next. *Perhaps the Camino is a starting point to give myself permission to explore how I want to live my life.*

The conversation with Patrick is most enjoyable and we've probably stopped longer than we intended, but here comes Mark hobbling towards us, relief on his face. Mark's plan was to stay here tonight, but we have managed to sweet talk him into continuing with us and I think he is happier with this decision, knowing we will provide a distraction from his agony. With another call to the albergue, he has secured a bed with his name.

Mark's pain is reflected in his face with each step he takes. I don't know how he is walking, but we can take our time, unwilling to leave this comrade behind.

A new wooden boardwalk directs us over a small waterway, then onto the now-dried river bed, leading us to Puente Villarente. Crossing beneath the stone arch of the roadway, we come out the other side to face an albergue advertising a pool.

The albergue itself is not all that inviting and not the one we reserved, but the thought of a refreshing dip in a pool has us question our reservations. Melanie is the only one with a bathing suit, but we all stand around, unsure of our next move until someone suggests we stick to our original plan. "Good idea."

The *Albergue San Pelayo* is a gift from heaven. It is a large cottage style house, and we enter the front door into a wide open foyer of flat stone and dark wood beams. The owner has us sit at a heavy wooden desk, the furniture fitting perfectly with the rustic charm.

After we are registered, we follow her on a tour of the premises. There is a sunken living room with massive leather couches calling out to me. To the left is a small, but modern kitchen, and a real dining room where we will eat together. Through the windows I spy the peaceful green backyard brightened with colourful flowers. I can lounge on the grass or sit at a patio table, protecting myself from the sun. Whatever the mood, this albergue has all the amenities to please.

Most importantly, I feel like a guest in someone's home.

A single bed costs 10 euros and we all indulge in the simple luxury, joined shortly by a sweet British fellow. James is a history teacher, but with his long hair pulled into a ponytail, I thought he might be a musician. *Note to self... don't judge someone by their looks.*

Today has been a longer than usual walk and I am hurting, desperate to put up my feet and chill. I am not alone in this backyard oasis. Surrounded by flowers and trees is a man with long blond greying hair and faded tattoos, claiming a section of the grass as his yoga mat.

He alternates from a state of meditation through various yoga poses, and I admire his ability to block out the world to attend to his own needs. In just his underwear, he is obviously very comfortable with who he is. *This is someone I want to meet.*

I don't notice him leave the garden, but when I mention him to Leen, she tells me she has him before. "He has an uncanny ability to sense when someone needs a healing touch."

Now I am even more determined to make his acquaintance, but I don't need to search him out, as he returns showered and dressed, joining me.

Jan is from Denmark and in no time, I feel completely at ease in his company, his faded light blue eyes sparkling as he speaks. This is his third Camino, and each one has helped him uncover something new about himself. This time he is walking for his *soul* purpose of helping others. My thoughts turn to Mark, suffering on his bed. When I mention this to Jan, he doesn't hesitate to get up and head to our room.

Hanging onto the door frame, I watch as Jan heats an oil between his hands. With his eyes on Mark's, Jan takes his foot ever so gently. Even the lightest of pressure must be excruciating, and my heart bursts each time Mark reflects his pain. But Jan stays focused on his face, slowly working his fingers under the foot, around the heel and towards Mark's calf. I hold my breath until I see Mark's body give in and relax.

I believe in the healing power of touch and have benefited from massage and Reiki treatments myself, but this is the first time I have been an observer, and the transformation is powerful. By the time he has worked on both feet, Mark has fallen into a deep sleep.

More than a little jealous, I would love a massage and I jokingly say, "Pick Me," waving my arm in the air, trying not to look too desperate. We return to the garden while Mark has a power nap, and Jan continues to share some of his life experiences. As I listen to him talk about his personal challenges and the death of his father, my admiration grows for this man who is filled with compassion for others, wanting to serve and inspire.

Melanie is quieter than her normal self, a bit withdrawn and deep in thought. I haven't spent a lot of time with her since we reconnected, but feel she has lost some of her spark along the way. From our conversations before we parted in Belorado, I know that she, too, carries burdens in her heart. Some were brought from home, but she also had to deal with the abrupt change in her Camino experience. She is a strong young woman who puts a lot of pressure on herself. I want to help her, but I am not sure I'm the one she needs right now.

Our hosts prepare a delicious dinner, and the conversation is light until Melanie looks over at Jan, tears in her eyes. "Will you help me?"

My heart is breaking and I know Leen and Mark are as surprised as I am to hear her words. Melanie and I are similar in that we don't often ask for help, but like me, she trusts Jan. He would have sensed her anxiety, perhaps waiting for her to speak up, and letting her make the decision to ask for support.

"Of course," he says, without hesitation or question.

After dinner, we all retreat to the backyard, where Jan invites Melanie to lay down on the soft grass. Pulling stones out of his leather pouch, he places them along her spine. He waits, head bowed, as though in prayer to his Higher Power. As soon as he starts massaging her legs, Melanie's tears flow, letting go of the weight that has been dragging her down. She remains on the grass after he is finished.

True to his healing nature, he gives Leen and I a massage as well. When he rubs my legs, the muscles are so tender and painful, I hold back the urge to holler. He feels me resisting, and looking into my eyes and smiling, he says, "Let it all out, Elizabeth."

Jan is generous with his wisdom. "As humans, we tend to avoid doing those things that are out of our comfort zone, that scare us or leave us feeling uncertain. But that is how we discover new things: allowing doors to open that wouldn't otherwise."

"We cannot hold a torch to light another's path without brightening our own."
Ben Sweetland

Day 17
21 km
August 20, 2015

Wide awake before Melanie and Leen, I quietly leave our shared room. James is standing in the living room, his sleeping bag on the couch, as he prepares his backpack. With his hair in a slept-in ponytail, he looks a little tired this morning. The look on my face prompts his kind reassurance.

"Don't worry about it," he says with a sleepy smile.

Thank you for not wanting me to feel bad. But I do. He is a gentle, kind-hearted soul and I hate the fact that my snoring forced him to escape our shared bedroom in the middle of the night.

Jan is already seated at the dining room table, smiling as he invites me over, James following suit. The owner has set up the kitchen island with baguettes, pastries, fresh fruit and an unlimited supply of coffee and juice. This morning I am in no rush to take my coffee outside for a smoke, preferring to sit at the table with these two gentlemen.

Jan and James will be travelling together this morning and part of me wishes I could join them. More time with Jan might allow me to better understand myself. Having discovered his role in this life, he's making the most of the gifts he has to offer. I desperately want to feel that way too.

The invitation isn't extended to walk with them and I'm not even sure I would have accepted it. Now that I have reconnected with Melanie and have made a new friend with Leen, I want to stay with them. Although Leen and I haven't had too many conversations, I feel we are two women searching for direction.

When James finishes eating, he excuses himself, leaving Jan and I alone at the table. Filled with respect for this Danish pilgrim, I am eager to soak up his wisdom. Not one for casual conversation, Jan gets to the heart of the matter... helping me find my way.

"You need to slow down, Elizabeth. Take breaks and remove your boots and socks when you stop." He knows I am a smoker, but obviously doesn't equate that to taking frequent breaks. I hang onto every word, knowing they are meant for me. "There is no rush."

But I have a flight to catch on September 7th, also known as Day 35. I have done the math, I know how many kilometres I need to walk each day to reach Santiago before my plane leaves the tarmac.

With patience, he reassures me that he understands the challenges of travelling solo, especially this kind of travel. "Don't worry about not finding a bed at the end of the day."

I admit I worry less when I am walking with others, but I know the traffic will increase as we get closer to Sarria. That means there will be more of us in search of accommodations.

Maybe he felt I was challenging his suggestions and needed to ask the big question. "Do you believe in God, Elizabeth?"

I don't hesitate to answer. "Yes, I do."

He looks at me, his faded blues eyes peering into my soul. "Are you sure?"

Do I believe in God?

Other than going to church with my aunt when I was a child, there were few introductions to religion, until I met my soon-to-be in-laws who were Salvation Army ministers.

My mom didn't attend church regularly, but she was certainly thankful, having struggled through four years in a sanatorium battling tuberculosis. She never expected to marry, let alone have a daughter *and* three grandsons. Every day was a gift and she thanked God for that.

My dad's beliefs were a little harder to pin down, as he never referred to *God*, but believed in the beauty and energy of nature. Maybe that's why he was such an avid gardener. As a young person, I wasn't interested in faith and by the time I started exploring my own belief system, my dad had died. My version of God can be defined as a godly divine force.

Seconds passed before I reply. "I don't go to church, but I do believe in a Higher Power."

With a smile on his face that lights up my heart, his words brand me. "Then don't worry! What is the worst that can happen?"

The dam that had been holding back my tears breaks, and with the flood, my doubts are washed away. *Wherever I end up, it is where I am meant to be.*

"You are never alone, Elizabeth. You are always being watched over."

It is no longer about the struggles I have endured on the Camino, but about all of those life events that left me questioning. Those significant moments when I asked, "Why is this happening?" I put my faith in a Higher Power, but have had moments when I questioned whether my belief was no more than a coping mechanism. More often than not, I have felt the embrace of invisible arms, reassuring me that I would be fine. I believe we all have a greater purpose, not only a need to enrich our lives with experiences, but also to have a positive effect on our surroundings.

Jan didn't need to say anything else. His work with me was done and now it was time to say *Goodbye*. I hesitate to pull myself away from his hug, but I know he has to go.

Melanie and Leen emerge into the hall, followed by Mark who is carrying his backpack.

"I'm taking the train to Santiago."

Mark is going back home to Switzerland. He made the decision some time between last night and this morning, offering no more of a reason than "I need to return." His eyes are sad as he looks at Melanie and Leen, hoping they understand. He is obviously torn, but in his heart he feels it is the right thing.

Melanie tries to hold back her tears. We nicknamed her the *Camino Police* because she doesn't want anyone giving up before they reach Santiago. In her eyes, that is the end goal. She has yet to embrace the idea that everyone has their own journey to take, with all of its detours and lessons along the way.

We head outside to send Mark on his way, Melanie holding on tightly, hoping she can convince him to stay.

I follow the girls back into the dining room. After refilling my coffee, I grab my cigarettes off the table and excuse myself to go out into the garden. I need a few minutes to gather my thoughts.

My eyes linger at the spot where I first saw Jan yesterday afternoon, as I begin to replay the last couple of days. If I had not run into Melanie, would I have walked 24 km to arrive at the same albergue as Jan? If we hadn't been chatting with Patrick in Mansilla de la Mulas, would Mark have caught up with us? Would he have made the same decision to go home?

I smile to myself. These events happened because they were meant to.

There have been many moments over the last two and a half weeks, directing me onto a path towards special friendships and challenges I needed to overcome. I am not the same woman I was when Pierre said goodbye to me at the Montreal airport. Slowly I am learning to trust, to see a little clearer, allowing a shift in my perspective.

On the trail, the conversation is limited, each of us in our own thoughts. Melanie and Leen are preoccupied with Mark's sudden departure and I am continuing to explore the thumbtacks of the last few weeks.

When the path is narrow, Leen takes the lead, her long legs moving her forward at a comfortable pace. Melanie holds the centre, oblivious to the trail, and I take the tail, stopping often for photos. The gap between us widens.

Leen stops so we can catch up. She has just received a text from Mark: his partner was admitted into the hospital. The hairs on my arms stand up, acknowledging the nudge he received to return home.

The fields of the Meseta countryside are swallowed up by apartment complexes and industrial lots. We are getting closer to the big city of León. The unwelcome introduction of a few hills slows my pace.

After 10 km we enter Puente Castro, the suburb of León, and stop to take a break. The girls are great for stopping with me, but the breaks are fewer than what I am accustomed to. Now I see how

Melanie bridged the 50 km gap between us. Overheated from the sun's reflection against the concrete and pavement, we indulge in a Magnum ice cream bar.

The peace and tranquility of the fields are forgotten in the chaos of the last major city centre before Santiago. My senses are assaulted by traffic lights and automobiles, tourist-packed alleys and sidewalks busy with admirers of the architecture. Despite my resistance to the noise and lack of any desire to visit the sites, I would be remiss not to acknowledge the grandeur of this Cathedral City.

Leen shares her knowledge of Gaudi, Spain's beloved and re-nown architect, who designed the *Casa Botines,* a castle worthy of a Disney princess. But I am not here as a tourist. These visual fas-cinations are just part of the scenery to be enjoyed and walked past.

I need to keep moving.

Melanie and Leen are giving themselves a shorter day today, to recharge and visit the cathedral, but I have only one thing in mind: to get out of León. The noise and busyness is unnerving, as it was in Santo Domingo, minus the excruciating pain. I bid them a heartfelt "Adiós, Chicas," hugging them tightly.

León is a large city and I am challenged with the task of fol-lowing the yellow arrows, stopping often to confirm I am headed in the right direction. With the last of the architecture behind me, I sit and regroup on an empty bench. Although I've lived and worked in urban centres, my preference is the tranquility of the country or the closer-knit familiarity of the suburbs.

One final double-check of the direction and I am out of here, my trusted FitBit showing the 6 km it took to get through the city.

The next town is an 8 km walk. My pack feels heavier as the sun beats down. The city was draining, but after leaving the sub-urbs I am left to walk through desolate industrial areas. There isn't a soul on the path, many opting to follow the stages and spend the evening in León.

By the time I arrive in La Virgen del Camino, I am exhausted to my core and absolutely famished. All I've had to eat is the continental breakfast this morning and the sinfully delicious ice cream, 14 km ago. At the first restaurant with a patio, I leave my backpack beside a table and head inside. The restaurant is empty, other than the 15-year-old boy behind the counter.

I know what I want. Time to practice my Spanish.

Belly full and desperate for a nap, I check back in with my young server, seeking directions to the municipal albergue. Aware of my not-so-fluent Spanish skills, he takes me back outside, pointing down the street. I am close to stopping for the day.

Not seeing the sign or turn off for the *Albergue D. Antonion y Dia Cinia*, I approach a man pushing a baby stroller, who walks me right in front of the building. This isn't the first time I have been hand-delivered, although I'm not sure I'll be able to find my way back to the main street for dinner.

A newer complex, this albergue has a clean utilitarian feel similar to a YMCA. There are several large dorm rooms, industrial washrooms with showers, a library with comfy chairs, a kitchen counter with a few appliances, and a couple of vending machines for my Coke addiction and tomorrow morning's coffee fix.

I haven't thought to buy any food for breakfast and the way I feel right now, I may not have the strength to head out for dinner. Exhausted, I lay down on the bottom bunk, doubtful I can stay awake long enough to write some emails. The journal can wait.

Waking from an unplanned nap, I drag myself out of bed, grab a Coke from the vending machine and head to the bench outside the front door. There is a large grassy area between our building and the road, fields to the right, and an assisted-living residence on the left.

The tenants come over to chat with the pilgrims who are smokers. One lady, whose English is quite remarkable, keeps asking me for a cigarette. I have given her two already, but she wants more. "Look," I said, pointing to the side of her head. "They are tucked behind your ears." That seems to appease her, as she wanders off in search of another pilgrim to charm.

Fidgety, I grab my journal and head to the comfy chair in the library. I still don't feel like updating it, but I fight the urge to procrastinate.

Pierre has responded to my email, bridging the gap between Spain and home. I didn't provide all the details of my experience with Jan, instead sending photos of León. I am not sure he has ever understood my need to search for something more. He doesn't dismiss it whenever I talk about it, but he doesn't encourage it either. Perhaps he feels it will pull me away from him, to discover there is more to my life than my wish for our *happily ever after*.

He could be right.

Back outside, I join Dave who is enjoying his own smoke. He is my age and in great shape, with a deep tan from all his walking under the sun. His hair is almost shaved to the scalp; he sports a single earring and a few tattoos, and is the friendliest of fellows. When he tells me he is from Brighton, England, I share my visit from a few years earlier.

"My uncle and aunt took me on a whirlwind tour, visiting Oxford and Leamington Spa on the way up to the Lake District, and York on our way back to their home in West Sussex. Afterwards we spent a day in Brighton, enjoying a nice lunch of *whale and chips* on the wharf." I laugh at my uncle's reference to the massive piece of fish we had on our plates.

Dave started his travels three months earlier, but not on the Camino Frances. When he arrived in Santiago, he continued on to Finisterre. Not ready to return home, he walked back to Santiago and took a train to Saint-Jean-Pied-de-Port. Now he's walking the Camino Frances.

"You're crazy, Dave!"

He tells me about an older German woman who has been walking the different Camino paths for eight years. After her husband passed away and the regular visits from her children and friends dwindled, she felt isolated. She decided to walk the Camino and that experience restored a sense of family. She is happiest travelling, meeting new people and building relationships.

"Apparently she goes home twice a year, to visit her children."

Dave doesn't sound all that crazy anymore.

A young man comes out asking if we can help him thread his blister. As he shows us the bottom of his foot, I wonder how he managed to walk. Dave offers, but doesn't have the necessary supplies, other than a lighter.

"I do."

Collecting my homemade First Aid kit, needle, thread, and some antiseptic wipes, I hand them over, but leave before Dave gets started. *I don't want to watch.*

Even though I have only had an apple and Clif Bar, I know I don't have the energy or desire to work my way back to the main street, and sit alone for a meal. I am going to bed.

With my cell plugged in, I take one last look at my emails. Ev's quote for the day has arrived.

"Don't waste today regretting yesterday instead of making a memory for tomorrow."

Laura Palmer

Day 18
25 km
August 21, 2015

There were no lullabies needed last night; I slept long and hard. I'm not asking anyone if I snored, I don't want to know. Still in my pyjamas, I head towards the vending machine in the kitchenette. With few options to choose from, I drop my euro into the coin slot, hoping the hot chocolate will give me the sugar boost I need. Weak from yesterday's long walk under the sun and my Camino-diet dinner, I need something in my belly. The small cup holds less than four ounces of watered down chocolatey not-so-goodness. Next cup will be coffee, but my expectations are low.

I'm going for a smoke.

An occupied sleeping bag blocks the concrete path near the front door. *Why would someone sleep outside?* It looks like it's seen better days, and within reach is a bag I imagine contains all this traveller's worldly possessions.

I sit quietly on the bench, sipping my drink and smoking my cigarette. There's no sign of movement until other pilgrims start filing out for their day, chatting as they detour around the body. An older man, disheveled and unshaven, pokes his head out the top of the bag.

"Buenos Dias, Amigo," I say.

He returns the greeting without a smile, turning his head towards the lawn. Curious what he is looking at, I follow his gaze towards a donkey... tied to a tree. I've been looking for a ride to carry me to Santiago and today is my lucky day! Daniel is from France. He and his 4-legged partner are working their way *back* from Santiago, travelling a total of 1600 km. *My ride is going in the wrong direction.*

It's slow going with a donkey, perhaps even slower than my own crawl, and Daniel has to plan ahead and look for alternate routes, as his furry friend won't cross any metallic walkways. *Is it the sound of the echoing hooves that spooks him?*

The worn bag beside Daniel is only part of the baggage they are carrying. Out of my line of sight are saddle bags and once they are packed up, the poor donkey is loaded. Maybe Daniel *is* carrying all of his possessions.

With no options for breakfast, I don't waste time getting ready. This morning I'm trying a new look. Another pilgrim folded her Buff into a headband, so I'm stealing her fashion statement. It still keeps the hair out of my face, but allows my wild, untamed curls free reign. I am calling it my *Kick Ass* look.

Out the albergue door, I don't need to worry about finding the Camino trail. I'm on it. There are a few hikers up ahead, but I am starting out alone. The morning is quiet until I reach the highway.

As the motorcycles speed by, my hand automatically raises in salute as each one passes. It's a perfect day for riding, and the sight of them leaves me with a pang of envy and homesickness. It would be incredible to travel across Spain on a Goldwing, my café con leche to-go in the cup holder, my arms propped on the seat that curves around my torso, and snapping more than enough photos as we ride into the wind. Jackets off, the sun warming our bodies, the wind burning our faces, and the only ache at the end of the day would be a numb backside.

My fantasy lets me escape the route for a while. There won't be any motorcycle trips this summer, at least not for me, but Pierre will get himself on the road for a few good day trips on the weekends.

My arrival in Valverde de la Virgen awakens my coffee craving, so I stop at the first café. With breakfast in hand, I join a Spanish family. Dad's English is strong enough for us to have a brief conversation, and he introduces me to his wife and teenage son. They have turned the Camino into a family vacation. *I wonder how that's working so far?*

When they leave, I refill my coffee, as I'm not too eager to continue. There are more people on the route now, but so far I haven't made any real connections. I no longer recognize anyone. It's like starting back on Day 1 with the loneliness amplified.

I need a pick-me-up, someone who can give me a boost.

A few kilometres before San Miguel del Camino, I am walking in tandem with a young fellow from Madrid. His English is about as proficient as my Spanish, so our communication is limited and we rely on hand gestures, taking advantage of our familiarity with the international language.

Up ahead we see something lying in the path, and we pick up our pace to investigate. A rolled sleeping bag has fallen off someone's backpack, most likely from the trio walking ahead. Without giving it a second thought, my partner picks it up, carrying it until we catch up. Sure enough, it belongs to the Dad I met earlier. In appreciation he offers to buy us a drink at our next pit stop.

Good deed done. Check.

I leave behind the Good Samaritan when he motions he is ready to take a break. *Buen Camino, Buddy*. I need someone that I can connect with or this is going to be a very long day.

The isolation intensifies as the trail narrows, surrounding me in trees and high bushes. The one constant on the path is a man in a red shirt, his straw hat pulled low to keep the sun off his face. He maintains a consistent pace, his head bent in thoughtful reflection. He passes me each time I stop to take a break and I take many, always offering a respectful nod. We never say anything to each other, but know the other is close by.

If I can't have anyone to talk with, at least I know Mr. Red Shirt is near.

With plenty of stops, I continue on with the goal of reaching Hospital de Orbigo, giving me a 25 km day. The sun is beating down and I'm starting to drag, even though the walking is fairly easy. It's during the last couple of kilometres that Mr. Red Shirt and I slow our pace, walking side by side in silence.

The entrance into Hospital de Orbigo is along a beautifully-built colourful stone bridge. Thick supporting arches dive deep into the sand floor. This is the second time I have walked over a dried waterway. Within the first few steps on the bridge, I discover the rounded stone surface difficult to walk on. The single strip of flat stone in the centre doesn't help either, as it's not quite wide enough for this pilgrim and her poles. I tread carefully, the tips of my poles slipping over the curved surface with each step.

Halfway across the bridge I take the off ramp towards the municipal pool and the newer *Albergue la Encina*. It doesn't take very many steps before I hear the music.

Ready to take ownership of one of the covered patio tables, I know my afternoon will be spent listening to the tunes blaring from across the street. Melanie would love this place, and I imagine her floating the afternoon away after another long day.

The hostess takes me past the industrial kitchen and down a small corridor to a room. Handing me the key, she knocks before entering. This is the first time, other than my night in a private room, that I am given a key. I suspect the bar may be a local hangout, especially since it's across the street from the pool.

The room is small yet modern, with two bunk beds and a private bathroom and shower. This is luxurious first class accomodations. My roommates are already settled, lying on the bottom bunks, listening to their own music.

Frances and Ann-Marie are friends from New Zealand, travelling together in part to celebrate their 50th birthdays. Totally relaxed, Frances is just out of the shower, a towel wrapped around her wet hair, at ease in her summer dress. Ann-Marie is chilling on her bed, selecting tunes from her cellphone.

With both lower bunks occupied, I attempt to beat around the *bunk bed bush.* "Top bunk... well, this will be a first. I hope I don't come crashing down on you in the middle of the night."

Ann-Marie is quick to react. "You can have my bed. No problem at all!" She quickly removes her gear from the lower bunk, climbs the ladder with ease, remaking her bed for the night.

"Thank you so much. To be honest, I'm not sure I could have gotten up and down." And there is a fair chance I could have killed her if the top bunk collapsed under my weight, Camino Diet or not.

Conversation begins easily, and both women welcome me. *This is just what I need this afternoon: women my age who speak English.* As I get myself settled, I listen to them chat, wondering what it's like to take this journey with a friend.

Ann-Marie's shoulder-length blonde hair and tan set off her strong athletic figure. I don't think we struggle through the same physical challenges. Frances seems like a take-me-as-I-am kind of woman. They are both friendly and I am delighted to be sharing the room with them, refraining from mentioning the potential risk of snoring.

While the girls head to the neighbouring pool, I take my time in the shower, washing away the layers of dirt and sweat. Having a bathroom to myself is a privilege that I'm taking full advantage of.

Laying on a thick coat of body cream, I'm thankful for my impulse purchase. *Now I am ready to kick back and relax.*

At the bar I order my usual, taking it outside. The waitress brings out a small plate of appetizers, or as we call them in Spain, *tapas*. The music next door is loud, the children's laughter louder: neither usual sounds on the Camino. As I hum along to the music, my thoughts drift to home and the two and a half weeks I have been gone.

I've clocked about 50 km over the last two days, and although extremely pleased with my efforts, they have been unbearably long days, without anyone to pass the time with. When Ann-Marie and Frances return from the pool feeling refreshed and full of life, I express my gratitude. "I can't tell you how happy I am to be sharing this room with you. It's been a long, lonely day."

Not wanting to spend another solo evening, I venture out of my comfort zone. "Would you lovely ladies mind if I joined you for dinner?" It is so liberating to ask. *What's the worst that can happen?* They are more than happy to accept my offer, suggesting we go for drinks first. *Why not? I don't have to drive.*

We cross the bridge and enter the hotel. Sitting on the balcony patio, we have the best view to take in the majesty of this incredible stone structure that crosses an expanse of white sand. I am treating myself tonight. "Una Sangria, por favor."

A familiar voice comes through the restaurant dining room, catching my attention. When I turn my head, I am shocked to see Melanie. Introducing her to the New Zealand gals, Melanie in turn, introduces us to 22-year-old Iris, who is cycling the Camino. I am always so happy to see Melanie with new friends; being alone pushes us to reach out to others.

We invite them to join us—the more the merrier. After looking at the prices on the hotel's menu, we finish our drinks and continue walking through town, in search of a restaurant with a Pilgrim's Menu.

We find one, and the waiter walks us through to the back, where we have an entire dining area to ourselves. Earlier than the traditional Spanish dinner hour, we have our waiter's full attention. With five beautiful women, he makes sure to check on us regularly.

Like many groups of new-found friends, we come from different backgrounds and bring unique expectations for this trip. Going around the table, we take turns talking about what brought us here. We have all experienced emotional upheavals and yet here we were, still walking, now sharing a meal together.

This is the bond between pilgrims: we can relate, appreciate, and empathize with what the other has gone through. It's an incredible connection; there's nothing to explain. Simply put, we get it.

"A journey is best measured
in friends, rather than miles."

Tim Cahill

Day 19
22 km
August 22, 2015

The music from the pool played *all* night long, making it hard to stay asleep for any length of time. In the pitch black of the night, I woke up to the silhouette of someone carrying a backpack. *Maybe I was dreaming.*

This morning, I quietly steal out of the bedroom in search of coffee, thankful the bar is already open for business. Outside, the patio chairs are still wet from last night's rain, so I scan the steps for a dry corner to sit. I need my coffee to wake me up, because I'm dead tired.

Across the street at the pool, the music is *still* playing.

By the time I return to the bedroom, Frances and Ann-Marie look half asleep as they get ready. My *Good Morning* is returned, followed by a well-intentioned, "Elizabeth...your snoring sounds like a freight train."

Time to play the shocked card, I blame it on being so tired after a long day yesterday. They don't need to know that this is a regular occurrence. In an attempt to change the subject, I tell them about my dream. My bubble bursts when Ann-Marie confesses she actually tried to find another bed. Without luck.

I seem to have developed a reputation. I am no longer *Elizabeth from Canada*, but *Elizabeth Who Snores*. I wonder how fast the pilgrim news travels across the Camino. Isn't it ironic that I was kept awake by the Spanish tunes and my New Zealand friends were kept awake by a Canadian one-woman-band? Thank goodness I have a charming personality.

The gals get a head start, uncertain if they will stop in Astorga or continue on. Seems one night with me might be all they're willing to commit to. Alone in the room, I can hear the private washroom calling my name. I'm actually surprised with how quickly I have adapted to sharing common facilities.

For as long as I can remember, I've avoided public washrooms, the pressure building in my belly and bowels, waiting until I get home to relieve myself. I didn't want to be the person responsible for leaving an unpleasant odour in an open stall. Almost three weeks on the Camino and I no longer worry about the sounds, as musical as they can be, or the smells. I'm in good company, even willing to hand toilet paper under the stall wall, if anyone is in need.

I'm tired but optimistic, thanks to the music still echoing through the air as I walk out of town, dodging puddles towards the damp open fields. The moving canvas of dark grey and bright blue accentuates the sparkling outlines of the thick white clouds.

The energy from above complements the smell of damp earth rising from my feet. The fields are a welcome sight, but I won't be in them long. I'm all about conserving energy, and the shorter, main route along the highway will shave off a kilometre. *One thousand metres.*

The first 12 km are painful as I pound the pavement. There are no towns or mobile canteens, so I resort to pit-stopping on rocks, refuelling on water and cigarettes. *I should have followed the more scenic route.* This is doing nothing for my morale.

In the first small town, I head towards the nearest café. I'm thirsty, hungry and my feet are throbbing. Melanie is sitting outside, as though waiting for me. *We finally have some time together, just the two of us.*

Seems Melanie wasn't the only friend staying in Hospital de Orbigo last night. "I saw Andreia and Sampaio this morning." Hearing that statement lights a spark within me. I was beginning to feel that I had lost sight of my pilgrim friends.

While we enjoy a snack, the New Zealand gals arrive, having followed the Alternate Route. A few minutes later, Leen, who I haven't seen since León, joins us. These ladies are my reward for the forced isolation of the morning. After a little socializing and knee-icing, Melanie and I decide to walk together to Astorga, neither planning on staying the night.

We think we're getting close when we come face to face with a tall mounted cross, with a multitude of stones piled on the concrete tiers of this memorial. What a beautiful vantage point for admiring the valley below. There is a steep hill to descend—my first real challenge since leaving the Meseta. Melanie is not bothered by the downhill, silently offering thanks that we aren't climbing, but she knows I'll need a few minutes to mentally prepare before descending.

I manage to make it to the bottom, but am surprised that Astorga is still a distance away. More walking leads us to a massive ramp structure that if miniaturized, would be a blast for kids to play upon. I've never seen anything like it and with all the hairpin turns, we are zig-zagging across the maze-like bridge. My mind drifts to Daniel and his donkey, who wouldn't have liked this one bit. I have to wonder if this was built to distract walkers or support steel manufacturing.

Before we even make it into the heart of the city, we're faced with a steep winding street. Flashback to Day 2 when my Australian friend and I struggled to reach the top of a hill, stopping often to catch our breath. This isn't as difficult or as far a climb, but it is going to be a workout. Melanie has her hands on her hips, head down, focused on each step, willing her body to make it to the top. Her ups are my downs.

The square buzzes with activity. Locals and tourists are in close proximity to each other, making it difficult to follow the yellow arrows.

Parked beside a building is a professionally painted motorcycle. It's a work of art and something Spider-man would be proud of. The front and sides are patterned bright red with black webbing. The top of the gas tank continues in red, accented by the electric royal blue of the sides of the bike. Even though Pierre and I have never been interested in having our own bikes painted, he will be impressed with this. There are more than a few crotch rockets parked in Astorga.

Melanie takes the lead and I do my best to stay close behind, weaving in and out of the moving mass, hoping my backpack isn't knocking anyone over. We're surrounded by buildings that remind me of Burgos: muted colours of peach, pink and yellow.

A festival is underway and a parade just about to start, with gigantic puppets strolling through the open square. As Melanie works her way through the crowds, we discover we have become part of the parade march. After several more detours to avoid the crowd and looming figures, we somehow wind up leading the march. Claustrophobia is setting in as we manoeuver through the alley tight with excited patrons.

To escape the madness, we head into a quieter quarter, where I see Andreia and Sampaio sitting outside a restaurant. "Hola, Amigos!" *It is so good to see you.*

My appetite ramps up as I stare at the homemade lasagne they have ordered. Hoping Melanie is as hungry as I am, I suggest we eat. "Do you mind if we have lunch?" She too, has worked up an appetite dodging the parade. *I'll have an order of Coke to go with my lunch, por favor.*

By the time we start to eat, Leen has found us. After I hug her tightly, I introduce her to my Brazilian family and pull over a chair so she can join us.

"Thank you, Elizabeth. I appreciate you introducing me."

I hadn't thought anything of it. "Why wouldn't I? There's plenty of Camino love to go around."

Yesterday was a bit depressing, thinking those I had met had moved on without me. But here I am this afternoon, recognizing so many, and jumping out of my chair when they approach to say hello. I'm in the *hug zone* and loving it.

For as long as I can remember I have been touchy-feely. It's my way of letting people know how much I care. On this journey, the *Warm Fuzzy* dial is cranked to High and I wouldn't change it if I could. These relationships are the threads that tie my experiences together.

After embracing the Italian couple, I sit back down with a smile. Leen turns towards me. "I wonder how you do it? You know so many people and are always so affectionate."

I have been blessed with opportunities to meet so many incredible individuals. I couldn't tell you the names of everyone, especially these Italians I first met 10 days ago in Hornillos del Camino, but there's a connection when we see one another. I don't try to understand it; I embrace it.

Bellies full and without stating our intentions, we continue walking together. There is no need to ask or question. If you want to continue, you put your pack on your back and you stay together, for as long as you want.

Five kilometres later, we arrive at the small town of Murias de Rechivaldo. The ranch-styled *Albergue-Casa las Aguedas* has no front door, but instead an arched open entrance, leading to an enclosed garden. The covered walkway joins the small artisan boutique on the right to the large bedroom on the left. Two levels of motel-styled rooms form a horseshoe complex around the garden.

In place of grass, the garden courtyard is covered with stones and has patio sets for anyone who wants to sit under the sun. On the facing wall is a bar where we can celebrate another successful day on the Camino. There will be no pilgrim menu for us; instead, we'll share a communal meal in the small dining area.

Many of the beds are already spoken for, so I find one near the far wall, pull out my shower bag and get ready to rinse away the day's grime. I take my showers at home for granted, but there is nothing quite as invigorating as standing under a strong stream of warm water, after sweating all day under the sun.

With my laundry in hand, I claim a patio table before heading to wash my clothes. There are several plastic bins to avoid a line up at the one sink. Clothes hung, the light bulb goes on. *I have an idea for my aching feet.*

At the outdoor bar, I order a Coke. I could have something with a bit more kick, but I've developed an addiction to the only beverage that really quenches my thirst. She offers me a complimentary bowl of nacho chips.

Snacks! Check!

"Do you mind if I use one of the laundry bins to soak my feet?" Nodding with understanding and looking over the counter at my Band-Aided toes, she raises her finger.

"Una momento." Filling a bin from the sink behind the bar, she adds a healthy dose of salt and then points to the freezer. *Would I like some ice?*

She gets an enthusiastic thumbs up from me. "You're awesome, Señora."

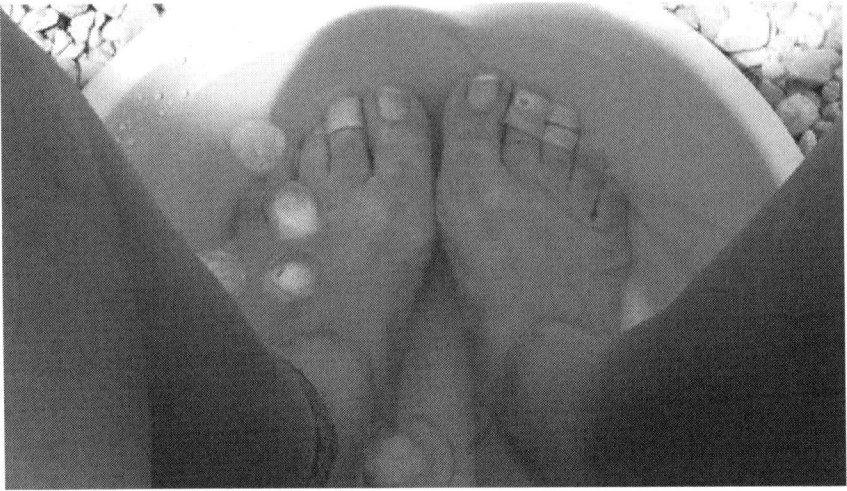

It takes me a few minutes to get both feet submerged in the icy water, but with my legs in the sun it feels heavenly. I'm going to be sitting here until the cubes melts. *Garçon, can I have another Coke?*

Refreshed and feeling like a new woman, I dump the water around the outside of the albergue. On my way back to the garden, I recognize a woman I had offered to share my body cream with in Virgen del Camino. With an exchange of smiles, she comes towards me.

Leaning in close, almost whispering, she says, "Can I talk to you?" The secrecy puts me on alert. "My husband and I are worried about you."

We shared a room that night and she wanted me to know that I stop breathing while sleeping. She seems very concerned, but I quickly put my hand on her arm, in reassurance. "I am so sorry! I have sleep apnea and without my CPAP I tend to snore. I apologize if I kept you awake."

"Don't worry about me. My husband snores as well. We just wanted to make sure you were aware."

She's a dentist and her husband a surgeon, both familiar with my situation. The fact that she felt compelled to bring this to my awareness, makes me self-conscious, but there's not a whole lot I can do about it. Maybe tomorrow morning I can blame her husband for the racket.

The dinner bell rings and we are invited around the long tables in the small *dining room*. Tonight's meal is salad, vegetarian lasagne, and yogurt with melon and fresh mint. Delicious!

"Twenty years from now you will be more disappointed by the things you didn't do than by the ones you did do.

Mark Twain

The couple sitting across from me are from Hawaii. They each took a leave of absence from their jobs, sold their home, put all their belongings in storage, and are now travelling the world. Caught up in their freedom and sense of adventure, I can't help but ask questions.

"How long will you be away from home?"

"Indefinitely."

They've been to Canada, Asia, Europe and are now walking the Camino. And they aren't done yet. They have no concrete itinerary and no time when they need to return home. They look so much in love, always touching each other, smiles lighting up their faces.

"Are you on your honeymoon?"

They exchange a look, as her hand caresses his tanned face. "We've been asked that before, but no." They are simply living their dream!

Frances drops by after dinner and has brought her map so we can review the next couple of days. I'm concerned about two mountain ranges that pose a risk, and am already contemplating Plan B. The first will be on Monday, Day 21. There will be several hills, a preview of what we can expect as we get closer to the mountainous region of Galicia. Tomorrow we will walk together. If we need to, we are open to other methods of transportation.

Day 20
22 km
August 23, 2015

There's a noticeable change to the morning. The sun is rising later, leaving the air too cool for just a t-shirt. *Maybe I shouldn't have shipped home the long sleeve.* This morning calls for rule breaking. I won't wear my white evening shirt to walk, but I need to keep warm and pull it over my ultrathin sports shirt to soften the early morning goosebumps.

Through the peaceful courtyard, I follow the smell of freshly-brewed coffee, and poke my head through the door of the small kitchen.

"Café con leche, por favor... Grande?" *Please let her have a large cup.*

She offers me a smile and picks up a cup, asking if this will do.

"Oh yes, muy bien, gracias Señora."

She hands me a cup full of frothy coffee; the heat and aroma are a comfort in the chilly air. Exceptional service at this albergue. I would definitely recommend staying here.

The morning is quiet, with just the soft clatter of dishes and a few pilgrims beginning their departure preparations. Frances will be arriving around 7:30 am, so I have plenty of time to contemplate my existence. Tomorrow will mark three weeks. It's mindblowing to know I am more than halfway done, and I no longer have any doubts that I will make it to Santiago.

The excitement about returning home is laced with mixed feelings about *leaving*. I absolutely want to be done with all this walking, having had enough after the first few days, but I don't want to lose my momentum. The time spent travelling through the raw beauty of the countryside has provided an opportunity to reconnect with myself, and I'm thankful for the peaceful thoughts I've entertained when walking through the forests, wheat fields and sunflower crops. In planning this journey, I hadn't given much thought to how nature would affect me.

I was certainly naïve to the physical challenges, but it didn't take long to receive a wake up call. I've gotten stronger out here, have pushed my body beyond anything I could have imagined, and even though I've been hurting since Day 1, that wasn't the real reason I wanted to call it quits.

It's the emotional hurdles that *almost* broke me, and yet that is where I found my greatest strength. Not only did I persevere, but I began searching for the root cause of my internal pain. Each day presents opportunities to go within and search for answers.

Our review of the map last night confirmed my anxieties about the mountain ranges we are heading into. Yesterday was a challenging walk and brought with it many of the pains I had endured reaching the Meseta. I hoped my body was in better shape, but my knees have been abused, the wear and tear a brutal assault, making the challenging terrain more difficult to endure.

I am not confident I can descend the steeper paths and am relieved to have a fellow peregrina who has the same philosophy as I. Frances and I will give our best effort and see how we feel, but we won't kill ourselves.

Melanie will join us this morning, but I know we won't end our day together. Still, I no longer worry about losing her. Our time together is not over. We are simply going at our own pace, trusting that we'll reconnect when the time is right. Until then, I have faith that everything will work out as it's meant to.

Frances, Leen, Melanie and I take a selfie. We are all feeling pretty good this morning and the group shot solidifies our hope for the day.

The brilliance of the early morning rising sun invites us towards the dirt path. A deep red glows behind a ceiling of cloud; the band of orange escapes to line the horizon. We have barely started to make tracks and I'm already stopping to take photos.

Leen has a solid pace and, with few breaks, will be ahead of us before too long. Melanie is quiet this morning, focused on her walking. Frances has taken the liberty to reserve us beds in Foncebadón, so we know we can take our time as we get to know one another better.

Even this early in the morning and with her knees bandaged to help with the pain, Frances has a vibrancy about her. Easy going, she seems to take each day as it comes, not out to prove anything. She is here to experience the Camino, with no real expectations or life-altering questions to figure out.

We match our pace, allowing us to chat comfortably, swapping stories about raising our sons. Although not consciously avoiding it, the topic of personal relationships doesn't enter the conversation.

Frances is not a smoker, but she appreciates a rest as much as I do and will happily stop in each of the small towns for a short break. The early morning temperature is still uncomfortably cool, and we stop after 4.5 km in Santa Catalina de Somoza to warm up in a quaint restaurant with a hot chocolate. This is the first time I haven't opted to bring my snack outside. That's how fresh it is.

The constant flow of the wheat fields is interrupted with an out of place tree or bush mid-field. A waist-high stone wall separates the field from the old paved road we travel. There's no sign of any cars, and we walk side by side, the asphalt jarring my knees. Frances feels it as well, continuing to walk when I stop to take photos, hesitant to lose her rhythm. It's easier to keep moving than to start walking again, even after the shortest of stops. *I get it.*

The route towards the mountains is uphill, sometimes a discrete unsuspecting incline, other times an in-your-face, *see if you can catch your breath and carry a conversation* climb. The scenery helps to distract the persistent burn in my quads and hamstrings. As we continue to climb, the wind turbines grace the top of the mountains, the terrain thick with trees.

The air is not warming up fast enough. *Why is it so cold in August?*

Our ears pick up the sound of pilgrim chatter and tunes as we enter El Ganso. *The Cowboy Bar* is the only café in town and by far the most interesting. It's a small establishment, and the outdoor tables and chairs are almost full with enthusiastic pilgrims, as the music encourages patrons to stop and shop.

I remove my pack and the cool air whips across my damp, warm back. Almost everyone is wearing a long layer, many adding a fleece, windbreaker, or both. *Except me.* This Canadian doesn't have either and I would rather be cold than soil the only shirt I have for the evenings.

I don't enter the store, resisting the purchase of a sweatshirt I'd only wear for a couple of hours and then have to carry. I'm not adding any more pounds. Besides, it's bound to warm up soon.

There are plenty of looks from the bundled pilgrims, who are probably wondering what I am trying to prove in a short sleeved shirt. Some ask if I'm cold, eyeing my nipples poking through my shirt. I certainly don't let on that I've come ill-prepared.

"I'm a hardy Canadian!"

Before leaving, I visit the roadside vendor, curious to see what handicrafts he has for sale. Gemstones, leather bracelets and necklaces, all homemade and definitely the type of jewellery I am drawn to, but they are a little more costly than I am willing to shell out.

"Sorry, Amigo."

We have another 7 km before arriving in Rabanal del Camino and that isn't even the end of our intended day. *God give me strength.* I am struggling to keep walking.

The path of red earth transitions into a narrow one of loose rock. A wire fence is covered in crosses of varying sizes, each created from small branches and decorated with coloured ribbons. I'm curious to know the history behind this memorial, as it isn't something a pilgrim could put together without being prepared.

By the time we reach Rabanal del Camino, I'm exhausted. It's been a difficult day of walking and we still have another 8 km before reaching Foncebadón. We're constantly walking uphill, occasionally dipping back down, only to continue climbing higher again. Ascending is a cardiac challenge, but descending is torture, and the shooting pain in my knee caps makes me resent the Camino.

The sky is dark as we approach Foncebadón from the valley.

Thankfully, Frances had the good sense to make us a reservation, because this little town has little to offer; the few buildings barely filling a city block. It starts to drizzle as we make our way up the hill towards our albergue.

As soon as we enter the building, I'm prepared to turn around and leave. Quicker than we can retreat, a young woman in her 20s, with her dreadlocks, tattoos and heavy eyeliner, notices us. Everyone looks to be under the age of 25, packed into the small living room like bees in a hive. The haze and lingering odour make me uncomfortable, and warning signs flash like a fire engine. The look on Frances' face tells me she feels the same way.

"Do you mind if we take a look at the room before making a decision?"

I know she is only being polite; we've already decided to flee at the first opportunity. It's a quick tour, returning with a *not-on-your-life* look. Voice lowered, she explains the state of the sleeping quarters. "The mattresses on the floor are packed so tightly together, there's barely space to move around."

I didn't even need to hear this. I'm not sleeping here tonight.

We want to let the young woman know we've changed our mind, but she is missing in action, even though Frances took no more than two minutes to scope it out. We hover at the desk, waiting to see if she'll return. With no one offering to help us, we leave.

High-tailing it up the muddy hill, we hear someone yelling at us. *Oh, she's back!*

"You are rude to leave after making a reservation."

We turn around in an attempt to excuse ourselves, calling back from the hill. "We tried to let someone know!"

She isn't interested in our excuses, dismissing us as ungrateful pilgrims. *Oh well, chalk it up to another experience.* We aren't going to lose sleep over it... as long as we can find another pair of beds.

Up and back down the same muddy hill, which is slipperier by the trip, we spot the newer albergue, nestled and somewhat hidden, near the top of the hill. It's not fancy, but spotless. The bedroom bunks are spaced out and there's a living room with a sofa and TV. The wood stove helps to diminish the chill in the air.

Tonight, the sexy red dress stays tucked within its Ziploc bag. Layers are needed to stay warm, so I pull out my long pants, clean wool socks, tank and white shirt. *If only I had a fleece.*

While a Spanish telenovela plays on the mounted television, I write in my journal. This is one of those afternoons when I wish I was home. I've lost track of which day of the week it is, asking Frances. *Sunday.*

Pierre and I would call this a *Sloth Day*. After a hearty breakfast, we would shower, get dressed and head to the grocery store for the essentials: cheese fondue, baguette, cretonne, paté, dried sausage, and bags of chips. Next stop would be to our little corner store, selecting at least 4 movies: an action, a horror, a romantic comedy and then a random, *let's see what this is like* movie. At the cash, I can count on him to buy me a roll of *Sweet Tarts*. Mid-afternoon will find us returning to bed and ultimately succumbing to a *post-amour* nap.

Today would be a perfect Sloth Day.

While my head is back in Ottawa, snuggled on the couch with Pierre, his text arrives. We have always had a synchronicity: our emails and texts cross in cyberspace as we think of each other. He reminds me that it is Sloth Day, and wishes I was there with him. My eyes tear as our texts bridge the miles that separate us.

He is still mid-morning and it's a beautiful summer day in Ottawa. There won't be a Sloth Day for either of us. *What I wouldn't give for a little time travel back home.*

With tummies growling, Frances and I are ready for dinner, but the sky is dark with rain. I dread having to head back outside, but ordering a pizza is out of the question and the vending machine doesn't offer anything to counter the calories I burned today. The path has turned to mud, and I slide down the hill in my sandals. It takes a couple of attempts to find the only option available, a Celtic medieval-themed restaurant.

The costumes of the staff complement the décor; the stone walls are decorated with light sconces, animal pelts, paintings, iron works, swords and crosses. The menu has only a few items to choose from, making the selection easy. My plate of deer stew and boiled potatoes must be 18 inches wide, enough to feed a small family. With a *clink* of our ceramic wine goblets, we toast our friendship.

The weather has become dismal over dinner, and the muddy road is more treacherous as we work our way back up the slippery slope. The rain chills me.

Executive decision made, we will taxi the couple of kilometres to La Cruz de Ferro in the morning. Once we visit the iron cross, we'll have the driver take us the 17 km to Molinaseca, avoiding the extremely steep climbs and descents, in the warmth and safety of an automobile.

"All journeys have secret destinations of which the traveller is unaware."

Martin Buber

Day 21
Taxi 19 km, 23 km
August 24, 2015

It's still dark outside when my internal alarm has me rising out of bed and heading to the balcony. Lights dance in the distance as people make their way up the hill towards Foncebadón.

As they battle the rain and steep muddy trail, these early morning pilgrims are working their way to La Cruz de Ferro, in anticipation of arriving for sunrise. Many will participate in the pilgrim ritual by adding their own stones to the base of the Iron Cross.

La Cruz de Ferro is 1504 metres above sea level, then the path drops about 1000 metres. Neither Frances nor I is comfortable attempting this serious trek and the weather has only served to reinforce our plans.

Alone on the balcony, I anticipate *my* moment at the cross. The three stones I collected along the route, remind me why I have carried them so far. My eyes spotted the largest on Day 1, as I walked the stoney trail outside Pamplona. It has been zipped in the side pocket of my backpack ever since, not forgotten but waiting for this day.

It's heavy, almost filling the span of my fingers, and worn smooth to the touch. A brown stone with accents of grey and red, it is the thick Y-shaped vein that catches my eye. On closer inspection, the marking resembles the *Wisdom* and *Life lines* on my right hand. This is *my* stone, and I hesitate to let it go along with the insecurity, uncertainty and doubt I have been carrying over the years.

The other two stones are white quartz: one with just a hint of orange, the other more so with black speckles. Compared to the larger smooth rock, these two are much smaller, jagged and sharp. They were not far from each other when I picked them up, thinking of Pierre and me: similar yet different. *Possibly in ways that matter the most.*

Strange thoughts to have about small rocks. For a fleeting moment I consider keeping them. *Am I ready to let go of the control I've been fighting to hold onto?*

Shortly after 8 am, Luis, our taxi driver, arrives in his minivan.

I smile in salute to the poncho-covered pilgrims as they cross the road to retreat back into the woods. As we descend the steep road, I share a glance with Frances. *I am so glad we decided to taxi!*

Luis gives us the tourist treatment, pointing out what we *would* be seeing if the fog wasn't so thick. I much prefer the safety and comfort of the van to battling the slippery rocks and climbing up through the trees, only to arrive winded, soaked and cold.

La Cruz de Ferro is on the right, a volcanic spill of stones rippling from the five-metre high pole. A simple iron cross sits at the peak, intimidating me before I even exit the van. There are fewer pilgrims than I expected; the others are still making their way up the muddy trail.

Instinctively, my hand feels for the stones in my pant pockets. A slow climb up the rocky slope feels like I am moving in slow motion, conscious of my relief that there are not more people here. I don't want to feel rushed in this ceremony.

Stones are left all along the Camino trail. They symbolize the letting go of sorrow—leaving behind the past and carrying on with a renewed sense of strength. The arrival at La Cruz de Ferro is a pivotal moment in my journey and personal growth. It's an opportunity to acknowledge my sadness, regrets, misdeeds, loss and heartache, giving the weight of these burdens to my Higher Power.

Luis is snapping photos and Frances is laying her own stone, but I try to maintain my focus. Handling the larger one, I roll my thumb over the Y. Before laying it down beside the pole, I let my lips linger on the cool mass. *May my journey continue to provide insight.* I have travelled 485 km with that one stone in my pack and now it is part of a collective healing, leaving a part of me at the cross. The two quartz stones are together as I let them go. *I trust that everything will work out as it is meant to.*

With one last look, I gives thanks for having made it this far.

The 1000 metre drop into Molinaseca is a dangerous one, even by vehicle. Mindful of those on the road, Luis slows down in the sharp turns. The mist is too thick to see down through the mountains, so all I can do is take his word that the view is outstanding. "The weather has been unseasonably cooler." *No kidding.*

By 9 am we have arrived in Molinaseca, the 34 euros providing a 19 km fast forward, right in time to meet Ann-Marie at the café. She is in great spirits, the healthy flush on her face an indicator that she is pleased with her morning workout. A hot cocoa and pastry is devoured in minutes, hopefully providing enough fuel to get me to Ponferrada, still 8 km away.

It's a challenging walk and it won't get any easier as we progress towards Galicia, but I'm thankful I didn't have to tackle that first stretch this morning. I can feel my feet and knees more than I would like as we cross the hills, but as the fog lifts, the view from this height is spectacular. There is so much green! The vineyards along the mountain side are lush. As the sky starts to clear, the sunshine warms the air. *It's about time!*

The residential area and industrial lots indicate our approach to Ponferrada. If I was walking alone, I would be stopping every kilometre. But with these ladies I'm working hard to keep up, the paved road assaulting my feet.

The worn and battle-scarred fortress of the Templar castle is more enticing to me than any of Gaudi's architecture. Part of me wants to enter and tour around, learn the history and acknowledge the battles, but instead I slow my pace.

In the city square we take a well-earned break, happy to stop. Frances and I have only walked 8 km this morning, not even half of the day done, but I am longing for the flat of the Meseta. *The next 2 weeks will be interesting.*

The gals are detouring to the post office, eager to send some items to Santiago for when they arrive. They are faster walkers than I am and will catch up quickly. Although missing the company, I can now slow my pace and stop whenever the urge arises.

As I make my way out of the city and through the suburbs, my energy dwindles, and self-talk is necessary to keep me moving. As my feet kick up the colourful leaves, I'm still surprised at how early in the season the trees have started to change.

Through Compostela, the path cuts right through the courtyard of the *Iglesia Santa Maria*, leaving me feeling like a trespasser as I head for the church bench for a smoke. *How am I going to get through the remaining 13 km?* I'm stopping more frequently, hoping a break will provide a recharge.

In the small town of Columbrianos I stop at a small restaurant to appease my nagging hunger. Ann-Marie and Frances should walk by at any time, so I'll take my lunch outside where I can keep an eye out for them. My bocadillo maker is busy chatting with a local, slowing down the sandwich making process. *Please hurry up*, I silently urge her, worrying the girls will pass before I get back outside. I need their company desperately.

It's a slow and solitary trek, my boots no longer feel like slippers, and the little energy I have gets more difficult to hold onto. Everything seems to be hurting today, and I've pinched my left shoulder.

My New Zealand friends are sitting outside a store enjoying a popsicle as I walk into Fuentes Nuevas. They don't seem to be as tired as I feel. Relieved to see them, I follow their lead, washing my own down with a Coke. The sugar gives me a little boost, but not as much as their company. Only six more kilometres before reaching our final destination of Cacabelos.

The route takes us through more vineyards, and we stop to sample some of the most succulent, fresh off the vine grapes. I

pose with a bunch dangling above my open mouth, and Frances takes photos of Spain's next wine supermodel. I am no longer complaining; my aches and loneliness forgotten in the moment. The fields that grace the mountain recharge me sufficiently to get to the end zone.

The *Albergue Municipal de Peregrinos* is my third monastery stay, once again proving to be a totally unique experience. Instead of rooms inside the building, these two-person cubbies form a horseshoe around the old church. Thin walls of pressed wood divide the tiny sleeping quarters. With only a small night table between the two cots, there is little room to move around. A gap at the top of the wall lets me eavesdrop on Ann-Marie and Frances chatting next door.

My German roommate arrives while I am sitting on a chair outside our door. I make my introduction right away, holding out my hand. "Hi. I'm Elizabeth, from Canada… and I snore." I thought it best to put it out at the start, so he knows what he's in for.

His smile reassures me that he isn't scared off. "That doesn't bother me at all... I have ear plugs."

From over the thin wall I hear Ann-Marie and Frances killing themselves laughing. They have first hand experience that my German roommate's ear plugs won't be enough to block the noise, nor will the thin wall do more than muffle the evening serenade.

The washrooms, showers and vending machines are right across from a common area with picnic tables, floor-standing clothes lines, and tubs where I can soak my feet. With my clothes hanging, I take advantage of the warm sun, my feet soothing in the cool water, but I am feeling unwell this afternoon. There will be no dinner tonight.

In an attempt to distract myself, I search my emails for Ev's daily quote which tends to reflect each day's events. Today's is no different, especially with the laying of my stones this morning.

"One's destination is never a place,

but a new way of seeing things."

Henry Miller

To ward off the chills that are taking over my body, I wrap myself tightly in a wool blanket, not caring about the potential risk of bed bugs.

At the patio tables, I meet my first Canadian. Bruno and I grew up in neighbouring towns, and although he is older than me, we reminisce about the landmarks. He and his wife Mary have been married 30 years and live in her homeland of Australia. *What a small world.*

They are generous in their offer to share their assortment of cheeses, baguette and wine, but I am feeling increasingly worse, excusing myself to head off to bed.

Tucked in before my German roommate retires, I have no trouble falling asleep, but wake in the middle of the night to use the washroom. As soon as I try to lift myself into a sitting position, an alarming sharp pain strikes my belly.

Nervously, I lay myself back down. *This isn't good!*

Trying to stay calm, I get up again. The pain is still there.

I don't think it's muscular, but it certainly has my attention, alerting me to a potential problem. *Is there something wrong with my kidneys?* I'm drinking gallons of water each day, but I never pee. There is no urge until I stop for the day. When I finally relieve myself, the urine is so concentrated the smell is almost pungent.

I make my way to the washroom, returning into our black room and lay myself down.

Do I need a doctor?

I fall back asleep before I can give it any more thought.

Day 22
17 km, Taxi 9 km
August 25, 2015

My first attempt at sitting up confirms the sharp pains have not magically disappeared. Sleep has lessened my panic, and I now blame it on the arduous routine. How can my body ignore the past three weeks?

Are we there yet?

My diet wasn't great before I left home, but meals are sporadic and the only vegetables I consume are in the occasional ensalada. I've been ignoring the minimal urination, blaming it on sweating all damn day. Now I wonder if my body is battling itself. Something was bound to let go, but I need it to hang on a bit longer.

There isn't any pain when I walk and it remains hidden when I prod my not-as-flabby belly; the pain only makes itself known when I rise from a horizontal position.

Physically and emotionally unstable, my body is telling me to stay in bed, but that's not a possibility.

I don't want to go.

After a short trip to the vending machine, I slowly retreat back to the chair outside my room, wool blanket around my shoulders, mini coffee in hand. My German roommate is long gone, and Frances and Ann-Marie are almost ready to leave. I won't be joining them this morning, choosing to remain here indefinitely.

My knees have been in pain since I started, but the achiness in my feet became noticeable after I changed the lacing of my boots. My British friend Dave showed me an alternative after spotting my missing toenails. I think it might be time to switch them back and see if that makes a difference. *That should kill another 10 minutes.*

What else can I do to stall? I check my emails. Melanie has sent one, adding a glimmer of sunshine to my grey mood. I haven't seen her in two days, since the morning we left Murias de Rechivaldo. In her email she writes that she walked 35 km yesterday, stopping in Companaraya.

That's only 6 km behind me. If we could walk together, we could balance one another, as our expectations and experiences are different.

I chose to take this journey on my own; she planned to walk with her best friend. I'm open to taking other forms of transportation if I feel it necessary; she will struggle along pushing herself, never considering a taxi or bus. We've been called to the Camino for different reasons.

I may be wrong, but I get the impression she needs to prove something to herself and perhaps some of the people in her life. She's determined to follow through with the pilgrim rituals: working her way to Finisterre to swim in the Atlantic Ocean and burn her clothes.

I, on the other hand, am looking for direction, not interested in going any farther than Santiago. I'd like to experience the opportunities that come my way, hopefully without killing myself. But, we have met for a reason and there will be more time to spend together, hopefully sooner rather than later.

My body and mind are on the same page, in no rush to move too fast. The breaks have started before I even get to the first town.

In Pieros, I crave a real coffee. The glass *tasse* is a work of edible art, a hot caramel-coloured beverage with an inch of foam at the top. It's almost too beautiful to drink, so I take my time, certain the first sip has left a frothy moustache. Bruno and Mary are in great spirits, enjoying their breakfast. Smiling faces help lift my mood during the short time we spend together.

At a highway crossroad I must choose a route. Uncertain which is shorter, I follow the other pilgrims, hoping they at least read the guidebook on which is the easiest trail. The path leads me through vineyards, and I pluck the grapes right off the vine. *This is food for my soul.*

I don't even notice I have fallen behind the others, and there is no loneliness, as Mother Nature is holding my hand. The terrain is challenging, with more than a few ups and downs, continuing along the dirt path, weaving through green fields and treed areas. The view of the valley and mountains from this elevation is spectacular.

In and out of small towns, I slow my pace to look around. On my left is a fenced-in garden of wildflowers, with signage covering five picket posts: *Look, Listen, Smile, Dream, Love.*

Thank you for the little reminder. *Don't stress, just enjoy the journey.*

Chestnut and mango trees grow in front yards. A small stone building, almost completely covered in vines, has one wall painted with a mural: *Bienvenidos a Villafranca.*

Once I'm out of the fields and onto the paved road, the larger than life mountain range is in my face. My feet and legs ache, but I am still moving, even though I'm struggling physically.

The city promises multiple cafés, but I'm also scanning for any familiar face. Leen appears within earshot, and I call out to her. Her body language suggests that she too is relieved to find a friendly face. She tells me over coffee that the scenic route I took is actually longer. My ignorance proved beneficial.

After devouring our snacks, we walk through the city together, but I am uncertain how much farther I want to continue. Entering the busy square, I hear my name called. Amidst the cluster of patio tables is Frances, waving her arms. I'm shocked to see her, certain they would be long gone.

"Ann-Marie told me you weren't feeling well this morning and I was worried about you." Hugging me, she continues. "I headed out of Villafranca, but something told me to come back and wait for you. I thought this would be the best place to find you."

My eyes start to well with tears. There is definitely a greater force at work along the Camino.

"How are you Elizabeth? Do you want to take a taxi part of the way?"

I didn't need to be asked twice, but realized that meant leaving Leen so soon after reconnecting. She needs the company as much as I do, so I invite her to join us. Her eyes reveal more than her words. Like Melanie, she will be walking the entire route.

The 10 km morning was tough and there is no way I can walk another fifteen. Frances has found an albergue that offers a taxi service and we are headed to find a ride. Having left Leen only minutes earlier, and still feeling shame for abandoning her for a taxi, I spot the telltale pink athletic shirt ahead, and it stops me in my tracks.

I recognize Melanie's stance: hands on her hips, head down, trudging slowly. "Melanie!"

The look on her face when she turns around could light up the Camino at midnight, but her body language tells the rest of her story.

"I am not sure if I am still enjoying myself, Elizabeth. I am alone and uncertain what I am doing here."

Memories of that dreadful day on the Meseta rush to the surface. I am torn as I hold her in my arms, hesitant to break the spell by telling her we are heading for a taxi. Quickly explaining Frances' reason for returning to wait for me, I encourage Melanie to come with us.

"Maybe you need a break? Some time off your feet? We are taking a taxi only as far as Trabadelo... only 9 km." From there, we will meet Ann-Marie, and continue walking.

I think Melanie is straddling the fence, considering the offer, proof of the struggles she is fighting to manage. But her strong disposition won't allow it. Her plan is to walk the next 9 km and stop for the night. In less than 30 minutes, I have let down two individuals I care deeply for. In an effort to soften the blow of continued isolation, I let her know that Leen is nearby.

"I am sorry, Melanie."

She understands, but knowing we cannot walk together is worse than if she had not seen me at all. My thoughts are of my own needs right now. *The need to stop walking.*

We say goodbye, leaving me to battle with my emotions. I keep telling myself to pay attention to the signs, but am questioning whether I should have stayed with Melanie and searched for Leen. We were all feeling similar this morning: *searching for a life buoy.*

I found it when I saw Leen, and relief washed over me knowing I was no longer alone. Then Frances appeared like the Coast Guard, offering a rescue. If Frances had not been there, I would have continued with Leen and we would have met up with Melanie, the three of us back together.

Instead, I left them both behind. *But Frances came back to wait for me.* She could have easily missed me, but she didn't, and I did extend the offer of a taxi to Melanie and Leen. I am only responsible for my own decisions.

The Camino is taking a toll on all of us.

A young local fellow stops to see if we require assistance. What a coincidence... he has a taxi on speed dial and calls someone to pick us up. We're a bit leery; for all we know he is in the habit of working with a partner to kidnap pilgrims. *There won't be much of a ransom buddy. You're taking your chances with these old gals.*

We look at each other wondering if we made the right decision. Five minutes later his friend shows up. No taxi logo, but we don't care as long as we are driving toward Trabadelo and not walking. We're taking our chances.

Arriving ahead of Ann-Marie, I have time to enjoy a cold Coke. She is all smiles as she walks towards us, her face glowing from the exertion and accomplishment. If I was in better shape, I might be more enthusiastic.

A pit stop in Portela de Valcarce has us chatting with Adrian, a Welsh fellow *without* a backpack. The conversation takes a more serious turn towards terrorism. Adrian works in defence and doesn't hesitate to share first-hand knowledge of other countries *behind the scenes* security. He is either full of shit or has intel that scares me.

He hasn't indicated that he is walking the Camino, but asks if we are stopping in Vega de Valcarce, suggesting the *Albergue Santa Magdalena*. The owner is a friend, a younger British fellow named Matthew. There would be no communication challenges should we decide to spend the night there.

With the last 3.5 km walked, we are standing outside the albergue, contemplating continuing toward the end of town. *Why?* I don't want to walk another step and this albergue came highly recommended.

"What do we have to lose?" Nothing like using Jan's influence for my own benefit.

We have the entire ground level bedroom to ourselves. Invited for a tour upstairs, we also have access to a modern living room, kitchen and dining room.

Before we even have a chance to wash up, Jen comes down to introduce herself. She is Matthew's girlfriend, an older American woman he met on the Camino. Enthusiastic about life, Jen tells us about how they met and maintained a long distance relationship. She seemed to appreciate having some women to talk to. Extremely friendly and welcoming, she encourages us to bring our dinner upstairs and join her, Matthew and Kiki, an older Spanish man who helps run the albergue.

A trip to the Super Mercado is on the agenda. I've been walking for 22 days and this is the first time I have stepped into a real grocery store. *My evenings and mornings would be easier if I started this habit.* We each purchase items for our communal dinner: tomatoes, sausages, salamis, cheese, baguette, Sangria and Doritos. In their dining room, we connect Ann-Marie's iPod, listen and sing as we enjoy each other's company. It feels like I am home, having dinner with my friends. My mood transforms from dark to bright.

"Travel and change of place impart new vigor to the mind."

Seneca

Frances and I have been reviewing the map again, planning another taxi for tomorrow morning, this time to the top of O'Cebreiro. From there we will walk the 9 km to Alto do Poio. The hardest descent is into Triacastela, which will account for one final taxi. It will be a short day of actual walking, saving the knees from further injury.

Sarria is only 23 km from tomorrow's resting stop. One more day and I'll only have 123 more km to walk.

It can't come fast enough.

Day 23
Taxi 22.5 km, 9 km
August 26, 2015

I slept like a baby, but my feet are aching. The tops are tender, the toes tight and tingly as I wiggle them, and I hesitate to even put them on the floor. The pains in my legs are continuous no matter what I try to do, and my kneecaps feel like they are rubbing against bone. Even at rest the throbbing travels down my shins. But I am not the only one suffering with aches and pains.

Fortunately, there is no rush this morning. Matthew has arranged for a taxi to arrive around 10:30 am, so Frances and I can take it easy while Ann-Marie climbs her way up to O'Cebreiro. She actually enjoys the thrill of a challenging trek. The more I get to know her, the more she inspires me with her physical stamina and endurance.

O'Cebreiro, which I refer to as *the big ass mountain*, is about 10 km away. Inasmuch as the uphill climbs are easier for me, there's an 800 metre increase in elevation. Today is one of the most challenging treks, up and down, but the descent into Tria-castela is described as brutal.

As this is my last day to consider alternate transportation, I am going to save my knees. Frances and I will taxi up the *big ass mountain*, hike to Alto do Poio, then taxi the remaining 12 km to our home base in Triacastela. I have no qualms with the layout of the day, in fact I'm relieved. If I can get through this, the remaining week and a half will be a walk in the park.

Our hosts have put out the kettle for tea and coffee, breads and baguette for toasting, assorted jams, peanut butter, and orange juice. There is no extra charge for this continental breakfast, but a small donation box sits on the kitchen counter.

The little balcony off the living room overlooks the main street and breadth of the mountains we are in. Coffee in one hand, lit Winston in the other, I find this is the perfect spot to consider the day ahead, while I gaze at the mountain peaks shrouded in heavy mist. The temperature is quite comfortable even though I am in my jammies, and I'm enjoying the tranquility of the still sleepy village.

The quiet of my reverie is broken by the sound of footsteps. I can't believe my eyes. Melanie is slowly making her way through Vega de Valcarce. Without thinking or concern for the volume of my voice, I call out with the enthusiasm she is accustomed to.

"Hola, Chica!"

Her head raises, her eyes searching for the familiar source high in the air. She is equally surprised to see me waving from above. *How is it that I am standing on the balcony at the exact time Melanie is walking by?*

"I'll meet you downstairs. Come to the side door."

Before she has the chance to get her hopes up, I share the taxi plan. Although she is disappointed, our impromptu breakfast helps to ease the loneliness she is battling. How I have missed our shared days of walking.

After Melanie leaves, Frances and I have forty minutes to get ready. In mid-dress, there's a knock at the door. Carlos, our taxi driver, has arrived 30 minutes early. As one hand pulls up my long pants, the other brushes my teeth, the frothy paste dripping onto the floor. In record prep time we are in the taxi.

Galicia is the final region and home to Santiago.

The drive up to O'Cebreiro is beautiful; the scenery breathtaking, especially for those exerting themselves with the climb. My eyes scan over the mountains and valley; I feel on top of the world.

Grateful for the ride, I feel a fleeting twinge of guilt linger as I step out of the taxi. Should I have pushed myself a bit further and attempted to walk here?

Let it go, Lizzie!

There are plenty of people visiting this busy hub of history and tourism. Celtic music pipes from one of the tourist shops and fills the damp, foggy air with magic. Amidst the old stone structures, I slowly turn 360 degrees, taking in the entirety of this community nestled on top of the mountain. A rounded stone structure reminds me of *The Hobbit* and the home of Bilbo Baggins.

Inside the church, I head towards the wall of bibles in more than a dozen different languages, all open to the same scripture: John 14.

"I am the way, the truth and the life."

For years I have been denying and even fighting against those feelings that something isn't right, that I am not where I should be or that I am betraying myself. That is part of the reason I came here: to remove myself from distractions and see how I feel.

This is my life, I'm seeking my truth and I will find my way.

I expected the weather to change in Galicia, advertised as a "welcome" climate from the hot days of the Meseta. Somewhere along the way, Mother Nature got her wires crossed, because this all-you-can-bear buffet of conditions is unwelcome. My major complaint, if *she* is listening, is the cold. Even with a mug of thick hot chocolate, I am shivering.

In the gift shop, I beeline to the sweatshirts hanging on the back wall. Fingering the soft inner fleece, I am tempted. *The weather will improve. I can get through another day.* My need for morning layers ranks as low as my need for breakfast. My only purchase is a tan leather bracelet with a couple of pearls and a small silver scallop shell.

Once we leave O'Cebreiro, the sun finally starts to peek out from behind the clouds, confirming my decision to pass on the sweatshirt. *I am a strong Canadian woman, able to handle temperature fluctuations.* At least that's what I tell people.

Walking alongside the stone rail, the valley is nestled far below along rolling hills, the elevated highway standing above the green carpet. The tops of the mountains are just out of reach. I am in the thick of it and the climbs up and down are merciless. At times the cliff edge drops straight down, and only tips of trees are visible.

At least the exertion creates body warmth, but I am losing stamina and struggling to continue. After more than three weeks of Camino Boot Camp, I am on the verge of tears, and my knees are in agony. *What am I doing?*

By the time we reach windy Alto do Poio, I am ready to collapse, while grey clouds threaten to burst open in the blink of an eye. The only shelter is a tiny restaurant at the top of the hill.

Thankful for the warmth, I point to what looks like a half-moon pie. "Do you know what this is, Frances?" *Meat pie.* I order my first empanada, swallowing it in a matter of minutes. The coffee warms me enough to brave the outside elements. Alone in the damp cold wind, I feel like an idiot in my t-shirt. I am pushed beyond my physical capabilities, my emotions tipping towards fragility.

The plan was for Frances and me to take another taxi to Triacastela. She's feeling stronger than she expected. "I think I am going to try and walk the rest of the way."

Now what?

As much as I need her moral support, there is absolutely no way I can make the trip into Triacastela on foot. Alone in the drizzle, I smoke my cigarette in the face of the defeating mountain. As I wait for a taxi, I chip away at what is left of my confidence and inner strength.

Who do I think I am, to come out here and walk 700 km?

The wind picks up, and my tears sting.

My young female taxi driver arrives, showing off her skills for the Formula One tryouts. As she defies the speed limit down the curves, my right foot presses hard against the floor. Thankfully she knows exactly where she is going, because I don't.

Just pull up in front and let me out. My day is done; my last taxi ridden. If the terrain doesn't improve greatly, I may not make it to Santiago.

Frances chose a charming stone albergue. There are several rooms, each with its own shower and bathroom. My room is empty when I enter, so I take the lower bunk closest to the door. Once the bathroom is free, I'll warm up under a hot shower, then relax outside at the patio table I spotted on the way in.

The shower door opens and a muscular, towel-wrapped pilgrim exits. My turn, I enter the cocoon of steam he left behind. The hot water works to take the edge off my chill and ease my tension, but my body temperature rises a few more degrees when I reach my bunk. The fellow who exited the shower is almost naked in the bunk beside mine. He is propped on one elbow as though posing for a magazine shoot, and I try to reign in my surprise at his wearing nothing more than a pair of scanty underwear.

He is a beautiful Italian cyclist and I am a tongue-tied Canadian, stumbling over my non-existent Italian. While I attempt to communicate with this Adonis, I hope my body language isn't as revealing as his nakedness. Through the quasi-conversation, he explains that his clothes are drying.

"No problemo," I say with a big smile. *Think I'll go find the hose and rinse them down.*

In short order, Frances surprises me as she pulls up in her own taxi. "You're here already Frances? How was it?" I am so proud of her for giving it her best effort. She wanted to tackle it and she did.

"The hills were more than I could manage. I should have taken the taxi with you!"

While I congratulate her on making the attempt, I stop berating myself for being unable to descend the unforgiving trail.

From the patio chair, I watch the flow of pilgrims on the street below, cheering them on as they pass behind our albergue. "Hola, Amigos!" Ann-Marie breaks from the crowd and comes up the hill waving, a huge smile on her face.

"I wasn't exactly sure where our albergue was, until I heard your voice."

Although she is not hurting as much as Frances and I are, she agrees that the trail "was wicked".

The dingy little diner we hope can offer us dinner, could use a bucket of soapy water and some elbow grease, but it's open and we are famished. Spaghetti, a warm baguette, salad and a glass of red wine seal the day.

Back at our albergue, I examine my map, penning out the rest of my trip. Each of the remaining towns and their kilometres is noted, making sure I will be able to end each day in a town that has at least a couple of albergues. There will be more pilgrims looking for beds, leaving me to play *Bunk Bed Roulette*. My journal page is filled with arrows, brackets and stars, but leaves me feeling reassured. With 123 km and ten days remaining, I have more than enough time. *I can stroll into Santiago!*

In the home stretch, I am glad a taxi or bus is no longer an option. They certainly helped me make my way across Spain, especially today, but I want to walk the rest of the way.

I want to walk?

Look how far I have come... I can make it the rest of the way on my own two feet.

"What seems to us as bitter trials are often blessings in disguise."
Oscar Wilde

Day 24
11 km
August 27, 2015

Oblivious to the sounds of my roommates getting ready, I have slept in.

The morning is dark and dreary, a threat of rain in the air as the thick fog masks the grandeur of the mountains. With no options for coffee or breakfast, there is little reason to delay my departure.

Frances and Ann-Marie are almost ready to leave, having decided to take the direct route to Sarria. I could follow them and walk the 23 km, including a pretty rough uphill climb. Or I can choose to travel fewer kilometres, stopping in Samos for the night, with the option to visit the historic monastery.

Still undecided, I listen to my body and lean towards a shorter day. It's doubtful I will see these two lovely New Zealand women again. I hug them tightly and thank them for our time spent together.

Initially, I invited myself into their friendship couple, but having found a comrade who was unopposed to taxis, I began spending more time with Frances, just the two of us. Had that not been the case, it's doubtful I would have travelled this far with them. Their pace is pretty strong with fewer breaks than I like to indulge in.

Whether you choose to take this journey alone or with a companion, there are undoubtedly challenges. I guess it depends on what you hope to get out of the experience, but I think my preference still lies with travelling solo.

When you have a partner, you have someone to brainstorm decisions. You aren't faced with total isolation, and there is always someone to talk to, dine with, and share the good and the not so good. The flip side is the need to be accommodating, flexible, and willing to adapt and adjust the pace of your day, and perhaps your entire trip. Frances and Ann-Marie have managed to balance each other's needs by going their separate ways when needed, but this is probably not an option for a romantic couple.

Would I leave Pierre behind in order to maintain my own pace or keep up with someone I had met? If Pierre did that to me, I would be hurt. Both parties need to adjust their expectations.

There is also the emotional rollercoaster that comes with walking the Camino: the physical challenges, the potential injuries that slow you down, the internal frustrations, the weather, and the sheer exhaustion of walking 20 or more kilometres a day. All of this can put stress on the relationship... or bring you closer together. All depends on the couple.

I've had to deal with my own loneliness and the all too regular spans of isolation, but I am glad to be doing this solo. It drives me outside of my comfort zone, that safe space where I feel confident and capable, allowing multiple opportunities to learn about myself, and to meet incredible people I might otherwise miss if I had a constant companion. I can connect with anyone I choose, for as long as it is comfortable and mutually beneficial. If I need time and space, I can walk alone. I can have a shorter day, hitch a ride on a donkey, taxi or bus, or I can go home.

There is more freedom when you are not committed to anyone else, but there's a price to pay. *And isn't that the same with life?*

Is that why some couples stay together when they are no longer happy or why a person remains in a job that is no longer fulfilling? Is it the fear of the unknown that keeps us stuck in a situation that might be restricting us from pursuing our own best interests?

I'm holding onto a little spark of hope that I may see Melanie in Samos. Last night she emailed me, writing that she stopped 12 km after our shared breakfast. She made it all the way up that *big ass mountain*. Hopefully she feels energized to continue with strength today.

I have no idea how far she'll go: it's more than 30 km to Samos. That would be an incredible feat, especially with the terrain she needs to hike across. I'm not holding my breath, but I know first hand how determined Melanie is when she has her mind set on something. If she feels reaching me will be a positive move, then she will give it her all.

There aren't many people on the road by the time I get my boots on, and I only walk as far as the first local restaurant bustling with activity. A coffee, a carb-laden pastry, and some interaction is needed before I really get started, so I join a couple on the patio.

They are on a tight schedule and cannot afford the extra kilometres of the alternate route to Samos. We have different agendas for the day, but they confirm the route is quite beautiful, especially if I enjoy walking through the woods.

A decision needs to be made sooner than expected, because at the end of the street is a crossroad. *Left toward Samos or right toward Sarria?*

Left it is.

Fewer distractions will have a positive effect on me, even with the likelihood of rain. Off the road and into the woods, it's just me and Mother Nature, with only the sounds of my boots and poles on the soft ground, and a trickling stream below.

Is this what they call living in the moment?

I'm getting more practice with the poncho, removing it each time the rain clears. By the end of the day I should be able to whip it on and off like a pro, ready to demonstrate the functionality of this huge, plastic body tent.

There are plenty of hills, reinforcing my decision to take the shorter route, even if I am on my own. With only 11 km to travel, I am taking my time, venturing in and out of small farming communities. I laugh at the irony of a *No Littering* sign that shows a squatting stick figure, when the road is littered with cattle manure.

I'm deep in thought, my eyes down to avoid tripping on the rocks and tree roots underfoot, when I raise my head, questioning the trail. The woodsy path I was following has changed to a paved road without my noticing. *When did that happen?*

A green pasture flanks my left, the tree-lined forest on my right. *Did I miss a yellow arrow?* I wasn't watching for any signs, assuming the path continued while my head floated in the clouds. A rich PEI-red tractor path moves deeper into the pasture, but doesn't look travelled except for machinery tracks. The alternative is this paved road that curves to the right in a hairpin turn, up out of sight. Neither option makes sense to me and there are no yellow indicators anywhere.

I backtrack about 30 feet, to see if perhaps I missed a sign nailed to a tree. *Nope.*

A few metres onto the farmer's trail doesn't feel right either.

I have been alone all morning, never feeling the isolation until now. A slow panic starts to bubble, my cheeks flushing as my heart skips a little faster. *Am I lost?*

My coping mechanism kicks in with lightning speed. It's time for a smoke. *Winston and I will brainstorm.*

If I listen carefully, I might hear the voices of my fellow pere-grinos approaching, but I know full well there isn't anyone out here with me. I haven't seen a soul since I made the left turn to-wards Samos. *Any chances of a vehicle driving down this road?*

There are no voices, no sounds, no animal sightings. It's eerily quiet, but no longer peaceful. My adrenaline is collecting speed, my heart pounding under my sweaty poncho. *Reassess the situa-tion, Lizzie.* The dirt path doesn't have any boot prints, but the paved road appeared out of nowhere.

I may have to buy a lotto ticket when I get home, because here comes a blue farm truck. It's time to use what's left of my assertive Canadian charm, flagging down the Spanish farmer and his son. As he winds down his window, I hope I can make myself understood with a simple "Camino?"

He talks quickly, and I barely understand what he's saying. He points behind him and mentions *tres*. A word I know: *the number 3*. From my translation, I walked 3 km past a right turn.

I point to the paved road. *Let's try this again.*

"Camino?"

He shakes his head *No*, thumbing backwards with his three fingers outstretched. I think he's telling me the paved road is just for cars; pilgrims use the trail 3 km back. *I don't think so.*

Tres time better be a charm.

"Camino?" pointing to the road with nervous determination.

As if unsure how to deal with a lost and emotionally unstable Canadian, he gives in, nodding reluctantly. My Spanish sucks, so I hope I understand correctly: follow the paved road, turn right at the highway. If the stars are aligned and my Camino guides are paying attention, I should somehow make my way back to the trail within 3 km.

He leaves me on the side of the road to fend for myself, the gears grinding as he prepares for the climb. Partially relieved he didn't offer me a ride, I still have to make my way up, taking it slowly, Melanie style. My calf and glute muscles are working double time, and I reach the highway out of breath and smothering under my poncho.

There is no sign of life in either direction. Maybe the map on my cell could help identify where I am, but it doesn't even pick up the Camino trail. Frustrated, I drop it back into the pocket of my money belt. *Just follow the farmer's directions.*

There are no cars, cyclists, sounds... nothing. *Where the hell is everyone? Is this highway even open?* What is worse? Stuck deep in the woods or along on an abandoned highway?

Inside a bus shelter, I pull off my poncho and drop my backpack on the bench. It's still raining, but I'm feeling claustrophobic, which does nothing to calm my nerves.

Sit down, drink some water, have a smoke!

Jan's words resurface: *What's the worst that can happen?*

With no one in sight, I have no other choice but to continue along the highway. The silence is broken with echoing voices coming up behind me: three cyclists are headed my way. As they come close, I yell out "Camino?" pointing forward.

Their thumbs-up are all the reassurance I need. Eyes sharp and holding onto my faith, I keep walking. In my peripheral vision I see a band of pilgrims on the left hand side of the highway, heading into the trees. *They must have just crossed.*

I laugh nervously. I'd been talking to myself this whole time, working through the situation and trying to hold onto my wits. I went from being lost and anxious, to comically relieved.

Although the others are well ahead of me, I am no longer alone, and celebrate my near arrival in Samos. The rain stops and the peeking sun encourages me to remove my poncho once and for all. Out of the trees at the crest of the town, the winding road gives a magnificent view of the grand *Monastery of San Xulian de Samos* below.

It is a massive complex with multiple tiered roofs, too many windows to count, and a courtyard in the center block. The monastery is nestled on a well-manicured lawn. As the road curves, the view shifts, and I stop often to admire the property. I must make an effort to visit the monastery while I am here. I certainly have plenty of time this afternoon.

Beside the albergue is a café with a busy patio. Once I drop my pack beside a vacant chair, I head inside for a coffee. After my adrenaline-pumping morning, I need to share.

An older couple from Denmark smiles and laughs as I recount my story and my multiple taxi trips. They are avid hikers, older than me, but much fitter. This is their first time walking the Camino, but they have had their share of interesting global adventures.

"The Inca Trail is brutal!" Their words, not mine. "The Peruvians consider the Camino *flatlands*."

No point in adding *Hike the Inca Trail* to my Bucket List.

Because this is a short day, I arrive so early that the *Val de Samos Albergue* is empty. My host brings me upstairs where I have my choice of bunk. There is a modern shower and bathroom, and the option to use one of their fresh clean towels. For three weeks I have been drying myself with a quick-dry, a not-quite-wide-enough, non-plush towel. *Of course I will use your towel, Señora. My body thanks you.*

The windows face the street, and I open one wide and stick my head out. Looks like the sun is drying the still-wet pavement. With the monastery literally steps away, I have options on how to spend my afternoon. With the morning isolation, I'm in search of company. Peregrinos, locals, I'm not picky at this point. Anyone can fill the void I am feeling, but the streets are empty.

At the end of town, I stop at a bench flanked by pilgrim statues. There is something to be said for just being... not walking, not thinking, just sitting here.

My hunger overtakes my thoughts and I walk back through town, stopping at the corner restaurant for lunch. Even as I sit outside with my piping hot tortilla, there's not a soul around. This could be a dreadfully long afternoon without any company.

Bored and needing something to do, I can't seem to motivate myself to go to the monastery. As I relax on my bottom bunk, I write in my journal, sending more emails than usual, just to feel connected. I try to rest but I haven't walked enough for my body to require it.

By 5 pm I'm restless, fidgeting on the bed. *I can't lay here any longer.* Back at the open window, I scan the area, shocked to see a pink-shirted peregrina. Melanie actually made it, and following close behind is Sampaio, my brother from a Brazilian mother.

Unable to contain my happiness, I wait for them to get closer to the main street, waving frantically from my window. "Hola, Amigos!"

They know my voice, a beacon through the air, producing smiles that light up their faces. Out of the albergue with no time to spare, I push through the front door and race into the street, not even bothering to check for passing cars. I cannot believe they are really here. Melanie has walked over 30 km to reach me and a good part of that was the challenging descent into Triacastela. Here she is, smiling and exhausted, standing in front of my albergue.

Our dear friend, Sampaio, stayed close to her the entire way. "I would see him often looking back, to make sure I was still in sight. He helped me to keep moving, even though we didn't really talk."

She refers to Sampaio as her *Guardian Angel*. Neither can really understand the other and there was probably a lot of international language during their walk together, but words are not needed when the heart is understood.

Sampaio is a beautiful soul. His gentle and genuine affection shines through, always ready with a big smile when he sees a fellow pilgrim. He makes Melanie and I feel safe and cared for. A man of great faith, he is a shepherd guiding his flock. Today, Melanie was his flock to protect and help arrive safely.

The poor girl is just exhausted. I certainly commend her stubborn character today. She walked so far to get here and that is a sign in itself. I doubt we will be parting ways, at least not for a while.

How blessed are we to have such strong friendships in so short a time. Being in the right places, at the exact moments, has created incredible opportunities. My heart overflows with love for these two people who have brought so much into my life. There is so much positive energy, you just need to be open to receiving it. With all of the love I am feeling this afternoon, I am hesitant to arrive in Santiago and end this journey.

"To travel is to take a journey into yourself."

Danny Kaye

Day 25
20 km
August 28, 2015

The most unexpected and disturbing dream yanked me from my sleep, but I didn't stay awake for long. But now that I am fully awake, the vividness of my sleeping memories haunt me as I try to rationalize why they are occuring. *Now*. I will need to spend some time thinking it through. Although I was asleep, I was reliving actual incidents in my life.

As we all get ready, I look at Melanie and Sampaio, and smile at my good fortune. *I still can't believe they are here!* They look tired, but I know better than to ask if they slept well.

With a relatively light day ahead of us, my exhausted friends and I can take our time this morning. A visit to the neighbouring café provides a good start; a buzz and enthusiasm is in the air as we chat with other pilgrims. The energy ignites my own.

From my calculations, we have about 14 km to Sarria, the 100 km mark.

Neither Melanie nor I plan on spending the night there, and Sampaio generally walks much further than that, so our plan is to continue on to the next town, an additional four kilometres. That's quite manageable, especially after my shorter day yesterday. I suspect Melanie will welcome the change of pace after walking more than a couple of 30+ km days this week.

The Spanish sun shines bright on my back, promising a warm day. There's a fair amount of pavement to be travelled, mostly in and out of the small towns, but the scenery changes regularly.

Surrounded by trees, we move along the tops of rolling hills, looking down into the valley below. The patches of greens and browns climb almost to the tops of the rounded peaks. The trail offers a tranquility even as we tackle the numerous hills, climbing single file along the narrow dirt path to reach the top.

It's not easy, but with Melanie and Sampaio I am keeping up and feeling confident. Their presence encourages me to give it my best effort. Even with fewer breaks, I still stop regularly to take photos, a sure sign of my contentedness.

When I struggle, physically or emotionally, my mind becomes preoccupied and focused on keeping my feet moving forward, and I often lose sight of the beauty that surrounds me. But when I feel positive, happy and energized, everything around me is more vibrant and alive, and I am determined to capture the feeling.

Melanie and I stay close together; Sampaio walks ahead. He is a strong walker, physically fit from his regular long distance cycling and running regimen at home. Like a true gentleman, he stays nearby, never out of eyesight. I catch him looking back when Melanie and I are quiet, just to make sure we are still there.

He now has two sheep in his flock.

We stop for breaks when we see a café, using our combined efforts of Spanish and English to continue getting to know one another. How much deeper our conversations would be if we spoke the same language. Sampaio is another pilgrim I can learn from.

With Sampaio out of earshot, Melanie tells me about *her* dream last night.

She's ready to settle down and start a family, and only needs to meet Mr. Right, that special someone who shares the same values and beliefs as her. Past heartaches have left her discouraged, wondering if she will ever meet her soul mate. Last night's dream instilled a sense of hope for the future and she just wants to share it with someone she trusts. I'm no dream analysis expert, but I've always felt it is our subconscience trying to send us a message.

She opened up the window to share my own dream. *Two actually.*

The first was a two-year-old memory when Pierre and I had to put our Gizzi down. The dream was as clear as that night on November 12th, 2013.

Gizzi was our baby, a 12-year-old schnauzer we had loved since a puppy. His health deteriorated suddenly; his capacity for understanding faltering and his behaviour changing almost overnight. It progressed to the point where he couldn't understand when I would call him from the patio door. Then, a couple of days before that sad night, he became extremely agitated, panting non-stop, unable to relax.

The vet offered to run some tests, but with his age and the description of symptoms, the doctor brought up the sensitive subject of euthanasia. Giving him a shot to help calm him, we went home. The following day, Pierre came home early and Gizzi's agitation had escalated, his body physically distressed.

Our hearts were breaking as we discussed our limited options before calling the vet again. We knew we wouldn't be returning home with our Giz and it made us sick. We were grieving before we even left the house.

What came to me in the early hours of this morning was not a dream. I relived those precious last minutes of Gizzi's life.

The doctor brought him into the care lounge, his body so relaxed they had to carry him, placing him in my arms. I held him, talking sweetly, telling him how much we loved him and how much happiness he brought into our lives. After a few minutes, the doctor returned, transferring Giz into Pierre's waiting arms. When we were ready to let go, the drug was injected.

My dream ended with the doctor telling us that our Giz was gone. We were both so distraught having to say goodbye, but we had each other to share in the grief and comfort. This was one of the saddest moments for us.

The next dream followed immediately. It was the night my mom died almost 10 years ago.

She had been in the nursing home for about a month, her dementia having taken away all of her capacities. For 10 days I sat there, almost around the clock, reading out loud, talking to her but getting little response, except the occasional flutter of her eyes and the rattle that escaped her throat.

On this particular evening, the nurses warned me that the time was drawing near. My aunt had been with me those last few days and Pierre was taking care of the kids at home. His daughter had also come down for the weekend. When I called to let him know, he raced to Mom's side.

Pierre always had a sweet spot for Mom and the feeling was mutual. He was so helpful during those four crazy years that had brought us to the nursing home. I'm not sure how I would have managed without his support.

My uncle and aunt from PEI showed up unexpectedly. Within a few minutes of their arrival, Mom's face changed. Her skin tone greyed, her face sinking within itself. She had been waiting for her little brother, holding on until his arrival, even though no one knew of his travel plans.

Everything sped up from that moment.

In my sleep, I replayed those final minutes, holding her hand, caressing her hair, my face right in front of hers. "We all love you so much Mom, but Dad is waiting for you. You don't have to hold on anymore." I knew she would watch over all of us. The dream ended with her taking that last breath, a memory seared into my brain that September night.

I had re-lived those two traumatic life changers that had left me scarred and doubting whether I had done everything in my power. I didn't know how to begin processing it until Melanie shared her own dream. I'm an over-analyzer, and often scrutinize details in an attempt to understand why something has occurred. This morning I've been trying to figure out why these two particular incidents came back to me now, of all times. These are memories of deep loss.

The last couple of years of my mom's life are a blur, many of the details I cannot remember, having lost her well before she took that last breath. My emotional states had me grieving for my mom, with little control over the aggression of her dementia.

The decision to put Gizzi down, our baby who offered unconditional love, who I could always count on to bring a smile to my face, was difficult. When he looked at me with his beautiful brown eyes, I knew I was loved, regardless of whatever else was happening in my life. I couldn't bear to see him suffer, but at the same time, hated to make that decision.

Perhaps these memories are to heal the old scars, to embrace the one emotion I may have unconsciously denied myself.

Forgiveness.

I like to think they are both travelling alongside me, helping to nudge me in the right direction. With Melanie's unfaltering faith in God, she agrees "they are here with you." Thankful to be able to talk it through with her, I feel lighter as we continue through the countryside.

Outside a small hamlet, a stone bridge leads us into another wooded wonderland. The symmetry of the trees lets me look right through the forest, each one lining up perfectly.

Back into the fields, we come across a farmhouse and small woman milking her cow. I can't hear any sounds and neither the woman nor the cow are moving, playing with my eyesight. Each step tricks my brain until we get close enough... and then we all have a good laugh. They are well crafted wooden cutouts giving an illusion.

Three weeks into the Camino, I'm still learning new strategies for descending hills. A local man ahead of me, busily chatting on his cellphone, is walking down the paved road... backwards. I give it a try. Call me crazy, but my knees don't hurt at all. That would have been handy knowledge weeks ago, although not a technique I could have tried on the rougher trails.

The time with my friends passes quickly. We take fewer breaks, but I'm happy to keep on trekking. The hills on our way to Sarria are challenging, but because we are together, they are not as daunting. The sun is out in full strength, and the temperature is back into the high 30s. It's a welcome change from the damp, cool, and rainier weather we've been experiencing the last four days.

Only 100 km to go!

Sarria is a popular starting stage for many, so there will be an influx of pilgrims on the trail, as well as more competition for beds after a long day of walking. Those beginning their Camino from this stage tend to have smaller packs and more bounce to their step. Those of us who have travelled a few weeks carry dusty, larger packs, our feet dragging, many suffering with injuries.

In an arena that offers so much opportunity to respect and care for your fellow man, it is unfortunate that some peregrinos look down on those who choose to limit their journey to the last 100 km, as though these seekers are less *authentic* in their quest. This seems somewhat ignorant when there are in fact more people who *don't* walk the entire 800 km.

So many individuals break their Camino into a multi-year adventure, start somewhere other than Saint-Jean-Pieds-de-Port, bus, taxi or leave the trail entirely and head home. I am having a hard time understanding why you would dismiss another person's journey, just because it is not as long or as painful as your own.

More than once I have caught myself saying, "Let's not forget that we are all peregrinos." As I am discovering, the distance travelled is not nearly as important as the time spent experiencing.

Even though we aren't spending the evening here, we have certainly earned an extended lunch. Along the boardwalk we find a restaurant perfect for people watching. There are more tourists here than pilgrims... *or are they cleaned-up pilgrims in tourist mode?*

Andreia is easily spotted with her wooden staff, bandaged knees, sunglasses and straw hat to protect her from the sun. I call out to her as we wave her over enthusiastically. Andreia left Triacastela this morning and although her pace is slow, she is still moving forward, delighted to be joining us in the last leg of the day.

We are all together as we bid *Adiós* to Sarria and head out of town.

The *Taberna do Camino* is the first albergue entering Barbadelo, situated directly across from a green pasture. A stone fence defines the large property, and the walkway through a thick well-manicured lawn welcomes us to our home for the night. Each cabin has about 8 bunk beds, a modern bathroom and shower.

In my eyes we have arrived at a Camino Resort, the first to offer so many amenities in such a well-designed and inviting atmosphere. They could easily charge more than the 9 euros for these luxury accomodations. There is no need to leave the premises for dinner. We can dine at the restaurant, order a drink from the bar, sit on the patio and listen to the music playing over the loudspeakers. What more could we ask for?

In the spacious backyard lies a large salt water pool that awaits christening from our sweaty and dusty bodies. Melanie's in heaven; her bathing suit ready for sporting. With our packs off, Andreia and I head to the back yard fully dressed. We are so hot from the day that we aren't even changing into cleaner clothes. Overeager and in need of cooling off, I am the the first one in, coaxing my Brazilian sister to join me. The salt water refreshes my body and spirit, while Melanie takes photos of me swimming across the pool.

My first swim. Check.

I've ordered a glass of sangria and a piece of chocolate queso for my dinner. Surrounded by the people I love, the happiness overflows inside of me. I can't hold it in, singing out loud to the tunes, not a care in the world.

I am in heaven!

Day 26
20 km
August 29, 2015

A wake before the others, I leave the cabin eager for my first coffee. A fellow peregrina sits cross-legged on the ledge of the stone wall, meditating in front of the rising sun. Part of me wants to join her in welcoming this new day, but I don't want to intrude on her quiet moment of reflection. The early morning dew christens my feet as I make my way up the lawn, and my senses are alert to the smell of damp grass and freshly ground coffee.

With my caffeine fix in hand, I witness the dawn from the comfort of a patio chair, while the music hangs softly in the light mist. This is the most serene I have felt, undisturbed by the few who have joined me to embrace the sunrise.

I can't believe I am sitting in Barbadelo, less than 100 km from Santiago. There were moments when I didn't think I would finish the day, let alone walk almost four weeks on my own, *but here I am*. With nine days left before my return flight, I have switched gears, no longer burdened by the urgency of a time-sensitive schedule.

A note of sadness rises. There were days I couldn't wait to be this close, but this morning I am hesitant to leave this peaceful oasis, wanting to hold onto the joy a while longer.

Two coffees and several smokes later, my friends are still not out. Opening the door to our cabin, I find the room is silent and the tension thick as I catch a few sidelong glances. I'd like to break the somber mood with, "Yes, I am probably the one that kept you up last night." Instead, I quickly gather my belongings and retreat outside, welcoming the fresh air.

Melanie, Sampaio and Andreia join me for breakfast, and my energy is a contrast to their sleepiness. Hopefully the music, coffee and food will recharge their batteries, because I am having trouble containing my enthusiasm.

Neighbouring pilgrims are unable to appreciate my good humour as I sing along to the tunes. They are either wondering what I added to my coffee (and where they can get some), or else we shared the cabin last night and they hope never to bunk with me again.

By the time we are done eating, my pilgrim family's mood has lightened. It is time for group photos, keepsakes to cherish this moment, not that I will need any reminders.

The time and coffee have worked me into a hurricane of energy and I quickly take the lead. My pace is strong, and my strides are long and determined. I catch myself humming the chorus to one of the last songs I heard.

My amigos pass me when I stop to take photos of the valley below, a plush green carpet disturbed only by the elevated highway standing high and proud, a centerpiece of the countryside. We have different rhythms: I do better on the uphill climb, and Melanie has power on the descents. Andreia is slow but steady, and Sampaio is consistently strong. We don't have to walk side by side to be together.

We are constantly climbing until the terrain flattens when we walk through hamlets, and we often share the road with cows and their master who rings his bell shouting words of encouragement. My heart is pumping wildly, and the beads of sweat sting my eyes. I would benefit from someone on the sidelines cheering me on.

Go Lizzie, you're doing great. Almost there. You can do it!

Through the more densely-wooded areas, my pace slows as I stumble around tree roots and unearthed rocks. My neck and shoulders strain, but my legs continue pushing me up the hill until I spot a large enough rock to sit on. My water bottles are emptying quickly, and my pack of Winstons dwindles. I'll need to stock up on both soon.

There is an influx of travellers and Melanie has made an acquaintance: a young German fellow named Daniel.

"You go on ahead Mel. I need to take a break." I am taking advantage of another pit stop and she would benefit from some time to get to know this young man.

"I'll wait for you at the next café, Elizabeth," her smile confirming my suspicions.

She is absent at the next stop, hopefully enjoying getting to know Daniel. That doesn't prevent me from stopping for a Coke and chatting with the others needing a break from the endless climb. My Brazilian friends arrive soon after.

Andrcia's pace is slower, especially on the rougher terrain, but she keeps moving forward. Her body never healed from the injuries she sustained four weeks ago, and the daily physical grind aggravates her condition. Focused and determined, this woman is no quitter, following no other agenda than her own. Through our quasi-chatting, she tells me she is a personal trainer. *That makes sense!*

A couple of hours after starting her walk with Daniel, I see Melanie sitting alone at a patio. Melanie and I have a relationship that is deeply-rooted; more than once she confides, "You are the most important person in my Camino." *The feeling is mutual, my friend.*

We came into each other's lives at the right time, balancing one another when it was most needed, and able to talk about *almost* anything. We've realized that the time we spent on our own was important for our overall experience, but now that we have reconnected it will be hard to say goodbye. *I can't think about that right now.*

She would like me to join her in walking to Finisterre. "I don't think so Melanie. I've had enough walking, and I hope to take shorter days from here on out."

Surprised by her willingness to change plans, she offers a compromise with a hint of hopefulness. "We could go by bus."

She is not ready to part ways either, but accepting her offer would require me to walk even more kilometres for the remaining days to Santiago. I am not sure how I feel about that. Finisterre was never part of my plan. I knew I would be on a time crunch, so I never entertained an extension after Santiago. It is doable with my revised schedule, but I am hesitant to commit.

"I can't make any promises, but will see how I feel each day. If I'm up to walking longer, I will." But I have convinced myself that shorter days is a better way to end the journey.

You said you would be open to whatever the Universe brings your way. That voice is getting easier to hear.

By the time the four of us arrive at a small gift shop, we are exhausted from the heat and exertion of the relentless ascension. With cold beverages in hand, we take possession of the few chairs lining the side of the building. Music filters through the outdoor speakers on the wings of an angel. As Bob Marley's *One Love* begins, Andreia and I start singing out loud. Melanie and Sampaio cannot resist joining in, our voices echoing the love we feel for one another. When the song ends, we drift back into our own thoughts.

In the arena of freedom and simple pleasures, I am overcome by the desire to stay in this moment forever. There have been many highs and lows along this dusty and often lonely trail, but moments like this remind me how incredible this journey has been. It seems I needed to pull myself out of my everyday world in order to see how simple life can be... *if I let it.*

My hesitation at wanting to leave the Camino stems from the acceptance that I am a *work in progress*, and there is still much work to be done.

This month of extreme physical demands, the hours of isolation, emotional chaos and situations that required resilience, have helped to push boundaries and tear down walls. I respect this woman who is walking on her own through Spain, meeting new people, gaining new perspectives, feeling connected to nature and this community of like-minded souls. I see a woman with a stronger self-confidence, learning to trust her voice and act on it.

With the increase of pilgrims comes an abundance of roadside vendors. We pass a bagpiper, a fruit stand and an artisan selling his wares, each offering a *cello* for our credential in exchange for a couple of euros. These pit stops help break the challenging walk into manageable stages, as we make our way towards the calm turquoise waters of Portomarín.

From the bridge in the valley, the elevated city awaits our arrival. Overheated and near the end of our endurance, the serenity of the still water is lost in the face of the gateway to Portomarín: a tall, steep stone staircase.

With no other option than to

climb it, we take our time sidestepping each stair, avoiding the temptation to look down. There will be no Rocky sequel filmed here this afternoon.

When we stop to catch our breath at the top of the staircase, we share a look of defeat. The street is literally straight up, right out of a San Francisco tourism commercial. Happy not to be driving a stick shift, this will take more energy than we have to offer, with gravity weighing us down.

Mid-way, our desperation forces us to turn around and head back to the only albergue we spotted on the first cross street. Thankful to have a place to stay, I've already decided I'll be spending the afternoon sitting on the front porch that overlooks the turquoise water.

While Melanie and I discuss evening plans, our attention is diverted by a phone conversation Sampaio is having. He is noticeably distressed, his voice cracking as he fights to hold back his tears.

Quietly moving to the porch to offer him some privacy, Andreia explains that he is talking to his wife, telling her about an incident earlier this week. It seems that Sampaio collapsed on the trail. We can't even imagine our strong friend being so vulnerable, even in these extreme conditions. Melanie and I had no idea; it had never come up in conversation. *How could it?*

When the call has ended, he comes out to join us, wiping his eyes. There is no need for any explanation, as our hugs reassure him that he is not alone. This is our cue to give space to Sampaio and Andreia, leaving them at the albergue, while Melanie and I attempt to climb up the street in search of dinner. We wander through the town square, visiting the vendor displays, and I take my own trip into the tobacco shop to stock up on my Winstons.

As I exit, I see Leen.

"I knew we would see each other again."

Tomorrow the five of us will walk together.

Day 27
17 km
August 30, 2015

The clock on the wall shows 1 am, and it torments me through my sleepless night. It could be due to the coffee I had with dinner, but more likely it's the lack of air circulation in our stifling little room. If I was home I'd be sleeping in the nude, but the thought of my already fragile reputation prevents me from becoming known as the *Canadian who Snores Naked*.

As the light starts to filter in through our curtained window, I reach for my FitBit to check the time. *Where is it?* An inside sweep of my bra causes panic. *It's not there.* Pat down my torso, search under my tank top, I'm shuffling in my lower bunk. I can't feel it. *Did I put it on after my shower?*

My heart races. *Oh God, I hope I haven't lost it.*

My routine is always the same once I stop for the day. It gives me a sense of control in an environment of unpredictables. Once I'm registered and claim my bunk, I unpack the two Ziploc bags I need for the shower: my toiletries and my clean clothes for the evening. Before even entering the shower, I remove my FitBit from my shorts and safeguard it in my money belt. The money belt goes into my Ziploc of clean clothes. Once I've washed off the dirt and sweat from the day, I dress, the Fitbit clipped inside my bra, the only discreet hiding place when wearing my sexy red dress.

The Ziploc bags are *always* hung *in* the shower stall, but these showers have a high wooden ledge, out of the stream of water and the bags were sealed closed. Now it's gone. *Did I put it in my money belt? Did I clip it into my bra after the shower? I can't remember.*

Now that everyone is awake, I get out of bed and remove my pillow and liner off the mattress, shaking them. I check my money belt, but it's not there either. In the now empty shower stall, I run my hand over the top of the shelf, but it's too high to reach all the way back. I lean against the counter to have a better view, but I can't see anything. Using an outdated, rolled up magazine from the lobby, I sweep it across the shelf.

Still no FitBit. *SHIT! What did I do with it?*

Although not the end of the world, it feels that way.

The FitBit was a Christmas present from Pierre, and has been my lifeline, a constant companion that I check regularly to see if I have walked enough to take a break. Depending on the reading, it may encourage me to keep walking or make the executive decision to stop, regardless of how far I have travelled. At the end of each day, I note the kilometres in my journal. My kilometres walked is not based on the guidebook, but on my FitBit. The act of checking it after a day of walking is ceremonial.

Back in our cramped bedroom, Melanie can sense I am frazzled, as I walk around aimlessly and agitated. "What's going on, Elizabeth?"

My friends jump on board the crazy train, in search of my missing FitBit. It is a lost cause and I am already feeling out of sync as I pack up my stuff.

Everyone is hesitating as we leave the albergue. Andreia and Sampaio will be continuing onto Palas de Rei, adding an additional 10 km to their day. Their schedule is tighter than mine, so today they need to walk as far as they can. At some point we will be parting ways, unlikely to see one another again.

It was bound to happen, but that doesn't make it any easier. My heart feels heavy at the thought and I distract myself by focusing on how fortunate I am to have spent so much time with them. *Don't push away the sadness.* The heartache is there for a reason... to remind me just how much they mean to me. With love comes pain and I've experienced my fair share of both, but isn't that the duality of life!

I'm certainly experiencing the duality on the Camino: the dread I feel most mornings of having to walk another day and the relief when I finally arrive at an albergue; the exhausting struggle to climb a steep hill and my amazement once I reach the top; the isolation of too much time on my own and the joy of being with others; and the gloom of an overcast grey sky and the sparkle as the sun breaks through the clouds.

Without the darkness there would be no light. *Who said that?*

We meet Leen at the top of the steep stone stairway. No one wants to climb the street to find a café, so there is no coffee or breakfast for the Musketeers. Aside from *Good Morning*, no one has much to say. Our group lacks energy and enthusiasm, making the walking slow in the smothering morning mist.

The walk towards Gonzar is long as we trudge slowly through the countryside. Leaving a wooded area, the mist is so heavy I can barely see the red path beneath my feet. We climb higher, and the heavy fog rises from the valley as the sun breaks free.

My body is sweating, and with no coffee or food, I'm overdue to stop when we finally arrive in Gonzar. The large enclosed canteen resembles the chip wagons Pierre and I have stopped at during road trips. *I'll have a couple of pogos with sweet mustard and a poutine, por favor.*

Conversation hangs in the air, and an unspoken sorrow draws out our final meal together.

Once everyone is done eating, we prepare to say goodbye, but my mind is elsewhere, contemplating my journey with these two incredible individuals.

Andreia and I met on Day 1, struggling to reach Alto del Perdón. After the successful climb up, we descended the hill together as she shared the insight she had already gained: *The Camino is talking to me.* As a green peregrina, I was struggling with the unexpected demands of the physical challenge, but her statement stayed top of mind. On and off, we have shared our journey, whether for a brief hug and smile, or getting to know each other once the walking was done.

The limitations of our verbal expression have never been an issue. We are connected by what is not said, by our smiles when we see each other. Andreia is my Camino Sister: she inspires me, loves me and encourages me to be my best self.

Leen and Melanie say their goodbyes to Andreia and Sampaio, knowing I am stalling until we are all ready to part ways.

Sampaio is a true pilgrim, sharing his heart and good nature with everyone he meets. Our first encounter was on Day 4, the afternoon that Andreia wanted each of us to share what had brought us to the Camino. As we spent more time together, our bond tightened. I always felt safe when he was close by, knowing he was watching out for me. He wants to maintain contact once we are home, friending me on Facebook.

Although we have trouble understanding each other, Sampaio, Andreia and I share an undeniable kinship and I am not ready to say goodbye.

The emotional Band-Aid rips off as we embrace with love to carry us through to the end of our journeys. Tears fall and Sampaio walks away first, wiping his eyes. Andreia and I draw out the parting with strength and courage. This is the time I wish we all spoke the same language, and I hope they know just how much they mean to me.

I realized early on that my journey was multifaceted. Not only would I learn about myself, but I would also develop incredible relationships with individuals I would not have met otherwise. With our intention to walk the Camino, we have crossed borders, creating friendships that will withstand the miles that separate our homelands.

With the goodbyes out of the way, we can walk alongside, pass or fall behind them, until they advance out of sight. The solemn morning encourages Melanie, Leen and me to make plans for one more night together. Tomorrow they will be picking up their pace, resulting in more goodbyes.

Melanie and I have had no further discussions about bussing to Finisterre. She knows that I am taking each day as it comes. We will see what tomorrow brings, but I am not ready for any more goodbyes.

We weave through the countryside, switching onto paved roads and through small towns, and the sun is now full strength and hot as hell. The last few kilometres are downhill, but I'm alternating between different styles to descend the hills. Today's tears are not due to physical pain.

Our albergue in Eirexe is conveniently located across from an already bustling restaurant with a large outside patio. *That's where we're heading once we wash up!*

Up the flight of stairs, we enter the cramped room where the bunk beds are pushed together like slices in a loaf of bread. Many of the beds are already spoken for, and I am the lucky recipient of one near the door. Melanie looks at me in all seriousness. "OK. You are sleeping here? I am going all the way over there," she says, pointing to a bunk on the other side of the room.

I am the only one laughing.

Leen takes a bunk close to me, much to Melanie's surprise. I am very fond of Leen, and I don't want my snoring to cause any issues between us. "If you hear me start to snore, tell me to 'Roll over, honey.' That's what my husband says to me and it usually works. But... you have to say it in a loving way."

She laughs, but I tell her I'm serious. Leen hasn't spent enough nights with me to know that she's taking her sleep into her own hands by bunking so close.

Melanie doesn't trust the trick will work. "I suggest you find a bed farther away, Leen!" That's what friends are for.

As I undress in the shower, I absentmindedly grab for the missing FitBit. Today's walk was dreadful and all I wanted to do was stop. Often. I did stop, but I'm sure I have more cigarettes in my pack because of the lost FitBit. We didn't even walk 20 km today, so I think I'll be able to manage without it. *What choice do I have anyway?*

We have earned an afternoon of leisure and have arrived early enough to enjoy socializing with our peers. It's a busy patio and the tables are full, so we invite ourselves to sit with Anna, from Logroño, who understands some English. She started walking in Sarria, with only five days to reach Santiago before she has to re-turn to work.

Hamburgers are on the menu. *Why not?* I need some home comfort after my morning of goodbyes. For a burger with only a few condiments, it is surprisingly tasty.

The patio is so busy with conversations that we almost miss the evening entertainment. A farmer has come down the street with his cows, stopping right in front of the patio tables, to have a slurp of the not-so-fresh water in the trough. I start filming. The farmer is oblivious to the crowd, herding his cows back down the road after a few minutes of refreshment.

As the sun starts to set, I walk out onto the grass in my bare feet, the damp softness cool beneath them. With arms outstretched and my body swaying, it can be easily mistaken as dancing, even though there is no music. It has been an emotional day, but my heart feels light. Melanie takes my phone and asks me to pose for some photographs. My body has changed: it's a little firmer and the tan is dark. My lost vanity returns.

I'm looking hot in my little red dress!

Day 28
27 km
August 31, 2015

"Did you ask me to 'roll over' last night, Leen?"
        In all seriousness, she starts telling me what happened after I layed down.

"I watched you put your hands behind your head and you started snoring almost immediately. I couldn't believe how quickly it started and thought to myself, *this is going to be a long night.*" With everyone still awake, she issued her first *roll over* command. "I didn't want to wake you up, but if anyone was going to sleep, I had to try. But you didn't react."

Leen probably wasn't loud enough to penetrate through the layers of my unconsciousness. We try to laugh it off.

"I'm sorry, Leen."

With a smile, she continues. "I tried it again, this time a little louder. *Roll over, honey!* I was shocked... you actually rolled onto your side."

A short term remedy, she needed to repeat this magic phrase a few more times, hoping to fall into her own coma during the quieter moments. My friend looks tired this morning. While I'm celebrating the small success, she reminds me that it was our last evening together anyway.

Unfortunately, that doesn't make me feel any better. Each day we spend together brings us closer. We haven't shared much of the personal challenges that brought us to the Camino, but we both accept we are here for a reason, and meeting each other has been a positive experience.

Leen is tall and fit, a strong walker who never seems to tire. Nor does she seem to be suffering, but perhaps she does it silently. She's an experienced hiker, and this isn't her first rodeo, but as we approach Santiago, her return flight to Belgium on September 3rd draws closer. She plans to pick up her pace today and cover as many kilometres as possible.

Leen and Melanie stay connected through *WhatsApp*, so when Leen moves ahead of us, she will let Melanie know what town she stops in. *Goodbyes* are imminent.

There have been too many days of struggling on my own, but I have walked enough to last a lifetime, and I'm prepared to simply stroll the rest of the way. Making that decision means saying goodbye to these women who have become my friends.

This is my 28th day of walking and the gloomy morning weighs on my heart as I consider the friendships that encouraged me to keep moving forward. Hundreds of *Hola, Amigos* and the true companionship of a chosen few have carried me to where I am today. The *Goodbyes* take a little piece of me, especially so close to the finish line.

We share one last quiet breakfast together, and I bury my emotions in the busyness of eating. Yesterday was difficult, saying goodbye to Andreia and Sampaio, and now I'm wishing my Belgian friend a *Buen Camino*. As Leen powers off towards the long day in front of her, Melanie and I continue together, our pace slow.

The sky hangs low and rain drizzles on and off, forcing me to cover my backpack. I'm chilled in my t-shirt by the time we stop for lunch, wishing I was *anywhere* else. Hungry and needing something substantial, I want another hamburger. It's undercooked, so I return to the counter showing the single bite and the raw meat tucked in the bun. He apologizes, reassuring me that it will only be a couple of minutes. True to his word he returns quickly with a seared patty, still raw inside.

I am disgusted, starving but turned off any alternatives. *Where's a bowl of spaghetti when I need it?* Still hungry, frustrated and cold, we abandon the tiny canteen. *I am ready to stop right now!*

The hamlets offer distractions to the walk, but I am not interested in visiting the old churches or peeking through the windows of ancient buildings. Fed up, I retreat to a bench whenever Melanie stops, seeking an escape from the day.

Within the warm earthy cocoon of a eucalyptus forest, I am transported out of my misery into the reassuring embrace of Mother Nature, the canopy above protecting us from the rain. The quiet eases my anxiety, lightening my mood.

Unwilling to say goodbye to Melanie, I am prepared to keep moving. "I will walk with you until I can't go any further."

Goodbyes delayed. Check.

As the day stretches out, I become more committed to staying with Melanie. We make a plan to reach Boente, where Leen is stopping for the night. A 27 km day will bring us ahead of schedule. Anna joins us, also planning to stop there.

"Let's make a reservation for the three of us."

Instead of stopping all the time, I am keeping up, walking more kilometres than I expected. "Why don't you come up with a plan for us to go to Finisterre! As long as we don't have to walk, I would love to join you."

She is delighted and I have to admit, so am I.

Part of my sour mood was realizing that I will be alone if I want to walk shorter days. It's time to be flexible, to accept the invitation for companionship, and the bonus trip post-Santiago. Finisterre had never been on my agenda, but the bus trip to Burgos and the couple of taxis, helped bring me ahead of schedule. Fewer kilometres each day might be easier physically, but I don't think I have the emotional strength for the loneliness.

We drag ourselves into Boente. As soon as we walk through the diner door of the *Os Albergue Meson Boente,* the red flags start waving. The store front windows of this 1950s style restaurant are grimy.

Behind the counter is a heavy-set fellow in a stained white t-shirt and black leather vest, his long grey ponytail and matching beard making him look more fierce than perhaps he is. Instead of a welcome, he eyes us with suspicion, as though patrons are few and far between.

He strokes his beard as he acknowledges our reservation, and asks for our national and pilgrim passports. With kohl-lined eyes, he examines our photos, then pulls out his ledger from beneath the counter. All I can see is thick gold jewelry dangling, solid rings on his large fingers, adding to the biker look he is pulling off.

While he takes care of the paperwork, I steal a look around the joint. The plastic-looking food in the refrigerated display case has a coat of greasy dust. *Why aren't we grabbing our passports and running for the door?*

I want him to hurry up and direct us to our room so we can distance ourselves from him, as I'm not liking this vibe. I don't know what I would have done if I had been alone. Late in the day and with so many people looking for beds, it was risky to walk away from a reservation. If the restaurant is any indication, I can only imagine what the sleeping arrangements are like.

After returning our passports, he leads us to the back of the building, and points out the rooms we are forbidden to enter.

"These are off limits." He is stern, making me question what he might have stashed behind the curtains.

Don't worry Señor, we aren't going to spend any more time here than absolutely necessary.

Up the stairs, he opens the door to a small room with two bunk beds. Melanie is silently wishing there was more space between us, but tonight she is willing to sacrifice her sleep for solidarity. There is safety in numbers.

Down the hall is a filthy single bathroom with a toilet, and a tub with a dangling shower hose. With no bracket to mount the hose and head, it will be challenging to wash my hair with one hand while rinsing with the other. My rat's nest is definitely a two-hand job. I *always* wear my sandals in the shower, but tonight it is a prerequisite. The toilet seat has a crack as wide as the San Andreas fault line, pinching my butt cheeks when I sit down.

We are adapting to our environment... we are only here to sleep. *Nothing more.*

Melanie messages Leen once we are showered. She is staying at the albergue down the street. In no time we are out the door to meet her for dinner, hoping the owner is gone by the time we return.

Leen thought *her* albergue was less than adequate, but after giving us a tour, we reassure her she is staying in a 5-Star establishment. The dining area is above par and her living quarters are fine, albeit cramped. There are a lot of pilgrims staying here and we are the only ones at *Chez le Creepy Albergue*.

Over dinner we get to know Anna a little better, everyone practicing the International Language.

Ready to return to our beds, we enter the dark albergue, the owner nowhere in sight. Quietly climbing the stairs, I'm eager to get into bed and fall asleep. I am done, wishing I was home.

"He who is outside his door already has the hardest part of the journey behind him."
Dutch Proverb

Day 29
25 km
September 1, 2015

S ometime in the night, an army of mosquitoes attacked, waking me with their incessant buzzing. The only way to escape was to pull the hood of my white shirt tight over my head and barricade myself inside my sleeping bag liner. This morning the albergue is silent, and the only thing on our minds is getting out.

In no time we race down the back fire escape and head to Leen's albergue for breakfast. We survived the night, but are exhausted.

The short trek has me chilled, and the warmth of the restaurant does little to help me shake it off. Thankful for a decent breakfast of toasted baguette, juice and coffee, my belly is full, but that is the only comfort I feel this morning.

The four of us are beginning together, but we'll likely lose Anna during the course of the morning. Our time with her has come to an end and I would prefer for Melanie, Leen and I to walk without distractions from anyone else. How I wish Leen and I had more time together. She has an air of calm about her, and yet I wonder if she recognizes this strength. We have never found it necessary to share too much of our private lives, understanding that we have each seen our fair share of personal trials.

She mentioned reading the *Celestine Prophecy* during her Camino.

"I've heard about that book. What are your thoughts?"

She takes her time to answer. "It's a book that needs to be read when the time is right."

My mood is grey like the weather, and my emotions are hard to pinpoint. My desperate longing to go home is laced with hesitation. This journey I spent so much time and energy preparing for, the month of walking with all the ups and downs, is coming to an end. *Shake it off Lizzie, you are tired and it's been a long month.*

Outside, everyone is bundled up except me. Being so close to the finish line, there is no way I am going to dirty my white shirt now. I have managed this far and it's the only *almost* long sleeve that I can wear at the end of the day. I'll brave the chilly air, but I wish I had a thick fleece to cover my goosebumped flesh. A little sunshine would brighten my spirits.

No sooner do we start walking when my back is damp beneath my pack. The wind has picked up, but the rain is holding off for now. Feels like a Canadian autumn morning—not at all what I signed up for when I chose the month of August to travel through Spain.

As soon as I remove my backpack at our first rest stop, the cold breeze leaves me exposed and shivering. My mother would say this is a great way to catch a cold. Thank goodness I am hearty and well-padded, although with a little less body insulation than when I started.

My pack is getting lighter now that the toiletries have dwindled and there are only a couple of Clif Bars remaining.

Since I gave Melanie the green light for Finisterre, she has been in planning mode and already has a tentative schedule. Her excitement fuels my own. If we walk farther today and to-morrow, the third would be a short 5 km into Santiago. An early arrival will give us time to meet up with Leen before at-tending the noon mass in the Cathedral. The following day we will bus to Finisterre and spend two days at the ocean.

Just as the many Camino routes have regained popularity, so has the extended trip to Finis-terre. The term *end of the world* comes from the Latin phrase *Finis Terrae*. For many, reaching the cliffs is the culminating act of their Camino.

Melanie is as happy as I am that we are ending our journey to-gether. I know the value of having spent time with my own thoughts and living the challenges and experiences of solo travel, but I want companionship for this last stage. We will celebrate our achievement and our friendship, by arriving in Santiago together.

Finisterre is a bonus! A well-deserved break at the beach, after a hard month of walking.

When I look back on events, I smile at how my trip has evolved. I have learned to go with the flow and follow the signs. Life has *not* been easy, but it *has* been simple. I feel as though I have lived a life's worth of experiences in these four weeks.

Reining in my dreamy thoughts, I come back to the present. I still have today and tomorrow to get through, and they are going to be long days.

The missing FitBit is now forgotten; I have adapted and am no longer checking for it. I don't seem to be stopping for as many photos, but that has more to do with the weather and my melancholy mood.

Melanie, Leen and I are spending more time side-by-side as we walk the path together. On other days, we let our pace carry us, but this morning we are sticking close to one another, sharing in the friendship for as long as possible. Each of us is quiet, absorbed in our own thoughts until one starts talking, breaking the trance.

One last 11 am selfie is all smiles.

The scenery brightens as the sky starts to clear. Through hamlets and fields of deep green, we travel over rolling hills spotted with houses. As though needing a final keepsake, I fall behind and call out to the girls, taking their photo just as they turn around. *These are my friends.* I'm not sure what it will be like to go home and not have them to share my thoughts with or to give each other support.

Melanie is not feeling well.

At first I thought her quiet mood was an emotional one, but she tells me she needs to stop, as her hips are in too much pain. We have walked 25 km and I could have stopped long ago, but was willing to keep going if that was the plan. I've made a commitment, letting her dictate when we've had enough.

Leen has slowed down her tempo and as the kilometres progressed, I just assumed we would spend one last night together. Change of plans. Leen is disappointed; she has to continue walking on her own and it is already late in the day. Now she runs the risk of not having a bed.

Melanie and I stopping means saying goodbye to her on short notice. I hold on tight. "See you in a couple of days my friend."

We are fortunate to get two of the few remaining beds available at the *El Albergue de Boni*. A crowd has already gathered in the common area, and our host, Boni, is ready to give us the royal tour. An animated fellow, he obviously enjoys his job of making peregrinos feel welcome. With a bit of dramatic flare, he identifies the bulletin board. "I know you will all be looking for access to WiFi."

Small cabins dot the backyard, but the showers are actually in a separate outside building. Much to my surprise, this is the best shower I have had. Hot water and a series of high pressure jets massage my spine, taking the chill away. As I exit the steamy room, the cold air confirms the need for long pants, my tank and my white top. I wish I had a sweatshirt or even a bug ridden wool blanket to pull over my shoulders. *Damn it's cold.*

I'm tired, my belly is upset, but I can't crash until my clothes are washed. In this damp air they will take forever to dry on the line. My eagerness to crawl into bed demands an executive decision: tonight I'm going full throttle clean. I search out Boni and lay on my Canadian charm.

"Can you show me how to operate the washer and dryer?"

He opens the washing machine with a key, takes out a couple of euros from the coin dispenser, and inserts them for my use. He gives me a little smile suggesting he has done his good deed for the day.

"Thank you so much!" I say, hugging him.

His gesture reminds me that I have been the recipient of many kind acts. Aside from the physical pain, the emotional battles, and the loneliness, I have been part of a supportive community this month.

The washing cycle is quick, and I hang my wet clothes until it's my turn to use the dryer. Just as I put my coins in, Melanie asks if I'm ready for dinner. Although I don't have an appetite, I do have to wait until my clothes are dry. *Why not?*

As we approach the end of our long driveway, we meet up with my Italian couple I last saw in Astorga, accompanied by a young woman with strawberry blond hair. We've never formally introduced ourselves, and I don't even know their names, but we always share a hug when we meet.

They look exhausted, but their companion, a pretty twenty-something Irish girl, seems on the verge of tears. It's 7:30 pm and the next albergue is about 6 km away. Although the Italian woman has limited English, her partner can speak quite well. "We have been walking all day." They have been unsuccessful in finding an albergue that can accommodate all three of them. This late in the day makes finding a single bed difficult, let alone three.

My heart aches for the younger girl. "Do you need a hug?" I ask, not waiting for her to reply. "It's going to be okay," I tell her soothingly.

She relaxes into my arms. "Oh... you smell so good." Her comment makes me laugh, as I've been washing *everything* with my multi-purpose Camp Soap.

I pull up my Excel spreadsheet on my cellphone, to compare with his own list of albergues. "Make some calls." He hesitates, not wanting to incur any charges. "Don't worry about that, there's no charge for me to call within Spain! I wouldn't care anyway." This is my opportunity to help.

I knew our albergue was full, but it didn't hurt to try. "There are no beds left." Just as we thought.

He calls the albergue they passed a kilometre back, and with only one bed left, he makes a reservation for their young friend. She is resisting, not wanting to leave this couple who have become her lifeline, their bond tightening with the exhaustion and now separation. I empathize, but she doesn't seem to have much more to give this day. What makes it harder is knowing her friends have to keep walking. No easy feat after the long day they have had.

The Italian couple put on a brave face. "We will be fine, don't worry. You must take this bed." She *wants* to stop and *needs* a bed, but doesn't want to say *Goodbye*. She starts to cry as they give her a final hug, nudging her back down the road.

Hugging me with thanks, they continue through town. *I wish I knew their names.*

Melanie and I walk down the road in search of a restaurant, but my head is whirling. "Thank you for encouraging me to go out for dinner." I share my thoughts about the *chance* meeting. Melanie and I don't believe in coincidence. Her need to stop in this town; my decision to use the washer and dryer, preventing me from going to bed early; her suggestion we get something to eat even though I wasn't hungry. Each of these little events led me to the street at the exact time this trio was walking by our albergue.

Fate intervened, just as it had for Melanie and me on countless occasions, and now leads us towards the finish line together. I don't question these events, but am fascinated with the seemingly random occurrences that connect us together.

By the time we return from dinner, my clothes are still warm in the dryer. Hunkered down in my bottom bunk, I count down until I can sleep in my own bed, snuggled in Pierre's arm, as I had seen the Italian couple that first evening.

"If you think you can do a thing or think you can't do a thing, you're right."
Henry Ford

Day 30
26 km
September 2, 2015

The cold penetrates the walls of our uninsulated cabin. I slept in the fetal position, clothed in multiple layers and wool socks, but it wasn't enough to keep me warm in my thin liner. It is too cold to hang out here, and there isn't even a vending machine to fill my coffee need.

Once we're all packed up, Melanie and I leave the albergue and head towards last night's restaurant. In only my t-shirt, I am freezing from the short walk, but still not willing to sacrifice my white shirt for anything more than sleeping.

Anxiety is already building towards this last full day of walking, a dread of the kilometres ahead and a sense of loss. *You will be home soon. Just a few more days.*

The protective warmth of the restaurant is a refuge from the cold. After 28 mornings I am finally eating a decent breakfast of toasted baguette, something I see Melanie order regularly. I *am* a slow learner. I could write a book highlighting all the things I could have done to make this journey a little easier, but I bet I'm one of a few who brought a dozen Clif Bars. There's no regrets over that decision, as they were lifesavers when there was nothing else available and I still have one or two left.

Melanie and I are tired this morning, and neither of us says too much. With only one other couple settled in front of the window, we have the place to ourselves and it's exactly what I need to ponder the many thoughts going through my mind.

My ear catches the music from a small TV mounted in the corner, a Spanish MTV playing videos. Although I can't make out the lyrics, it's obviously a love song. Staring at the set, I watch the story of an elderly man tormented by thoughts of a forever lost love unfold.

Compelled to search for her, he embarks on a journey, scouring the depths of the city on his electric scooter. His quest brings him into social arenas unlikely for a man of his age and lifestyle. But he is on a mission, searching *everywhere*! Those he meets feel and empathize with his undying love, encouraging him to continue looking for his soul mate. These connections seem to be the most human touch he has had in a long time, and they feed his soul. In the end, he finds her.

I didn't need to understand the words of the song; the images were enough to stir my own emotions.

Whether it's my love for Pierre, or my desire to be loved so deeply that a man would search high and low for me, my heart feels like a heavy brick in my chest. Last night Pierre and I had quite a few email exchanges. Now that we are closer to reuniting, I find myself missing him even more; missing all the good we have together. I can't wait to see him, to feel his arms around me... to feel his love.

Will our relationship be different when I get home? So much has happened, in his life too, that I can't imagine it will be the same.

This trip has had a profound impact on how I view myself; the challenges have built my inner strength. I'm not the same woman I was when I left, and yet I feel there is much waiting for me when I get home. More inner dialogue, more exploration, and more action based on what feels right. This journey wasn't about Pierre and me: it was about discovering myself. My commitment to a *happily ever after* hasn't changed.

All I have wanted is to be loved as much as I love.

Maybe it's just the sleepless night and the realization that this is my last full day of walking, but my thoughts shoot off in all directions. My chest is tight, the tears well in my eyes, and I'm afraid to blink or pull them away from the TV. I want to let it out, but at the same time, I want to hold onto this mixed bag of emotions.

I need this time to just feel.

Melanie sees me focused and eats her own breakfast quietly. We can read each other pretty well by now; she knows when to give me my space and when to ask if I'm alright. For now I'm letting the wave wash over me, glad she is sitting across the table. Once the feelings subside, I bring my eyes to hers, smile and release the tears.

"I think I'm homesick." I can't share anything more. We will talk about it later. *Maybe.* Melanie doesn't know the history that brought me to Spain.

We have a full day ahead of us, about 25 km before we arrive in Monte do Gozo. I flash back to my first day and how unprepared I was for the reality of this challenge. As the weeks passed, I often questioned what I was doing here, to the extreme of planning my escape route that dark day on the Meseta. Here I am, one day away from arriving in Santiago.

Before we leave the restaurant, I take a photo of the two of us.

Random thoughts cross my mind. *Document the last day. Pay attention. Be present. Avoid going on autopilot.*

You are almost there, Lizzie!

The thought of being near the end makes me want to sit back down and order another coffee. This morning's stalling is about prolonging, rather than resisting.

The air is still cool, but as the sun rises higher, I see promise in the day. The forests provide a tranquil landscape and help me reset my thoughts. It is just Melanie and me walking through the treed areas. Sometimes we are together, other times I fall back to take a photo, but neither of us is walking too fast.

Melanie, too, is having mixed feelings about arriving in Santiago. Returning to regular life is not something either of us are too eager to do just yet. Strange that I have spent all month wishing I didn't have to walk another day and now I find myself resenting the end.

This journey will change once we reach Santiago. *What are the next steps?* I won't be able to go back to my past behaviours; I'm just not the same person anymore.

With plenty of towns every couple of kilometres, I find the most peace when we return to the woods, like a caterpillar in the safety of her cocoon, waiting to transform into a butterfly.

I don't need to suggest breaks: Melanie is quite happy to stop in each of the small towns, and we treat ourselves to a snack and hot beverage. My favourite is the thick hot chocolate, a sweet goodness that warms my core.

At lunch we take extra time, and I snap a photo of my tasty ensalada. It's a work of art, if perhaps a few too many slices of Spanish onion. I think Melanie has photographed every meal she has eaten, but she is also a little more adventurous than I am. A vegetarian, she is trying all the seafood offerings. I admire her eagerness to indulge, but my palate is less courageous.

The mileage stones counting down our arrival appear every couple of kilometres, an encouraging reminder that every step brings us closer. A few pairs of hiking boots hang over a telephone wire above our heads, a more powerful sign than a stone reading 15.5 km.

I'm not parting with my hikers: they have treated me well. I look down at the small dusty maple leaf badges I sewed near the toes. My physical pain is not a result of my footwear, but my lack of strength, the insufficient training, and an ignorance to the benefits of stretching at the end of each day.

Another note in the book of Could-Haves.

Melanie has reserved two beds at the albergue in Monte del Gozo, so we can take our time. Our pace is slow as we delay our arrival. It's been a long, emotional day, filled with self-reflection and little conversation.

The large monument on the *Hill of Joy* comes into sight, the crown at the top of the climb. The four sides of the concrete base are painted in murals to celebrate the pilgrim arrival in Santiago, visible in the valley below. The *Albergue Monte do Gozo* is an enormous complex, a mini village that can accommodate 400 souls in 20 dorm buildings that stretch down the steep hill. Only one building is open. Perhaps the seasonal rush has come to an end.

The last full day of walking is done!

We make polite introductions, but I'm less inclined to develop meaningful relationships. After I wash up, I head outside to a bench, joined by another peregrino who has spent the last month seeking answers after his girlfriend cheated on him. He doesn't hesitate to tell me he is angry and feels betrayed, but the *her loss* attitude tells me he has worked through his feelings. Interesting, the things people share when they don't know you.

Melanie is ready for dinner, but there is nothing onsite. We have only two options: we can backtrack to the last town or descend the steep hill towards a cafeteria. Down it is, and my knees jar with each step. My Crocs offer little support as my feet slip forward.

The cafeteria leaves much to be desired and the menu even less. Neither of the two *international* options leaves me hopeful of sleeping on a full tummy. The schnitzel is unappetizing and an insult to Austria. I can't even finish it, but my belly is still rumbling. Back at the albergue, I devour one of my remaining Clif Bars. There was a reason I had a couple left.

As the sun sets, I gaze out onto the valley and Santiago. I have walked over 25 km today, the last day of extremes. My head hasn't been on the trail, but on the journey. My dragging was to delay our arrival, rather than resist the challenges, aches and pains. Few photos were taken other than the shots of Melanie and me, and the wooded areas that surrounded us.

So much for avoiding autopilot.

The relief of nearing the end is bittersweet. Part of me wishes I could catch a plane right after tomorrow's noon mass and wrap the entire adventure up. The urge to go home battles my desire to stay indefinitely. *I'm not sure I'm ready to finish.* It's been such a hard journey, but wasn't that the purpose?

The future depends on me.

Maybe I am doubting my ability to maintain the momentum once I leave the Camino, and that everything I have learned about myself will get lost in the routine and sameness that I'd become accustomed to.

My comfort zone.

It would be easier to stay here, but this is training camp. Now I need to put on my big girl pants and live my life. These are intimidating contemplations after such a long day, but the flow of my thoughts intrigues me. It seems safer to question life when I am so far away from it.

"Happiness is an attitude.
We either make ourselves miserable,
or happy and strong.
The amount of work is the same."
Francesca Reigler

Day 31
5 km
September 3, 2015

O ne last morning selfie for the record. *Smile.*

As I read through my journal last night, the most I had walked in three consecutive days was 70 km, so the 78 km that Melanie and I crossed is a personal best. A strong finish to an incredible month.

My friend by my side helped pass the time, and without my FitBit I had no idea how far we walked, until we added it up at the end of each day. Between the exertion, inadequate sleeps, and insufficient calorie intake, my battery is running low this morning.

I feel lost, unable to anticipate the day with only an hour or so of walking until we arrive.

The End.

This started out as a month to escape my day-to-day life. In short order, it became the need to get through each kilometre of the day. I had to break it down into manageable chunks. Day One, Week One, One Fifth, One Third, Last Week, Last Full Day. Now it's the last five kilometres. *Then what?*

The temperature is comfortable—the cold mornings have been left behind. *Hallelujah!*

My pack feels heavy on my back as I descend the steep hill again. Sharp pains in my knees are an immediate reminder of the month of physical demands and the toll it's taken. That is one thing I won't miss: the daily assault on my body. It will be nice to have the pack off and not *have* to walk. Will I ever do anything like this again? *Hell no.*

Mother Nature's serenity is long gone, replaced with an ugly industrial landscape. The numerous Santiago signs are a turn off, even though I photograph them. We agree to stop for breakfast as we enter the business district, obviously delaying our arrival. Even Melanie is resisting the urge to continue on.

"Do you want another cigarette, Elizabeth?"

We are quiet, consumed within our own thoughts.

What will it feel like when I cross the threshold? Relief that I'm done? Proud that I made it? Happy to be going home?

The descent into the city is gradual, but the closer we get, the more people we see. My excitement peaks as we approach a busy intersection, the sidewalk engraved beneath our feet: *Europe was made on the pilgrim road to Compostela.* The Camino is listed as one of UNESCO's World Heritage Sites and I have walked it. *Add that to the resumé.*

The stone arch gateway is up ahead, leading us into the Plaza do Obradoiro, the meeting point for newly arriving pilgrims. *The Finish Line.* The entrance into the massive main square is intimidating. Flanked by ancient architecture, we are awed by this site worth beholding. But what comes forefront in my thoughts is the emptiness.

Where is everyone? The euphoria that had been building escapes like a deflating balloon.

Melanie runs to the centre to take it all in.

The cathedral is under construction, and some of the renovations are hidden behind a screened image of the masterpiece. The surrounding blue scaffolding is offensive. Whatever emotions I was expecting, they are not what I am experiencing in this moment. *There isn't a wisp of energy here.* After 30 days of walking, I feel let down.

I pull out my camera to hide my emotions, but I am embarrassed, as though I'm missing something that only I cannot find.

With each 90 degree turn I photograph the history that surrounds me. *The Colegio de San Jerónimo,* the *Palacio de Rajoy* and the *Parador Hotel* that was once upon a time the *Hostal de los Reyes Católicos.*

Melanie offers to take a photo of me.

"No thanks, that's alright."

The sight of Leen coming towards us lifts my spirits. She looks like a tourist without her backpack. "How does it feel to be done?"

Difficult to answer, I'm hesitant to share my thoughts. "I feel disappointed somehow, especially after the month I had. This isn't what I expected."

Pierre has always cheered me on from the sidelines, waiting at the finish with open arms. *Is that what I'm missing?*

Leen arrived yesterday, and shares her first-hand knowledge of the next steps.

"Let's go to the Pilgrims Office first. There's always a long lineup. After you get your compostela, we can go to the Post Office to store your packs, because you can't enter the cathedral with them."

It's helpful that she knows exactly where to go, and we waste no time finding our way. The Pilgrims Office is tucked at the end of an alley, and there's already a long queue. This is a great place to reconnect with others, but I'm not expecting any of my own reunions. Anyone else I met this month has already arrived in Santiago and probably returned home.

Thank God I am not here alone.

With so many pilgrims ahead of and behind me, my senses finally awaken through the energy of others. The electricity in the air intoxicates me, drifting into my own thoughts, as I consider where I am and the path I took to arrive.

A random conversation about the Camino; a marital breakdown that fast-forwarded a need to escape; 30 days of challenges, experiences and relationships... thumbtack moments that delivered me to this lineup in order to receive my compostela, a Latin document that until now meant little.

Sampaio appears out of nowhere with his unmistakable huge smile, his arms wide open to embrace me. Confused, I was sure he and Andreia were already on their way home, but I have my arms wrapped around him, flooded with emotions. Tears of joy slide down my face.

Still in shock, I take my place at the front of the line as Melanie snaps a photo of me before I enter the office. I hand over my national passport and pilgrim credential, as the tears dampen my face. "What brought you to the Camino?"

Lady, we would need a lot more time for me to tell you the story. "Spiritual and Other." That's all she wants to know.

The Latin document bearing my name holds an unexpected significance. It's not a finish line participant medal, nor is it proof that I walked the Camino.

It is a sign. If I can do this, I can do anything. My destiny is in my hands.

Andreia is waiting for me as I exit the Pilgrim Office. There are no words to say to this woman who has shared my journey since Day One. A fresh river of tears flow as I hold onto her tightly, my heart full of love.

To have my Brazilian friends join Melanie and Leen, as my journey comes to an end, is better than anything I could have hoped for. The spark that I lacked when I first arrived in the empty square now burns brightly. Strangers in the line offer to take group photos for us, puffy faces and all. The people who shared in my journey are my Camino.

Goodbyes to Andreia and Sampaio are heartfelt, and I'm so happy we had this last opportunity to see each other.

Leen directs us to the *correos* through a confusing maze of small, winding streets. With our packs in storage for the day, we have the freedom to move around the city with ease. Hopefully, Melanie has a better sense of direction than I, as we still need to make our way back here later today, before finding the seminary where we'll spend the night. She did a great job planning our arrival, as we still have time to have breakfast with Leen before she leaves to catch her plane back to Belgium.

On the steps of the cathedral, people are laughing, crying and hugging, as they celebrate the completion of their journey. This is the loving energy I expected when I first arrived, and the perfect venue for saying *Goodbye* to Leen. Pulling away from her embrace, her tears invite my own. The love and warmth of our friendship will carry us forward to new beginnings. We will stay in touch and who knows, maybe one day we will see each other again.

After one last wave as Leen walks away, Melanie and I hug before heading up the steps of the *Catedral de Santiago de Compostela*.

Scenes from the movie *The Way* flash in my mind. I have been looking forward to entering this sacred space, and becoming part of the collective experience. Eager to feel the worn stone pillar beneath the statue of St. James, I ask one of the guides about it.

"Sorry. It is blocked off for the renovations."

What? I'd been looking forward to placing my hand where so many had laid theirs, envisioning an experience similar to La Cruz de Ferro, as I absorbed the vibrations of past peregrinos. *I guess I will have to return.*

The seats are filling up as people stream in. There are perhaps more tourists than pilgrims, but the exhausted travellers are easy to spot with their deeply tanned faces anticipating this culminating experience. We sit down in a front row at the side, but Melanie's eyes continue scanning for a more optimal location. She pulls my arm to follow, bringing us into a vacant first row, right in front of the altar. Several rows behind us are already full. "Do you think this is reserved?"

Melanie isn't worried about that, taking ownership of the pew, as others quickly follow in behind. The Italian couple is nearby, and we wave them towards us while squeezing down to make room.

Mass is a serious affair, and the rules of admission are shared in multiple languages. Cameras are not permitted once the service begins and violators will be asked to leave. My eyes and ears are alert, and my heart and spirit are open as my body starts to tingle.

Here I am in the grand cathedral in Santiago, part of a community of individuals who have travelled many kilometres, challenging themselves and conquering the physical, emotional and spiritual demands of their individual pilgrimage.

Emotions wash over me while polaroids of my experiences skip across my mind's eye. Those moments that left me wondering why, left my heart aching, pushed me in unexpected directions, and those that brought me great happiness.

Life has detoured to lead me right here, sitting in the cathedral with tears streaming down my cheeks. My heart is overflowing, full of love for those who share my life journey and love for myself. Every step has brought me to this moment of peace and light.

When the service ends, it's difficult to switch gears. I have found the beginning of what I have been searching for, and I'm now ready to go home with these feelings intact. I no longer feel like a pilgrim, but I am certainly not a tourist. I'm unsure where I fit in.

We tour around the city, finding our way through the maze of streets and into the museum and gift shops. This feels like autopilot, not paying attention, simply following Melanie. The busyness of the streets and passing tourists are a sensory overload, and I already miss the calm of the forest. Even as I sit under the warm sun outside a café, I feel out of place. Without my backpack at my feet and with no destination to reach, I am caught between two worlds.

Another gift shop visit and I finally buy myself a sweatshirt, a memento that will keep me warm on the coast. Not really needing it, I put it on anyway as we search for the tourist office to get the bus schedule. We retrace our steps to the post office and retrieve our packs. I am emotionally drained, but the day is far from over. We need to climb through the streets to the seminary. If I still had my FitBit, it would probably read over 10 km walked today.

The air has cooled down a bit, and I'm glad to have my cozy navy blue sweatshirt, and the new soft fleece is warm against my brown skin. I travelled through cold Galicia weather without one, only to pick one up for my last few days in Spain.

At a cost of only 15 euros, we book a bed for Sunday night as well. It's a massive complex with several floors, each with multiple corridors through sectioned wings making it easy to get disoriented. The shower stalls in the communal washrooms are so small, I can barely turn around.

Without an elevator, I'm taking the stairs each time I want to go outside. *I thought I was done walking.*

Exhausted, I could easily opt out of returning to the city centre for dinner. I still have a Clif Bar I can munch on, and could wash it down with a Coke from the vending machine, but that is a ridiculous idea. Thank goodness for Melanie and her enthusiasm for exploring.

After a bit of down time, we return through the maze of streets in time to catch a 45-minute trolley ride. Even with the limited leg space it is enjoyable, and I learn so much more about Santiago than if we had been on foot and left to our own devices. Fueled with a decent dinner and a strong coffee, we revisit this morning's path into the plaza. The setting sun casts a golden glow on the ancient architecture.

It's a laborious climb as we work our way back up the streets for the second time today. The evening comes to an end, as we sit on lawn chairs and watch the pink glow close in on the horizon.

"The will to win, the desire to succeed, the urge to reach your full potential… these are the keys that will unlock the door to personal excellence."
Confucius

Day 32
September 4, 2015

My alarm not only wakes me, but reminds me that I am alone in my bedroom, momentarily missing the community a room full of strangers provides. Although we have put an end to the 20 km hikes, my morning routine still requires time to contemplate the day. I made sure to give myself an extra hour before we leave for the bus station.

The descent along the paved streets assaults my knees again, a reminder that the journey is not yet over. Marj and Joanie are going to be disappointed when I refuse our weekend walks back home, but I have no desire to continue those outings for at least the next month. Maybe two. *Maybe indefinitely.*

Melanie is a dynamo. Not only can she get the WiFi from a bartender without even ordering a drink, but she has a keen sense of direction, and navigates us through the maze of quiet stone streets. We have no trouble finding the station, and the only minor hiccup is the discovery that my return ticket differs from hers. With my newly-found big girl pants, I *politely* push myself back into the front of the line to get it corrected.

Taking charge. Check.

With enough time to enjoy breakfast, my newly-adopted morning meal of toasted baguette, orange juice and café con leche, is the perfect start to the day. How did I ever manage to walk several kilometres without anything to eat or drink?

Those days are over! Two days at the beach will be a complete change of pace and I am excited for it.

Many pilgrims continue their journey after arriving in Santiago, by walking the additional 90 km through woods and coastal towns to Finisterre. They may have the same intentions as Melanie: to swim in the Atlantic ocean, to visit the cape at sunrise, then burn their clothes in a ceremonial final act. This extension of my Camino is an unexpected welcome, but I won't be burning anything. I'll be the acting Fire Warden.

We cruise along the highway in a tour bus, and the couple of hours fly by as we weave in and out of fishing villages, the bright sun twinkling atop the ocean. I cannot believe how well my cellphone takes photos through the glass pane. The white sandy beaches and turquoise waters are such a contrast from the last month.

Our bus stops right in the midst of this quaint coastal community. From my seat window I see Patrick, the German fellow who is tenting his way along the Camino, sitting with a group of people. It never dawned on me that I might see some of my fellow peregrinos here.

We hurry across the street where he is joined by Helena, his pretty blond companion, and Karen, the Australian who has been travelling for four years. They walked from Santiago, arriving yesterday. Over a refreshing cold beverage, we discuss getting together during the next couple of days.

"Melanie and I are hoping to stay at the *Albergue Do Mar*, although we haven't made any reservations."

I keep referencing Finisterre, so Patrick politely corrects me. "This community is actually Fisterra. Cape Finisterre is a 3 km walk. Absolutely beautiful. We are planning on hiking there tomorrow to watch the sun rise."

Melanie and I plan to walk to the cape tomorrow too, but probably not that early in the morning.

The scent of salt is heavy in the air, a familiar memory from my many visits to the east coast of Canada where I often travelled to visit family. After we sat on the bus for a couple of hours, my pack now feels heavy. Fortunately, we shouldn't have far to walk since our albergue is near the water.

Down the street towards the beach, we see the distinctive pools of greens and blues that look like separate bodies of water melting together to join the depths of the ocean. The albergue we discovered online is right at the water's edge as promised, resembling a North American beach-front motel.

For 12 euros each, we will share our ocean-facing room with up to a dozen other pilgrims. With a nod of agreement, we reserve a bed for tomorrow night as well. I'm patting myself on the back for jumping on board Melanie's Finisterre invitation, but I need to get this pack off and remove my boots and socks, to claim my holiday status.

The glass bedroom wall overlooks a breathtaking view of the Atlantic ocean. Once I claim my lower bunk, as far from Melanie as physically possible, I head out the connecting patio door onto the spacious balcony.

This is what dreams are made of.

Melanie allows little down time today, as she's eager to hit the beach. Uncertain how long we'll be relaxing on the white sands, we need to stock up on beach snacks. Shopping on a hungry belly is never wise and this time is no exception. As a complement to Melanie's full wheel of Santiago cheese, I include a couple of baguettes, some fruit, pop, and a bottle of Sangria to be enjoyed sometime over the next two days.

I am on vacation after all.

With my beach gear stuffed in my orange daypack, I now wish I'd brought a bathing suit. It wouldn't have guaranteed a dive in the ocean as the air is a little cooler here, but I might have ventured in if well equipped.

My Crocs come off as soon as I hit the sand, and I expect my feet to sink down through the exfoliating grains. But the sand offers no cushion, shocking me with its hard surface. Barefoot, I pound my way along the white beach, stepping on the occasional pebble or shell, adding insult to the tenderness. Still, it's a small price to pay to stroll through the waves, collecting washed up shells.

So this is what all the fuss is about.

The beach carries on for miles, while the salty wind whips my hair into my face. I am ready to stop anytime. I didn't sign up for *more* walking. Coming towards us is a fellow in his shorts and t-shirt, sandals in hand.

"If you keep walking around the cove, you'll find the perfect spot out of the wind. There are several large rocks you need to cross," he says, pointing ahead, "but it's worth the extra hike."

I can see the boulders in the distance. "How much farther?"

He doesn't sugar coat the answer. "About an hour."

Melanie and I look at each other. We still need to make our way *back* to the albergue. Being no more eager than I to keep walking, she's quick to decide. "Let's save that for tomorrow."

My quick-dry towel is not quite long enough to lay on, but in true pilgrim spirit, Melanie shares the yoga mat she has carried over 800 km. As soon as our treats are spread out, we start digging into the cheese with thick chunks we tear from the baguette. There may be a price to pay for our gluttony, but it feels so good to indulge.

I could easily zone out watching the diamonds sparkle along the water.

The ocean is cold, and I'm only brave enough to go in up to my calves. *Hopefully this will soothe my aching feet.* While Melanie checks off her pilgrim to-do list, I assume the role as her unofficial videographer.

Once swim time is over, I let myself relax, closing my eyes to embrace the sun's kiss while the gritty wind caresses me. Had Melanie not given me the nudge, I wouldn't be here right now.

On a holiday buzz, I've renamed our albergue *The Beach House*. After I shower off the salt and sand, I can feel my belly fighting the mass amounts of cheese. *Oh dear.* I'm tempted to curl up and stay in bed, but so far there's no need to hover near the toilet. Besides, there's a harbour sunset waiting for me and Melanie is craving a seafood dinner.

My lack of appetite gives her carte blanche to choose our restaurant, where she can continue her mission of sampling Spain's delicacies. The colourful wharf is lined with restaurants, each boasting their menu in large faded wall posters. We pass the length a couple of times before she decides.

Eeny Meeny Miny Moe.

We finally find a place, and Melanie orders a fish soup which tells me she is no longer feeling adventurous. I order the usual spaghetti for myself, and I hope the pasta will settle the upset. The waitress places a large tureen in front of her, but after the first sip Melanie's face turns up, an obvious sign that she regrets her selection. She's unable to eat more than half of a small soup bowl. The spaghetti is no better, drowning in orange grease.

Melanie looks at my meal with disgust. "Are you going to eat that?"

Neither of us is bothered to order anything else, both meals still intact by the time we ask for the bill. Our waitress looks at us queerly and Melanie isn't shy to state her displeasure. "It wasn't very good!"

Mucho Gracias for the crappy dinner Señorita.

The salt air is refreshing us as we head out to the end of the pier to take in the view. My mind is no longer focused on my upset belly. It is soothed by the water, wind and setting sun. My identification as a pilgrim is disappearing.

"Don't cry because it is over.
Smile because it happened."
Dr. Seuss

Day 33
September 5, 2015

As soon as my toes touch the floor, I feel the aftermath of my barefoot walk along the beach. I'm not complaining. How can I, when the rising sun spotlights an invitation towards a beautiful day?

Out onto the balcony in my pyjamas and sweatshirt, I gaze at the ocean horizon as the light glistens over the water. Now this is the perfect way to begin a day of appreciation and gratitude. As I sit with my knees pulled into my chest, the excited anticipation of visiting the end of the world starts to bubble.

My tender feet resist the confines of my hikers, but my Crocs are inadequate footwear for manoeuvring over the cliff boulders.

The lightweight pack feels non-existent on my back, compared to the 20 odd pounds I've been carrying around the last month.

It's only 3 km to reach Point 0.00, the end of my journey.

We follow the ocean towards the hill. The green pools are left behind, as diamonds scatter over the deeper, darker waters. There is the lighthouse and the edge of the bluff, the tour buses and busy souvenir shops. My trance is broken by the influx of people, and I pick up my pace towards the peninsula, the cliff beckoning me to find a quiet spot for my thoughts.

Tourists hover close to the top where it feels safer, but some venture along the worn path leading down to the stone cross. The pilgrims are the ones navigating their way over rocks, descending past the cross towards the tall pole at the tip of the peninsula. Adorned with flags, clothes, and boots, it's impossible to miss.

Cautiously, I make my way over the massive rocks; the wind cleansing me as I face the great expanse of ocean. With my arms outstretched, I embrace the surrounding energy. At the edge of the world, I have never felt more free.

A cyclist carries his bike *all* the way down to the flagpole. I hold my breath, hoping he doesn't miss a step, slip or fall, especially with his hands full. He makes it look simple, and he receives a chain of support from others on the way back up, when the footing is more precarious.

Mid-way down, there's a perfect vantage point off to the side that shelters me from the noise and activity. My hair flies unharnessed in the wind, matching my thoughts as I revisit the last 32 days. *Look at what challenged you, what you accomplished, and the incredible people you met, as you searched for yourself.*

I could sit here all afternoon, absorbing and replaying my journey, the perfect end to an incredible experience. Thoughts float along the twinkling water as I look out onto the endless ocean. My reverie is disturbed as Melanie comes to join me, determined to burn her socks. Finding a spot out of the wind, I pass her my lighter before filming her finale.

"How are you feeling at this moment, Melanie?"

She takes off in a stream of German, explaining to her viewers where she is, what she is doing and why. I love her enthusiasm for all things pilgrim and her desire to share every step of the way with her family and friends.

I'm not a regular user of social media, and I had no intention to post daily updates. Other than my family, close friends and coworkers, the world didn't know what I was up to. My preference was to journal each day. People, places, aches and pains, emotional storms, reasons to leave... it was all written down. After my first meltdown, I started sharing more intimate thoughts, desperate to break down the walls I had built to protect myself. By sharing my vulnerability and weakness, I let others in, their support helping to carry me.

Melanie's shadow crosses me.

"I need a bit more time."

She understands, giving me space with my thoughts as she walks towards the other side of the cliff.

Similar to La Cruz de Ferro and the mass at the Cathedral, this is a place of introspection and healing. This is the final song, the last scene, the moment that ties it all together. This part is completed; the rest will follow once I return home.

As I make my way back to the top, I leave a part of myself behind.

Now I'm ready to tackle the gift shop and vendor stalls! Clam shells of different shapes and sizes hang on coloured string. The same, but different, like each pilgrim and the journey he or she travels. This is the symbol I want to bring home, the perfect memento to share with those I love. *Am I now a tourist?*

The timing feels right for the journey to end. I am more than ready to go home now, having accomplished all that I can. *Here.* The time has come to move forward with my new sense of self. Eager to see my family and friends, I can't wait to share my experience with others. If they thought they were done hearing about the Camino, they are in for a surprise. With experience brings a stronger passion.

At the busy wharf, my appetite awakens. We have a personal pizza each, but it's more that we can eat, and the remains are on the table when a middle-aged woman walks towards us, having spied our lunch.

"Is it tasty?"

Almost done and with leftovers to spare, I say, "Why don't you come and join us?"

Not quite sure how to respond, she hesitates for a moment before pulling out a chair. She looks at both of us with a smile. "This is the Camino way, isn't it? Taking care of each other."

Deb is from Australia and in her late fifties, and she's on a one-day return bus trip from Santiago, stopping in each of the coastal towns towards Finisterre. She came about this journey through a sequence of events after her 25-year marriage ended. Comfortable in our company, she shares her life story, at least the part that brought her here. With a small section of the French route completed, she hopes to return one day. For now, it has provided her with the strength she needs to move forward.

Back at our *Beach House,* I am no longer interested in walking along the white sands. "I'm going to stay here this afternoon, park myself on the balcony and have a glass of sangria."

After my dirty clothes are washed and hanging to dry in the warm wind, I sit beneath the sun as the ocean caresses the beach. Two young American peregrinas join me, their tired faces lighting up as they take in the view. They are clearly ragged from their walk here, and I invite them to share in my sweet beverage.

With only one more full day to go, I offer some of my supplies to my two new friends. After wrapping up the loose ends, I have no reason to stay. My experiences have been reconciled on the cliff of Cape Finisterre.

Melanie returns from the beach sooner than expected. "I will be ready to leave on the morning bus, Elizabeth, if you're fine with that."

We don't belong here anymore.

Melanie has reunited with fellow peregrina, Kirsten, and we are all having dinner together. We give a wide berth to last night's restaurant, and this time, our dinner and company are excellent. Stepping outside with an after meal coffee, I take a seat at the patio and people watch while I smoke my cigarette. There's a group of men sitting together near the end of the wharf.

Is that Jan?

Unsure, I leave the patio, taking a few steps to get a closer look. I can't see well enough, cursing my poor eyesight.

I excuse myself to Kirsten, pulling Melanie away to come outside with me.

"I don't think it's him."

Really? I don't pursue it, but it's bugging me. How I would love to see Jan one more time.

Our waitress comes by the table with shooter glasses of complimentary Spanish liquor. Kirsten and I take one, surprised when Melanie does the same. She is not a drinker. Perhaps she thinks it is an unwritten rite. As we toast to friends made along the Camino, it doesn't take long for Melanie to feel the punch. With her head spinning and heart pounding, she starts to panic.

"Stay calm, Melanie." I reassure her that the feeling will pass.

It's difficult for Kirsten and I to contain our smiles.

"Tres cafés por favor." I encourage Melanie to drink hers. She's not a coffee drinker either, but it takes the edge of her buzz.

Karen joins us for an herbal tea. When I mention my possible *Jan sighting*, she confirms that he is here. I rush back outside to see if he is still there.

Shoot. I should have walked up closer to get a better look, but I've now lost the opportunity to reconnect one last time. Jan's words of wisdom acted as a catalyst to shift my perspective, helping me cope with the remainder of my walk. His words are never far from my mind. *What's the worst that can happen?*

Either Melanie's drink or dinner hasn't agreed with her, and we hurry back to the *Beach House*. The situation escalates to a Defcon One, entering an unknown albergue to use the washroom, only to exit moments later because all they had was a sheet for a door. Kirsten and I empathize, but her determination to get there quickly is entertaining.

Another day done. One left before I head home.

It can't get here soon enough.

"Success is getting what you want. Happiness is wanting what you get."

Dale Carnegie

Day 34
September 6, 2015

Just before I tucked myself in my liner last night, I opened the picture window blinds, hoping the rising sun would wake me again this morning. In the pitch black, I hear the American girls prepare for their hike up to Finisterre. With the wool blanket from my bed wrapped around my still sleepy body, I head onto the balcony.

Alone in the wind, my last Spanish sunrise blesses me with her early morning light. By the time the sun has lifted off the horizon, we are a small group of peregrinos witnessing the dawn of a new day. *My last day.*

I am not sad to leave. *It's time.*

A little dog has deemed himself ambassador of farewells, following us up the street towards the bus stop. There are contradictory stories about the dogs on the Camino. Some warn pilgrims to be wary, to stay out of the way of packs; others tell of dogs leading or following pilgrims, guardians of the Camino. Our new friend is just a small dog, not malicious or fearful, just someone's curious pet.

I can't help but remark that this is the first and only dog I have seen, and it's escorting me on my last day, as though wishing me a *Buen Camino*.

We are on the road by 11:30 am, barely seeing the time or landmarks go by before arriving.

Back in Santiago, I feel the weight of my backpack drag me down as we begin the climb towards our seminary. It didn't take long for my body to forget the effort required. *How did I manage to carry it for so many days?*

By the time we arrive I am beat and need a break, recalling the many pit stops I took during these past thirty-one days. *Would I have travelled further each day, met the same people, had the same experiences, if I had taken fewer breaks?* Everything could have been different.

There are so many negligible choices we make each and every day. Without any awareness, they alter our course. People we may or may not meet, situations we may encounter or bypass completely, simply because we are in a different time and place.

Playing back to Day 2, I remember too clearly how exhausted I was before I had even finished the day. My extended breaks left me without a bed, forcing me to fast forward to Estella. Had I arrived at the albergue 30 minutes earlier, I would have stayed in Villatuerta. Would I have met Alfdis and Hermann, Antònio, Sampaio, Melanie, Julie, my Danish Trio, Christophe, Leen, Jan, or Frances and Ann-Marie? Would I have even made it to Finisterre? *Who knows?*

The list of events and their connections is a long one. All the stops, the smokes, the bus and taxis, and time spent chatting with new friends, brought me here. *Right now.*

After a short rest, we clean up and change into something more comfortable, then head back down those same streets we climbed an hour earlier. This is my last night here, so I'm channeling my enthusiasm, ready to experience Santiago.

The streets are narrow, and the old stone buildings are so high it is easy to lose my bearings, but Melanie knows the direction. We walked so many loops when we first arrived, she has a map in her mind and knows exactly where we are going. *Shopping!*

Stores, souvenir shops, restaurants and cafés line the streets. Newly-arrived pilgrims absorb the impact of their arrival. The tourists, dressed in their fancier clothes, kids in tow or couples hand in hand, are on vacation.

I am neither, but no longer struggling to find my place. *I know who I am.*

We take another tour through the Cathedral, but this time I am not distracted by my emotions. With every turn there is another corridor, a hidden chapel, an alcove to explore. The stained glass windows, the carvings, the gold, the altar itself… a magnificent centerpiece. There is too much to take in with one short visit.

Down the small stone steps of a sunken corridor, I stand in front of the tomb of Saint James. Slightly ashamed, I should know more of his story and have a deeper understanding of how the Camino became the route for those seeking forgiveness, because I have become part of that story. I am a member of a community of souls who made their way to Santiago in search of freedom.

I don't feel like a visitor on holiday, because I never considered this month a vacation. It was a quest to take myself away from the normal and place myself in unfamiliar territory, not only geographically, but also emotionally and spiritually. I had an idea of what I wanted. To walk each day alone with my thoughts, to experience solo travel, and hopefully get a glimpse into who I really am on the inside.

Santiago was the end destination, but never the goal.

The journey was getting here and it became so much more than anything I had entertained. As I look back, the trials were often more than I wanted, but exactly what I needed.

Tomorrow morning I will leave the Camino. It will be a long day of travelling, returning to my life a little wiser, definitely more in tune with myself, and committed to bringing the freedom and love I found here, back home.

Melanie and I are both ready to leave Spain, but that also means saying *Goodbye*. I keep pushing those thoughts aside. We have gone through so much together, have been there for one another when it really mattered. It will be hard to let go.

But isn't that part of any journey? Our life is impacted by those we meet, especially when the connection has significant meaning.

We stop at a patio bar for one last Spanish Sangria. We will be sitting here a while, as I sip it slowly, giving us time to talk. This is not the first time we discuss divine timing: when we met, unexpected partings, individual struggles, and how we continued to find each other. We laugh about my snoring, the meals that left us hungry, and our trip to Finisterre.

My emotions are running high, but I need her to know how much she means to me. "Thank you for being such a big part of my journey. I wouldn't have wanted it to end any other way than with you."

Melanie doesn't need to say anything for me to know she feels the same way. "You are the most important person on my Camino, Elizabeth."

There is so much more I want to say, but the words are caught in my throat, and I'm afraid I will cry uncontrollably. It's hard to rein back my feelings when preparing to part ways. Best to just take some selfies and let them speak for themselves.

In honour of my love of spaghetti, we choose an Italian restaurant for our last meal. The chef-owner is from Italy and the ambiance of the music transports us out of Spain. He happily answers Melanie's questions, recommending the negro pasta for her, but I stick to my tried and true favourite. It is even better than Pierre's and that is a compliment to the chef.

Touring the streets one last time, we know we are delaying the inevitable and fighting the urge to return to the albergue and pack up.

After one last climb up the streets, we sit outside to watch our final sun set. Once we enter the albergue door, we know that will be the end. Hugging, crying, and holding on tight, we promise to keep in touch.

Prepared to repack my bag and get rid of anything that I don't need, I go through my money belt. While throwing out paper receipts and sorting through my remaining cash, I find my FitBit. I laugh to myself, tempted to knock on Melanie's door and show her. *Isn't this interesting?*

My money belt has been around my waist since I left Ottawa. There are two zippered compartments. One is rarely opened, containing my credit and bank cards, and my Canadian funds. The other is accessed all the time, holding my Canadian Passport, credential, euros and cellphone. The zipper broke long ago from so much wear and tear. My FitBit was always placed in that used compartment, but it appears that afternoon in Portomarín I tucked it deeply in the second one. I never saw it, even though I had searched both sections.

How's that for a sign?

Ready to call it a night, I read the *Pilgrim's Prayer* on the cover of the postcard Melanie gave me as we said good night. I had been delaying, holding off until I was ready to climb into bed. The note she leaves on the back fills my eyes with tears.

Pilgrim's Prayer

Although I may have travelled all the roads, crossed mountains and valleys from East to West, if I have not discovered the freedom to be myself, I have arrived nowhere.

Although I may have shared all of my possessions with people of other languages and cultures; made friends with Pilgrims of a thousand paths, or shared an albergue with saints and princes, if I am not capable of forgiving my neighbor tomorrow, I have arrived nowhere.

Although I may have carried my pack from beginning to end and waited for every Pilgrim in need of encouragement, or given my bed to one who arrived later than I, given my bottle of water in exchange for nothing; if upon returning to my home and work, I am not able to create brotherhood or to make happiness, peace and unity, I have arrived nowhere.

Although I may have had food and water each day, and enjoyed a roof and shower every night; or may have had my injuries well attended, if I have not discovered in all that the love of God, I have arrived nowhere.

Although I may have seen all the monuments and contemplated the best sunsets; although I may have learned a greeting in every language or tasted clean water from every fountain; if I have not discovered who is the author of so much free beauty and so much peace, I have arrived nowhere.

If from today I do not continue walking on your path, searching and living according to what I have learned; if from today I do not see in every person, friend or foe a companion on the Camino; if from today I cannot recognize God, the God of Jesus of Nazareth as the one God of my life, I have arrived nowhere.

Author Unknown

I pull a page from the back of my journal and begin writing her a note. All the things that I cannot tell her to her face, I can put in words. I will slip it under her door before I leave.

Epilogue:
The Journey Continues

Those 34 days of experiences along the Camino de Santiago de Compostela provided a unique opportunity to learn about myself. While the Boot Camp forced me to stretch the boundaries of my physical limitations, the hardships offered a garden in which to tend to my inner growth. With each step, I moved forward, often dragging myself along the yellow-arrowed trail.

It was now up to me to continue with new strength and insight. I alone am responsible for ensuring I make conscious choices, that I block the noise in order to listen to my inner voice, that I acknowledge my feelings for what they are, and most importantly, that I respect myself to take the necessary steps towards true happiness.

Even if it means going outside of my comfort zone.

The return home was exhausting. I fell asleep at the Madrid airport while I waited for my flight to Montreal.

Pierre was eagerly waiting with a *Welcome Home* balloon when I walked through the gates. I couldn't get into his arms fast enough, happy to finally see my husband after five weeks. I could barely catch my breath. *Where to start? How much to tell?*

Having shared so much of the journey in emails and texts, he was familiar with the highlights, but I had also kept certain experiences to myself. They were mine to hold in my heart. A balancing act was needed, and I had to be considerate. I wasn't the only one who had lived that month.

My enthusiasm needed to be restrained.

We had missed each other and truth be told, I was happy to return to the familiar. We quickly settled into a routine, partly new and recharged. There was a comfort in being able to slip right back into what I knew, but I was also itching to stand on these legs that had carried me for a month on my own. Legs that had gotten stronger and wanted to keep moving. *Figuratively.*

My knees and feet had taken a toll and were resistant to any upright position. There would be no weekend walks or hikes for as long as I could avoid it, and I was forced to descend the stairs sideways. Indeed, I had put myself to the test. *And I had come out stronger.*

Happy to be back in Pierre's arms, I also hoped our separation had changed us. Five weeks apart gave us plenty of time to think. *Were we meant to be together, soul mates dedicated to one another?* I still held onto that dream of a *Happily Ever After*, but I didn't want to return to the same life. I wanted new and improved; a relationship that had grown from the miles apart. *Was I asking too much?*

Returning to work the day after my return, my colleagues embraced me, happy to see I had survived. They had been enthusiastic before I left, and many of them continued to support me on the trail with emails of encouragement. But they were worried too, especially when I declared my need to return home.

I was asked the same question by many. "Would you do it again?"

Not only could I barely walk, but it had been the most challenging month of my life. It had also been the most incredible and I wanted to share the experiences. The Camino was all I could talk about.

As I slipped back into my day-to-day routine, I felt the void my fellow travellers had filled: complicity, understanding and empathy. Staying in touch with my Camino family became paramount to holding onto the spark that still burned.

Between Facebook messages with Andreia, Sampaio, Leen, Henrik, Frances, Julie and Antònio, I could maintain those friendships and watch their lives unfold in real time. Emails with Alfdis and Hermann, Julie and Melanie, allowed us to share longer threads of updates, reminisce on our shared journeys, and the steps we were still walking to find our way.

Still, I struggled as I adapted to life back home. I was different; a foreigner in my own homeland.

Pierre and I were on a high, but as with any drug, it tapered off. Within months we were back to where we had been all too often, wrapped in a safety net that prevented us from being truly happy. Now more in tune to my own needs, I paid attention to my thoughts and those feelings in the depth of my belly that told me I was falling back into a pattern. In place of the warm caterpillar cocoon, I felt restricted by invisible chains.

I tried to resist the urge to over-analyze or fight the signs that were hard to ignore, but so far away from the Camino, my actions carried heavier risks than simply not having a bed for a night. The unknown was uncertain; that uncertainty was uncomfortable.

Jan's words were never far. *What is the worst that can happen?*

By the Spring of 2016 we split up. *Here we go again.*

The pain of previous breakups returned, but I was able to manage my emotions and my expectations. I let go of the control I thought I had. There was no use in fighting. Pierre and I were great communicators when life was good, but we seemed less willing to compromise when threatened by storms.

Although I missed and grieved much of that lost life I had with Pierre, I was able to move forward. Accepting this change in circumstances allowed new doors to open.

When a Reiki Workshop presented itself, I jumped on it. My experience with Jan influenced my desire for a more hands-on role in my own healing. Self-treatments became part of my weekly routine, and I felt empowered each time I invoked the energy of the universe. After a month I noticed myself hopping down the stairs to my apartment; I was no longer descending sideways.

On Mother's Day, Pierre and I reconnected. I would be lying if I didn't confess how happy I was to hear from him. I missed my best friend. The cozy comfort zone was luring me while I tried to find balance living a single life, but all the positive memories pulled me in like a magnet.

We needed a new approach if a relationship together was to work, and I would hold onto my big girl pants and not settle for anything less than what I needed. *Or wanted.*

It only took a month before it became crystal clear that we desired different things. We had held onto the idea of being soul mates for so long, fighting to find our way back to one another, that we were blind to the illusion of security. The threat of being single had kept us trapped in a relationship that had exceeded its lifespan.

Over two decades we had raised a family, overcome tragedy, enjoyed motorcycle road trips, and shared intimate moments. But we had also had more than our fair share of heartaches, hurting one another time and again. Even though we loved each other, we had passed the stage of being able to make one another happy and we both knew it.

With one final decision, we hugged and parted ways, knowing we had made the right decision for the both of us. Driving back to my apartment, I told myself it was for the best. There were no tears. Within my heavy heart, I let go. Unaware of what the universe had in store for me, I would never find out until I opened myself up to the possibilities.

With too much time on my idle hands, I worked at staying busy.

At the end of July, as the first anniversary of my Camino drew near, I knew what I needed to do. Since my return I had wanted to share the magic I'd discovered along that yellow-arrowed trail. More than once I tried to put my thoughts on paper, but I needed quiet *and* time when I wrote, neither of which I had.

Eager to relive that incredible month, I started a blog.

It became a daily project in which I relived those 34 days, sharing the adventure with my friends. While the blog became therapeutic for me, I had planted a seed in others. Sharing my story was exactly what I needed to get through those first few months without Pierre.

Trying to stay conscious of the signs and the connections that moved me forward, I acted on a radio advertisement for the local Distress Centre. Volunteers were needed on the 24/7 crisis line. This opportunity would allow me to give back, fill up my social calendar, and connect me with like-minded individuals. It might even open doors to a new career.

By winter, I felt ready for another change and started looking at condos. After several home visits, the doubts surfaced. Uncertain what the future held, and eager to remain open to all possibilities, something suggested the time wasn't right to put down financial roots. As though fate waited to intervene, my son Andrew asked if I wanted to move in with him. We have always been very close and after several conversations we agreed. No commitment, no pressure. I could stay for as long as I wanted, giving me time to figure out my next steps.

We would cohabitate; mom was moving in with her eldest son. Not at all what I expected to be doing in my early 50s, but I was game. The opportunity presented itself and we both felt comfortable with the decision. All of my material possessions were stored in boxes, tucked away in his basement. Painting the master bedroom a light blue, I created a peaceful, uncluttered oasis in my small square footage. With the exception of some books, my clothes and bathroom items, everything else was out of sight. Everything. I had no photos, keepsakes, or dust collectors.

My life had once again been simplified. Although keeping more than a backpack and two changes of clothes, I had only what I felt I needed. The collection of stuff that had tallied up my life was out of sight. *Another fresh start.*

Four hours each weekend was dedicated to volunteering, often overnight. The commitment helped plan for those occasions when I didn't want to find myself alone.

New Year's Eve on the phone in the call centre. Check.

The annual fundraiser of the Distress Centre just happened to fall on my birthday and I pulled in all of my resources to contribute to its success, soliciting over $5,000 in auctionable items. In style, with a brand new dress, my toes painted coral, hair in its first ever updo, and my two dearest friends on my arms, I rang in my 52nd birthday.

The butterfly had emerged.

Yes, everything was coming together. Still single and at the same job, but I was making progress. *One step at a time.*

My confidence spurred me to start dipping my toes in the dating pool. The thought had been lingering since the previous summer, but I wasn't ready then. There was still a lot of gardening to do in my own backyard.

In early May 2017, I bit the bullet and went online. The first smiley face caught me off guard. *What the heck. Send a smile back.* And so it started. I'm not sure which excited me more: that men were interested in me or that I was interested in someone other than Pierre.

One special man spun my world, the flutters returning each time we saw each other. *Could there be something here?* Our timing was off and unfortunately, he needed to tend to his own garden before being ready to commit to a new relationship. So often I questioned why he was even brought into my life. It took many months before I realized that I met him to learn that I was ready to love again. There were no longings or lingering feelings for Pierre.

My heart was free.

Work was still an area that left me unsatisfied, but I never had the guts to move forward. I loved the people I worked with, many having supported me during my trek through northern Spain. My boys told me more than once, "If you don't like it, you know what to do." They were right, but I kept holding on, waiting for something to change, a stronger sign than my own unhappiness. But, there was something else I was meant to pursue.

Once I made the decision, the chains were released, and I was free to take the next step to move forward. *Into the unknown.*

It was time to make a list, so I dusted off my red leather portfolio.

Write a book about my journey along the Camino.

Travel, maybe volunteer abroad.

Goals penned, I transferred all the content from my blog, unpacked my travel journal and opened my laptop folder of Camino photos.

I was on a new journey; another thumbtack in my roadmap.

Elizabeth Hale

During the summer of 2015, Elizabeth Hale walked the Camino de Santiago in search of freedom. She continues to pay attention to the signs, and trusts that everything will work out as it is meant to. You will find her living in Ottawa, until the journey takes her elsewhere.

Contacts:
trustingthesigns@gmail.com
www.tinyurl.com/trustingthesigns

28890862R00187

Made in the USA
Middletown, DE
20 December 2018